# Ritual Scenes on the Two Coffins of *Pꜣ-dj-ỉmn* in Cairo Museum

Eltayeb Sayed Abbas

BAR International Series 2603
2014

Published in 2016 by
BAR Publishing, Oxford

BAR International Series 2603

*Ritual Scenes on the Two Coffins of P3-dj-imn in Cairo Museum*

ISBN 978 1 4073 1235 4



BAR Publishing is the trading name of British Archaeological Reports (Oxford) Ltd. British Archaeological Reports was first incorporated in 1974 to publish the BAR Series, International and British. In 1992 Hadrian Books Ltd became part of the BAR group. This volume was originally published by Archaeopress in conjunction with British Archaeological Reports (Oxford) Ltd / Hadrian Books Ltd, the Series principal publisher, in 2014. This present volume is published by BAR Publishing, 2016.

Printed in England

BAR
PUBLISHING

BAR titles are available from:

BAR Publishing
122 Banbury Rd, Oxford, OX2 7BP, UK
EMAIL info@barpublishing.com
PHONE +44 (0)1865 310431
FAX +44 (0)1865 316916
www.barpublishing.com

**Table of Contents**


**Preface** ........ iv
**List of Abbreviations** ........ v
**List of Plates** ........ vii
**Chapter One:**
**Introduction** ........ 1
1.1. Methodology ........ 1
1.2. Egyptian Coffins as Ritual Machines ........ 2
1.3. The 21st Dynasty and the Rise of the Priests of Amun in Thebes ........ 9
1.4. The Archaeological Context of the Coffin Ensemble of *P3-dj-jmn* ........ 10
1.5. The Coffin Ensemble of *P3-dj-jmn* ........ 13
**Chapter Two:**
**The Outer Coffin of *P3-dj-jmn* (CG 6080-6081)** ........ 14
2.1. The Lid of the Outer Coffin (CG 6080) ........ 14
2.1.1. General Description of the Lid ........ 14
2.1.2. The Upper Part of the Lid ........ 14
2.1.2.1. Commenatry and Analysis ........ 15
2.1.3. The Middle Part of the Lid ........ 15
2.1.3.1. Commentary and Analysis ........ 16
2.1.4. The Register under the Figure of the Goddess Nut ........ 16
2.1.4.1. Commentary and Analysis ........ 17
2.1.5. The Lower Part of the Lid ........ 18
2.1.5.1. The Middle of the Lower Part of the Lid ........ 18
2.1.5.1.1. Commentary and Analysis ........ 18
2.1.5.2. The Scenes on the Left Side ........ 19
2.1.5.3. The Scenes on the Right Side ........ 20
2.1.6. The Borders of the Lid ........ 21
2.2. The Lid Decorations: Conclusion ........ 21
2.3. The Case of the Outer Coffin of *P3-dj-jmn* (CG 6081) ........ 22
2.3.1. Exterior Decorations and Texts ........ 22
2.3.1.1. The External Left Side Wall ........ 22
2.3.1.1.1. Scene A (near the head) ........ 23
2.3.1.1.1.1. Commentary and Analysis ........ 23
2.3.1.1.2. Scene B (near the shoulder) ........ 23
2.3.1.1.2.1. Commentary and Analysis ........ 24
2.3.1.1.3. Scene C (near the hips) ........ 25
2.3.1.1.3.1. Commentary and Analysis ........ 26
2.3.1.1.4. Scene D (near the legs) ........ 26
2.3.1.1.4.1. Commentary and Analysis ........ 27
2.3.1.2. The External Right Side Wall ........ 28
2.3.1.2.1. Scene A (near the head) ........ 28
2.3.1.2.1.1. Commentary and Analysis ........ 28
2.3.1.2.2. Scene B (near the shoulder) ........ 29
2.3.1.2.2.1. Commentary and Analysis ........ 29
2.3.1.2.3. Scene C (near the hips) ........
2.3.1.2.3.1. Commentary and Analysis ........ 30
2.3.1.2.4. Scene D (near the legs) ........ 30
2.3.1.2.4.1 Commentary and Analysis ........ 30
2.4. The Interior Decorations of the Outer Case ........ 31
2.4.1. The Decorations on the Floor Board ........ 31
2.4.1.1. Commentary and Analysis ........ 33
2.4.2. The Decorations on the Two Inner walls ........ 34
2.5. The Outer Coffin of *P3-dj-jmn*: Conclusion ........ 36
**Chapter Three:**
**The Inner Coffin of *P3-dj-jmn*** ........ 37
3.1. The Lid of the Inner Coffin (CG 6082) ........ 37
3.1.1. General Description of the Lid ........ 37
3.1.2. The Decorations under the Collar and the Clenched hands ........ 37
3.1.2.1. Commentary and Analysis ........ 38

3.1.3. The Middle Part of the Lid........ 40
3.1.3.1. Commentary and Analysis........ 41
3.1.4. The Lower Part of the Lid........ 42
3.1.4.1. The Speeches of the Gods and Goddess On the Middle Part of the Lower Lid........ 42
3.1.4.1.1. Commentary and Analysis........ 43
3.1.4.2. The Decorations and Texts on the Lower Part of the Lid........ 44
3.1.4.2.1. The First Register........ 44
3.1.4.2.2. The Second Register........ 44
3.1.4.2.3. The Third Register........ 45
3.1.4.2. 4.The Fourth Register........ 45
3.1.5. The Decorations and Texts at the edge of the Feet........ 46
3.1.6. The Texts on the Borders of the Lid........ 46
3.1.6.1. Commentary and Analysis........ 47
3.2. The Lid's Decoration as Representation of the *Stundenwachen* and the Journey to Sais........ 47
3.3. The Case of the Inner Coffin of *P3-dj-jmn*........ 50
3.3.1. Exterior Decorations and Texts........ 50
3.3.1.1. Scene Behind the Head........ 51
3.3.1.1.1. Commentary and Analysis........ 51
3.3.1.2. External Left Side Wall........ 51
3.3.1.2.1. Scene A (near the head)........ 51
3.3.1.2.1. Commentary and Analysis........ 52
3.3.1.2.2. Scene B (near the shoulders)........ 52
3.3.1.2.2.1. Commentary and Analysis........ 53
3.3.1.2.3. Scene C (near the hips)........ 54
3.3.1.2.3.1. Commentary and Analysis........ 55
3.3.1.2.4. Scene D (near the legs)........ 55
3.3.1.2.4.1. Commentary and Analysis........ 56
3.3.1.2. The External Right side Wall........ 56
3.3.1.2.1. Scene A (near the head)........ 57
3.3.1.2.1.1. Commentary and Analysis........ 57
3.3.1.2.2. Scene B (near the shoulder)........ 57
3.3.1.2.2.1. Commentary and Analysis........ 58
3.3.1.2.3. Scene C (near the hips)........ 58
3.3.1.2.3.1. Commentary and Analysis........ 59
3.3.1.2.4. Scenes D (near the legs and the Part under the Feet)........ 59
3.3.1.2.4.1. Commentary and Analysis........ 60
3.3.2. The Inner Decorations of the Inner Case........ 60
3.3.2.1. The Decorations on the Floor board........ 60
3.3.2.1.1. Commentary and Analysis........ 61
3.3.2.2. The Right Side Inner Wall........ 62
3.3.2.3. The Left Side Inner Wall........ 62
3.3.2.3.1. Commentary and Analysis........ 63
3.4. The Inner Coffin's Case Decorations and the Hall of the Judgment........ 63
**3.5. The Mummy Cover of *P3-dj-jmn***........ 65
3.5.1. The Mummy Cover (CG 6078)........ 65
3.5.1.1. The Upper Part of the Mummy Cover........ 65
3.5.1.1.1. Commentary and Analysis........ 65
3.5.1.2. The Middle Part of The Mummy Cover........ 66
3.5.1.2.1. The First Register........ 66
3.5.1.2.2. The Second Register........ 66
3.5.1.2.3. The Third Register........ 66
3.5.1.2.4. Commentary and Analysis........ 66
3.5.1.3. The Lower Part of the Lid........ 67
3.5.1.3.1. The First Register........ 67
3.5.1.3.2. The Second Register........ 68
3.5.1.3.3. The Third Register........ 68
3.5.1.3.4. The Fourth Register........ 68

3.5.1.3.5. Commentary and Analysis....................................................... 69
**Chapter Four:**
**Conclusion**
4.1. Coffin Texts and Coffin Images: Towards a better Understanding of the Ritual Images on the 21st Dynasty Coffins of *P3-dj-jmn*......................................................... 70
4.2. The Outer Coffin of *P3-dj-jmn* ................................................................ 73
4.2.1. The Lid of the Outer Coffin as Representation of the Funeral Procession........... 73
4.2.2. The Case of the Outer Coffin and the Burial Rites...................................... 75
4.2.3. The Floor Board of the Case of the Outer Coffin and the *ḳbḥw* Offering Ritual..... 77
4.3. The Inner Coffin and the Judgment of the Dead............................................... 78
4.3.1. The Ritual of the Judgment of the Dead on the Lid of the Inner Coffin............ 79
4.3.2. The Case of the Inner Coffin as the Hall of the Judgment of the Dead.......... 80
4.3.3. The Floor Board of the Case of the Inner Coffin and the Embrace of the Goddess of the West...................................................................................... 82
4.4. The Mummy Cover......................................................................... 82
4.5. Ritual Images and Ritual Texts.............................................................. 83
**Bibliography**......................................................................................... 85
**Plates**

## Preface

This study deals with the significance of ritual scenes on the 21st Dynasty coffins. Scenes referring to certain rituals were placed in particular places on the coffins for both religious and ritual purposes. The images on these coffins will be studied as texts referring to the passage of the deceased to the next life. The aim of this study is also to argue how the Middle Kingdom Coffin Texts were replaced at this later date by the images on the coffins. Images and representations on these coffins will be related to Middle and New Kingdoms ritual texts and rites of passage. The study will focus on a group of coffins belonging to the priest *P3-di-imn,* and date to the reign of the High Priest Pinudjem II. They were found in 1891 at the tomb of Bab el-Gassus, as part of the find generally known as the Second Find of Deir el-Bahri. Excavated by Daressy and Bouriant, they were numbered and acquisitioned to the Egyptian Museum in Cairo. Recently Niwiniski has provided a primary publication of the whole group of these coffins in Cairo Museum.[1] This study will consider the decorations of these coffins as evidence for ritual practice in the 21st Dynasty itself, but also for the long continuity of ritual practice during the rites of passage in Egyptian religion. It will also consider attitudes to the coffin, not merely as an object, but as part of and objectification of those rites, and its role as descendant of the mortuary literature and the tomb decoration of earlier periods, towards a better understanding of the material mortuary record of ancient Egypt.

I would like to express my deepest thanks to the Binational Fulbright Commission in Egypt. A grant of this foundation enabled me to visit the United States and to write this book. I also would like to thank the director of the Egyptian Museum in Cairo for allowing me to take photos for the two coffins of *P3-dj-jmn*. I should also thank the Department of Egyptology and Ancient Western Asian Studies at Brown University for hosting me as a visiting scholar for nine months and for their generous help and support.

I must thank Professor Allen James P. for his generous help, valuable advice, encouragement, and for reading and correcting my English manuscript. I should further mention the generous hospitality of Susan Allen, who has been a great support for me during my stay at Brown University.

My eternal thanks go to my parents, my wife and my two kids Hana and Omar who have been supportive over the last years.

[1] Niwinski, *Catalogue General of Egyptian Antiquities of the Cairo Museum Numbers 6069-6082, The Second Find of Deir El-Bahri (Coffins)*, 2nd vol. 1st Fascicle, Cairo, 1999.

## List of Abbreviations

| | |
|---|---|
| ÄA | Ägyptologische Abhandlungen, Wiesbaden |
| ASAÉ | *Annales du Service des Antiquités de l'Égypte*, Cairo |
| AV | Archäologische Veröffentlichungen, Deutsches Archäologisches Instituts, Abteilung Kairo, Mainz am Rhein |
| BAe | Bibliotheca Aegyptiaca, Brussels |
| BAR | British Archaeological Reports International Series, Oxford |
| *BD* | Book of the Dead |
| BdÉ | Bibliothèque d'Étude, Institut Français d'Archéologie Orientale, Cairo |
| *BIFAO* | *Bulletin de l'Institut Français d'Archéologie Orientale*, Cairo |
| *BiOr* | *Bibliotheca Orientalis*, Leiden |
| *BOREAS* | BOREAS. Uppsala Studies in the Ancient Mediterranean and Near Eastern Civilizations, Uppsala |
| BSAE | British School of Archaeology in Egypt |
| *BSFE* | *Bulletin de la Société Française d'Égyptologie*, Paris |
| *CdÉ* | *Chronique d'Égypte*, Brussels |
| Ch. | Chapter |
| Col(s) | Column(s) |
| CT | Coffin Text |
| *CT* | De Buck, A., *The Ancient Egyptian Coffin Texts*, 7 vols, Chicago, 1935-1961. |
| DAIK | Deutsches Archäologisches Instituts, Abteilung Kairo, Mainz |
| *DE* | *Discussions in Egyptology*, Oxford |
| EES | The Egyptian Exploration Society, London |
| *Essays te Velde* | Van Dijk, J. (ed.), *Essays on Ancient Egypt in Honour of Hermann te Velde,* Groningen, 1997. |
| EU | Egyptologische Uitgaven, Leiden |
| Fig(s). | Figure(s) |
| *Fs Irmtraut Munro* | B. Backes, M. Müller-Roth and S. Sthör (eds), *Ausgestattet mit den Schriften des Thot; Festschrift für Irmtraut Munro zu ihrem 65. Geburtstag*, SAT 14, Wiesbaden, 2009. |
| *Fs Hornung* | Bordbeck, A. (ed.), *Ein ägyptisches Glasperlenspiel, Ägyptologische Beiträge für Erik Hornung aus seinem Schülerkreis,* Berlin, 1998. |
| *Fs Stadelmann* | H. Guksch and D. Polz (eds), *Stationen. Beiträge zur Kulturgeschichte Ägyptens: Rainer Stadelmann gewidmet*, Mainz am Rhein, 1998. |
| *GM* | Göttinger Miszellen: Beiträge zur ägyptologischen Diskussion, Göttingen |
| HAT | Handschriften des Altägyptischen Totenbuches |
| *Hommages Fayza Haikal* | N. Grimal, A. Kamel and C. May-Sheikholeslami (eds), *Hommages à Fayza Haikal,* BdÉ 138, Cairo, 2003. |

| | |
|---|---|
| *Hommages Lecalnt* | C. Berger, G. Clere and N. Grimal (eds), *Hommages à Jean Leclant*, 4 vols, BdÉ 106, Cairo, 1994. |
| *JARCE* | *Journal of the American Research Center in Egypt*, New York |
| *JEA* | *Journal of Egyptian Archaeology*, London |
| *JEOL* | *Jaarbericht van het Vooraziatisch Genootschap (Gezelschap) „Ex Orient Lux"*, Leiden |
| *JNES* | *Journal of Near Eastern Studies*, Chicago |
| *LÄ* | W. Helck, E. Otto and W. Westendorf (eds), *Lexikon der Ägyptologie*, 7 vols, Wiesbaden, 1972-1992. |
| MÄS | Müncher Ägyptologische Studien, Berlin/Munich/Mainz am Rhein |
| *MDAIK* | *Mitteilungen des Deutschen Archäologischen Instituts, Abteilung Kairo*, Mainz |
| MESS | Memoir of the Egypt Exploration Society |
| MIFAO | Mémoires publiés par les Membres de l'Institut Français d'Archéologie Orientale du Caire, Cairo |
| OBO | Orbis Biblicus et Orientalis, Freiburg/Göttingen |
| OIP | Oriental Institute Publication (Chicago, 1924-present) |
| OLA | Orienatalia Lovaniensia Analecta, Leuven |
| P | Papyrus |
| Pl(s) | Plate(s) |
| PT | Pyramid Text |
| *Pyr* | Sethe, K., *Die altägyptischen Pyramidentexte*, 3 vols, Lepizig, 1908-1922; reprint, Hildesheim 1960. |
| *RÄRG* | Bonnet, H., *Reallexikon der ägyptischen Religionsgeschichte*, Berlin, 1999. |
| *RdÉ* | *Revue d'Égyptologie*, Paris |
| SAGA | Studien zur Archäologie und Geschichte Altägyptens, Heidelberg |
| *SAK* | *Studien zur altägyptischen Kultur*, Hamburg |
| SAT | Studien zum Altägyptischen Totenbuch, Wiesbaden |
| *Studies Redford* | G. N. Knoppers and A. Hirsch (eds), *Egypt, Israel, and the Ancient Mediterranean World: Studies in Honor of Donald B. Redford*, Ledien and Boston, 2004. |
| Theben | Theben, Mainz |
| TT | Theban Tomb |
| *Urk* I | Sethe, K., *Urkunden des Alten Reichs*, Leipzig, 1903. |
| *Urk* IV | Sethe, K., *Urkunden des Neuen Reichs, historische-biographische Urkunden*, Heft 1-16, Leipzig, 1906-1909, continued by Helck, W., Heft 17-22, Berlin, 1955-1958. |
| WAW | Writings from the Ancient World, Society of Biblical Literature, Atlanta |
| *Wb* | A. Erman and H. Grapow (eds), *Wörterbuch der ägyptischen Sprache*, 7 vols and 5 Belegstellen, Leipzig and Berlin, 1926-1963. |
| WVDOG | Wissenschaftliche Veröffentlichungen der Deutschen Orientgesellschaft (Leipzig, then Berlin, then Saarbrücken, then Saarwellingen 1900 present) |
| YES | Yale Egyptological Studies, New Haven |
| *ZÄS* | *Zeitschrift für ägyptische Sprache und Altertumskunde*, Berlin |

**List of Plates**


| | |
|---|---|
| The Lid of the Outer Coffin | Pl. 1 |
| The External Left Side Wall of the Case of the Outer Coffin | Pl. II. 1 |
| The External right Side Wall of the Case of the Outer Coffin | Pl. II. 2 |
| The Inner Decorations of the Case of the Outer Coffin | Pl. III |
| The Lid of the Inner Coffin | Pl. IV |
| The External Left Side Wall of the Case of the Inner Coffin | Pl. V.1 |
| The External Right Side Wall of the Case of the Inner Coffin | Pl. V.2 |
| The Inner Decorations of the Case of the Inner Coffin | Pl. VI |
| The Mummy Cover | Pl. VII |

# Chapter One

## *Introduction*

### *1.1. Methodology*

During the 21st Dynasty new iconographic compositions were introduced and were placed on coffin sides. The 21st Dynasty coffins can serve as a miniature for the tomb, at a time when richly decorated tombs were no longer built.[1] Instead of on the walls of the tombs,[2] ritual and hereafter scenes were placed on the inner and outer sides of the coffins and also on papyri.[3] The decorations on the coffin's sides not only include representations of the underworld scenes as found on the walls of royal tombs,[4] they also have vignettes of the New Kingdom Book of the Dead.[5] The 21st Dynasty coffins and their antecedent coffins of the 18th and 19th Dynasties have depictions of the funeral scenes, which are well preserved on the walls of the tombs and also preserved in texts.[6] As with the Middle Kingdom coffins, the 21st Dynasty coffins served as a universe for the deceased and also reflect the rituals performed for him from the moment of his death until his burial. The only difference between the Middle Kingdom coffin and that of the 21st Dynasty is that the latter has more decorative elements than the former. These decorative elements replaced the ritual texts in the rites of passage.

Since the 1891 discovery by Daressy and Bouriant of the tomb at Bab El-Gassus,[7] which is better known as the Second Find of Deir El-Bahri, a considerable amount of work has been done on the coffins of the 21st Dynasty that were found inside the tomb However, most of this is typological study, the most important being the work done by Niwinski on the 21st Dynasty coffins and that of René Van Walsem on the Coffin of Djedmonthuiufankh in the National Museum of Antiquities at Leiden.[8] The images and scenes on these coffins do not serve only as decorative elements: their ritualistic functions are more important. Some studies consider only parts of the coffin decorations; others, individual scenes.[9] This book will not, then, be a typological study, and will not aim to deal with a typology of all coffins dating to the 21st Dynasty, but will compare the decorations on the coffins of *P3-dj-jmn* with that of the Middle Kingdom coffins, in order to show how the scenes work together to mediate the passage of the deceased to the next life. The best approach for this is to concentrate on the images and texts of a particular group of coffins, to examine their specific texts and images as a group. For this I will examine the coffin ensemble of a priest called *P3-di-imn*, dating to the reign of the High Priest Pinudjem II.

The two coffins of *P3-dj-jmn* were found in 1891 at the tomb of Bab el-Gassus. Excavated by Daressy and Bouriant, they were numbered and acquisitioned to the Egyptian Museum in Cairo. Recently Niwinski has provided a primary publication of the whole group of these coffins in Cairo Museum.[10]

Not much is known about the priest *P3-dj-jmn*, but his titles show that he was a High Priest of Amun who knew the mysteries in the Theban temples. According to Niwinski, *P3-dj-jmn* was a theologian who was concerned with the cult of *Š3j*, the personification of destiny, in one of the sanctuaries of Amun in Thebes. He has a funerary papyrus in the Egyptian Museum no. 23.4.40.1 which has been found together with his coffin.[11]

The coffins of *P3-di-imn* are important here because they have all the images and texts necessary to carry out this study. For instance, the outer lid is decorated with the image of the sky goddess Nut spreading her wings and protecting the deceased; she acts here as the mother as well as the protector of the deceased. The inner lid is decorated with the image of Osiris on his funeral bier, and Isis and Nephthys are depicted at the foot and the head of the bier. In the middle, the goddess Nut is depicted, while the corners of the lid are decorated with the images of the Sons of Horus acting as the supporters of the sky goddess Nut. All these are the ritual images that will be studied in this book.

The images and texts on these coffins will be dealt with as texts referring to the rites of passage. My plan is to analyse the location of the scenes and texts on the coffins to show how the placing of the images on certain parts of the coffin has to do with the rites of the passage as in the Middle and New Kingdoms coffins.

---

[1] Niwinski, *21st Dynasty Coffins from Thebes*, 15.

[2] The scene of the sky goddess Nut supporting the sky and separated from the earth god Geb by Shu, which is well known in the royal tombs, is found on the Cairo coffin CG 6153: Niwinski, *The Second Find of Deir El-Bahri*, 98, fig. 132.

[3] Most of these coffins included also religious papyri found inside them. These contained vignettes from different chapters of the Book of the Dead: Niwinski, in: Backes et al, *Totenbuch-Forschungen*, 260-2; in: Uehlinger (ed.), *Images as Media*, 21.

[4] On the coffin of Pinudjem II from Cairo Museum (JE 26197), there are depictions of a solar boat being dragged along the ways of the netherworld, and Apep is shown speared with knives. This depiction of the scene resembles the motif that is found in the Eleventh Hour of the Book of the Gates: Niwinski, *21st Dynasty Coffins from Thebes*, 115 (coffin No. 65). On the vignettes from the Book of the Dead on the Coffin of Pinudjem II and his wives, see Niwinski, in: Backes et al, *Totenbuch-Forschungen*, 255.

[5] Niwinski, in: Backes et al, *Totenbuch-Forschungen*, 245-64.

[6] On what Niwinski called the white coffins, which date to the 18th Dynasty, there are depictions of burial rites, scenes of mourners, mummy transport, and offerings before the deceased: Niwinski, *21st Dynasty Coffins from Thebes*, 11.

[7] Niwinski, *JEA* 70 (1989), 73-81. For the most recent discussion of the TT 320 and the royal cache see, Graefe et al, *The Royal Cache TT 320*.

[8] Van Walsem, R., *The Coffin of Djedmonthuiufankh*; Niwinski, *21st Dynasty Coffins from Thebes*.

[9] Niwinski, *GM* 49 (1981), 47-59; *GM* 65 (1983), 75-90; '*GM* 109 (1989), 53-66; in: Altenmüller et al, *Linguistik, Philologie, Religion. Akten des Vierten Internationalen Ägyptologen-Kongresses*, III, 305-14; *BiOr* 53 (1996), 324-63; in: Uehlinger (ed.), *Images as Media*, 21-43; In: *Fs Irmtraut Munro*, 133-62; Heyne, in: *Fs Hornung*, 57-68; Singleton, in: Strudwick and Taylor (eds), *The Theban Necropolis*, 83-7: Sousa, *JARCE* 46 (2010), 189-204; Englund, *BOREAS* 6 (1974), 37-69; *Medelhavsmuseet Bulletin* 20 (1985), 33-41.

[10] Niwinski, *The Second Find of Deir El-Bahri*.

[11] Niwinski, *The Second Find of Deir El-Bahri*, 21.

The scenes of the judgment of the dead on the coffins, for instance, are related to the Coffin Text spell 335 and Book of the Dead chapter 125. I will try to demonstrate that instead of presenting the judgment of the dead ritual in texts for recitation, the ritual is illustrated, and the iconographic depiction of the ritual plays the same role as the texts presented for recitation. The same occurs on the New Kingdom private tomb walls where pictorial representation of Chapter 125 of the Book of the Dead was placed on certain parts of the tomb walls for ritualistic purposes. Both the architecture of these tombs and the placing of the spells and images on the walls mediate the passage of the deceased to the next life.[12] The nature of this scene on the coffin, as representation of a recitation, may be confirmed by the fact that it is here preceded by *ḏd mdw* 'recitations'. This raises the questions of whether and when there were ritual texts recited and performed with the depiction of the ritual, and whether the representation of the ritual in captions on the sides of the coffin can replace the texts intended for recitation.

Another instance is the depiction of Osiris on his bier, attended and protected by Isis and Nephthys. This depiction refers to the roles of the two goddesses as kites protecting the deceased. It is a key for all the rituals performed for him in the night before burial, or what is known as the *Stundenwachen*. On the Middle and New Kingdoms coffins, these rituals are preserved in texts, while on the 21st Dynasty coffins, the rituals are kept in vignettes and captions placed on the sides of the coffin.[13] This depiction of the two kites on the head and foot of the deceased is well expressed in a Middle Kingdom liturgy in which Osiris is awakened by the two goddesses in the resurrection ritual and in what is better known as the *Stndenwachen.*[14]

My plan is to argue how certain images and texts were placed on purpose in specific areas on the coffin, implying that the texts and images worked together to ensure an eternal life for the deceased who is placed within the coffin. This will require the arrangement of individual scenes and grouping them together in sequences of scenes, as the basis for reconstruction of the rituals from the images and the texts. It will also require a full and systematic description and analysis of the decorative program on the coffin of *P3-di-imn*. As it is impossible to reconstruct a ritual from a single spell in Middle Kingdom Coffin Texts, it is also impossible to reconstruct a ritual from a single scene on the 21st Dynasty and the Late Period coffins. My plan here is to reconstruct the rituals on these coffins by analysis of the contexts of individual scenes, their relationship to the surrounding scenes, and the way in which they fit the whole decorative program on each coffin. The scenes that will be dealt with in detail in this book include depictions of the sky goddess Nut and how they can be related to the funeral procession, the scene of the judgment of the dead, the scene of Isis and Nephthys attending the bier, and the scene of the Four Sons of Horus. Some other scenes which are related to the chapters of the Book of the Dead will be considered.

In my study of the coffin ensemble of *P3-dj-jmn*, the arrangement and the distribution of the scenes on the different parts of coffins will be considered to determine if there are specific rules for their placement on the coffin sides. It will also be argued that the attributes on an individual coffin can make allusion to more than one religious concept, and that they were skilfully integrated to create a coherent religious and ritualistic entity. How can the coffin be considered as a microcosm for the deceased during this period? How was the Egyptian vision of the cosmos considered in the orientation of the scenes and texts on these coffins? Is the coffin a ritual machine as it was during the Middle Kingdom?

The texts placed on coffins have always been considered as a reflection of the coffin's use as a ritual machine. In the 21st Dynasty such ritual texts are replaced by images covering all the inner and outer surfaces of the coffin. The important question here is how to interpret these images and whether we can consider them as texts referring to the rite of passage or merely as referring to mythological ideas. These are the most important questions that this book is about.

### *1.2. Egyptian Coffins as Ritual Machines*

Before proceeding to the Egyptian coffins as ritual machines, it is important first to give a brief introduction about the Egyptian coffins and their symbolism. The Pyramid, the tomb, and the coffin, all serve as a metaphor for the cosmos, which the dead inhabit and pass through. The key point of interest here is where the observable inhabited parts of the world merge with the invisible 'Otherworld', and how the Egyptians envisaged and ordered the physical world (sky, earth, and horizon) within this wider cosmos. The proper organization of the Egyptian cosmos was of great importance and it displays a fixed form during rituals connected with birth and rebirth, death and resurrection, as well as when the Egyptians created their own ritual landscape of pyramids, coffins and tombs. These ritual landscapes were envisaged or mirrored as microcosms of macrocosms.[15]

Of all the tomb equipment, the coffin can be described as the most important object that was endowed with symbolism and symbolic significance. The coffin can be interpreted as an eternal house for the deceased and his spirit who were supposed to be placed within it to rest. As an eternal house of the deceased, the coffin carried some of the architectural elements of the tomb. The development of tomb design during the different periods of Egyptian history had its effect on the coffin design and also decorations, where both were considered as dwelling

12 Saleh, *Das Totenbuch in den thebanischen Beamtengräbern*.
13 Niwinski argues that these depictions will equip the deceased magically, and ensure his protection and resurrection in the hereafter: Niwinski, *21st Dynasty Coffins from Thebes*, 15.
14 Assmann, *Totenlitrugien I*.
15 Raven, *JEA* 94 (2005), 37.

houses for the deceased.[16] For instance, the false door in the tomb had a religious function, which was to enable the spirit to go through it to consume the offerings presented for the deceased. These false doors with the palace facade were placed on the coffin sides during the early periods. The soul could then leave the body and the coffin and consume the offerings presented in the tomb. This concept was also developed later in the offering lists on the coffin sides. These offerings to the deceased were presented both in images, as object frieze, and in the words of the Coffin Texts. By having both on the coffin sides, the deceased within the coffin was equipped with everything needed for the passage into the hereafter. Spells inscribed on the coffin form liturgies recited for the deceased eternally by virtue of their presence. The deceased did not need either physical offerings placed in front of the offering niche and the false door, or the repeated performance of offering rituals, because their presence in texts guaranteed their eternal validity.

Hayes argues that the architecture of the coffin makes it looks as a house in itself. The horizontal bands at the edge of the sarcophagus serve as lintels and the vertical columns serve as supporting pilasters. Even the arrangement of the panels on the coffin and sarcophagus are derived from the facade of the palace, the dwelling houses of the ancient Egyptians.[17]

In the early stages of Egyptian coffins, the form, texts and images created for the deceased the space in which to be reborn. In this concept, the coffin also served as a tomb for its inhabitant. It was a place from which he started his journey to the hereafter and in which he was equipped with what is necessary for the journey. In this sphere in which the deceased dwells, he is surrounded by gods and goddesses and other divinities providing him with all protection. The coffin represented the realm and the natural cycle in which the deceased would participate and play a major role. For that reason the coffin was identified with Nut, mother of Osiris, in whose body he — both god and deceased — will be reborn again.

During different periods, the tomb was a model from which the coffin borrowed most of its architectural elements. In the early dynastic period and before the invention of large tombs, the deceased was buried in a deep rectangular pit lined with mud brick, with monumental mounds of dirt above. The body buried within these pits was simply placed on the ground. During the same period, the rectangular shaped sarcophagus appeared and shared the features of these tombs. The deceased was placed within these sarcophagi in the same way he was buried in the rectangular tomb.

After the tomb and coffin began to appear together, the coffin became one of the most important pieces of tomb equipment and shared the forms and decorations of the tomb itself.[18] For instance, mastabas and coffins of the early dynastic period share the decoration of the palace facade. The decoration on Middle Kingdom coffins was also inspired by that on the tomb walls of the 4th and 5th Dynasties.[19] Images and texts on the walls of these tombs were copied and placed on the coffin sides of that period. In the New Kingdom, the decorations and texts on the private tomb walls of Tell El-Amarna inspired the yellow type anthropoid coffins in vogue from the New Kingdom until the Late Period.[20] During the New Kingdom, the burial chambers of some kings of the 18th Dynasty were designed in the shape of a cartouche and so was the sarcophagus of this period.[21] In the 21st Dynasty, richly decorated tombs disappeared and all the decoration and scenes that had been on their walls were placed on the coffin sides; the coffin that served as a tomb as well as a coffin.

The coffin can be also considered as a substitute for the body itself. The earliest coffins were rectangular in shape and carried images and texts, and thus the coffin became effective equipment for the deceased. The body as the focal point of all the rituals carried on the coffin acquired a new stable and eternal state. In this perfect state of being, the deceased became a *sꜥḥ* as the result of enveloping the body in wrappings and covering the face and chest with golden skin, wigs, and collars. These new images, produced in wood and cartonnage and placed around the body, developed into the anthropoid coffin.[22] The earliest such coffins acted as a replacement for the body or as a shell.[23] They were decorated simply or not at all. They carried no images and the inscriptions on them were very simple, in most cases consisting of an offering formula (*ḥtp-dj-nsw*).

During the New Kingdom, anthropoid coffins continued to carry the same symbolism and function of the Middle Kingdom rectangular coffins, and with shaping it in the deceased's face, the coffin was considered as eternal body for the deceased.[24] These anthropoid coffins also resemble the *sꜥḥ* or the elevated and divine image of the deceased.[25] They were considered as replacement for the body of the deceased in his perfect status, the status of being like the resurrected Osiris or being an *ꜣḫ* (transfigured spirit).[26]

Beginning in the Old Kingdom, the coffin was associated with different symbolic objects. An important association was with the bed. The deceased within the coffin is surrounded by divine images and texts and protected by goddesses and gods, and the coffin can refer to the

[16] Taylor, *Death and the Afterlife in ancient Egypt*, 148.
[17] Hayes, *Royal Sarcophagi of the XVIII Dynasty*, 62.
[18] Bettum, *Death as an Eternal Process*, 21.

[19] Willems, in: *Essays te Velde*, 239.
[20] Bettum, *Death as an Eternal Process*, 21.
[21] Hayes, *Royal Sarcophagi of the XVIII Dynasty*, 9, pl. XVIII-XIX.
[22] Taylor, in: Davies (ed), *Colour and Painting in Ancient Egypt*, 164-5.
[23] Schneider, *Shabits* I, 64-5
[24] Taylor, in: Davies (ed), *Colour and Painting in Ancient Egypt*, 165.
[25] Taylor, in: Davies (ed), *Colour and Painting in Ancient Egypt*, 164; for the coffin as a temple, royal palace, and bed, see, Bettum, *Death as an Eternal Process*, 24-31.
[26] For more discussion on the coffin as a substitute for the body, see Bettum, *Death as an Eternal Process*, 36-8.

identification of the deceased with Osiris. For that reason, the deceased is sometimes represented lying on a bed of mummification, as is shown in the vignettes of BD 151 and later in BD 182. In its role as a bed, the coffin since the Middle Kingdom was provided with a headrest, which could be placed beside the coffin or painted on the frieze object near the head of the deceased.[27] The bed symbolism of the coffin is also reflected in the idea of the bier on which the body of the deceased inside the coffin was placed during the night of the *Stundenwachen.*[28]

Some parts of the coffin can also be identified with certain divinities. The coffin as a whole can be a personification of the sky goddess Nut, mother of Osiris, who covers and protects his body with her wings. That is the image behind the address to Nut on some coffins, in which the deceased asks his mother Nut to spread her wings over him and to make him like the Imperishable Stars. Nut features here as the womb of a mother in which the deceased travels and through which he will be reborn again as the son of Nut or simply as Osiris or Re. Placing Nut on the lid of the coffin, spreading her wings, is a kind of divine protection against the chaotic forces threatening the deceased within the coffin, embodied in the two gods Seth and Apophis. As Billing argues, water and space are the prominent aspects of the sky goddess Nut and these are the basic elements that link the goddess as sky goddess and cosmic mother of the deceased.[29]

The coffin can refer to the sun god Re and could also represent the entire universe of which the deceased forms a part. The decorations on the lid, for instance, might reflect solar aspects. The deceased's journey from his house to his tomb, referred to in images and texts, is parallel to the journey of the sun god Re from the east to the west of the sky and it also resembles the journey of Osiris in his *Henu* barque.[30]

The coffin represents a microcosm for the deceased. It also represents heaven and earth and alludes to the rejuvenating cycle of death and rebirth. The most important functions of all Egyptian coffins during different periods are not only magical but ritualistic. The placing of the body of the deceased inside the coffin and the orientation of the burial itself has an impact on the distribution of the texts and images on the coffin sides and on the relation between the body of the deceased inside the coffin and the orientation of cosmos. There are two important concepts that played important roles in the placing of texts and images on the coffin sides: the orientation of the whole body and the orientation of the head of the deceased within the coffin. Raven simplifies the position of the bodies in the ancient Egyptian burials in two clear patterns that are easily distinguished.[31] In this respect, he argues that there are two main periods. The first stretches from the later Predynastic Period to the end of the Middle Kingdom,[32] when the body of the deceased was laid on its left side, crouching or extended, and the head was oriented towards the north.[33] The second period appeared from the New Kingdom to the late Ptolemaic Period, where the common position of the head was toward the west.[34] This leads to the conclusion that in both cases the deceased is looking to the east: in the first case, through lying on his left side; in the other, the deceased raises his head when the coffin is in a standing position. The positioning of the deceased in the centre of the cosmos was reflected in the coffin decorations in all periods, and in rectangular coffins as well as anthropoid. The placing of the texts and images around the body of the deceased also played an important role in the ritual use of the coffin.

Harco Willems has defined Middle Kingdom coffins as ritual machines.[35]As such, the ideal coffin should carry all that is necessary for the performance of rituals on or for the deceased: the elements necessary for the performance of funerary rituals. These ritual elements include texts, equipment, actions, and speech. All these ritual elements are found written or pictured on Middle Kingdom coffins, both in the words of the Coffin Texts and in the vignettes of the object frieze. Together these comprise liturgies recited for the deceased in the night before burial or on the day of funeral.[36]

The decorative program and the texts on Middle Kingdom coffins have played an important role in the understanding of how the funerary rituals were performed for the deceased:[37] how, when and by whom the ritual might be performed. The decorations on these coffins consist of text bands, and usually relate to the placing of the body of the deceased on its left side, facing east.[38] The back, west side of the coffin is inscribed with texts for Anubis as the patron of the western desert, and thus good burial for the deceased in the west is ensured.[39] On the front, eastern side, an invocation offering is inscribed for Osiris as provider of offerings and thus connected with the east. From the reign of Sesostris I, Isis and Nephthys are depicted at the foot and head ends, respectively. Willems argues that the placing of these two goddesses on these sides of the coffin has a ritual background, derived from their roles as female mourners (mythologically identified as kites) during the burial rites.[40] Isis as the widow of the deceased was represented on the coffin facing him; Nephthys protects him from behind and thus was represented on the back.[41] The position of Neith and Serqet is less clear as they appeared

[27] Willems, *Chests of Life*, 202, 9; Taylor, *Death and Afterlife in ancient Egypt*, 107-8.

[28] Ikram and Dodson, *The Mummy in Ancient Egypt*, 107; Willems, in: *Essay te Velde*, 358-9.

[29] Billing, *Nut*, 10-2.

[30] Assmann, *Death and Salvation*, 267.

[31] Raven, *JEA* 94 (2005), 40.

[32] Mace, *The Early Dynastic Cemeteries of Nag-ed-Der* II, 31-2.

[33] Bourriau, in: Willems (ed.), *Social Aspects*, 1-20.

[34] Brunton, *Qau and Badari* III, 23; Schäfer, *Priestergräber und andere Grabfunde vom Totentempl des Ne-user-re*, 16; Quibell and Hayter, *Teti Pyramid, North Side*, 3; Giddy, *The Anubieion at Saqqara II*, 35.

[35] Willems,*Chests of Life*, 148-60.

[36] Assmann, *Totenliturgien* I.

[37] Willems, in Willems (ed.), *The World of the Coffin Texts*. 203-7.

[38] Willems, *The Coffin of Heqata*, 364; *Chests of Life*, 122-4;

[39] Willems, *Chests of Life*, 124.

[40] Willems, *Chests of Life*, 134.

[41] Willems, *Chests of Life*, 135.

once or twice on the left (south-east) and Serqet on the right (south-west) of the coffin. These column gods feature among the Great Ennead who forms protection around the body of the deceased Osiris. Their role is to pronounce a judgment of the Dead. Their role with the Four Sons of Horus is clear in the *Stundenwachen*.[42]

During the reigns of Sesostris II and III, the Four Sons of Horus were depicted on the edge columns, along the corners of the two long sides of the coffin, as protectors of the deceased.[43] Imsety and Hapi are connected with the northern (head) end, and Duamutef and Qebehsnuef with southern end (at the foot).[44] This is corroborated by the association of Imsety and Hapi with the two hands or arms of the deceased, and Duamutef and Qebehsenuef with the feet or legs. Imsety and Hapi are equated with the souls of Pe (Buto in the north) and Duamutef and Qebehsenuef with the souls of Nekhen in the south (CT spells 157-158). They were later depicted wearing the crowns of Upper and Lower Egypt respectively.[45] The lid is identified with the sky goddess Nut and the Four Sons of Horus represent the poles that support the sky, which ensures the connection between the placing of the body within the coffin and the direction of the cosmos.[46] The Four Sons of Horus have their connection with the canopic jars and the protection of the intestines of the body of the deceased. Their connection with the intestines of the body is clear since the Old Kingdom Pyramid Texts, where, for instance. PT spell 338 reads:

*ḥpj dwꜣ-mwt=f jmstj ḳbḥ-snw=f dr=sn ḥḳr pn ntj m ẖt nt N jbt tn ntj m sptj N*

Hapj, Duamutef, Amesti and Qebehsenuef drive away the hunger that is in the belly of N and the thirst that is on the lips of N.[47]

This spell connects the Four Sons of Horus with preventing hunger and thirst to the deceased. They were also connected with the ascent of the king to the sky, a well known theme in PT § 1092, 1338/9, and 1828; since Horus himself refers to the sky, any one of his sons might also have a celestial role. This role of the Four Sons of Horus on Middle Kingdom coffins is clear when they are described as column gods and are named at the four corners of the coffins. With the lid of the coffin being identified with the goddess Nut, the Four Sons of Horus would be the supporters of the sky.[48]

One of the most important decorative elements on Middle Kingdom coffins is the object frieze: simply a register showing the items and the implements to be offered to the deceased during ritual. The objects within the register are usually depicted standing on tables, accompanied by explanatory labels, which may occur in a register above the objects or distributed among them.[49] The object frieze and the placing of the spell on the coffin can provide information on the performance of certain rituals. It helps to explain the religious texts inscribed on the inner and outer parts of Middle Kingdom coffins.[50]

During the New Kingdom, coffins were decorated with images and inscribed with ritual texts. Although the burial orientation during this period changed from the north-south axis to the west-east axis, the coffins of this period follow the same decoration patterns of the Middle Kingdom coffins. Isis is still shown at the foot end and Nephthys at the head end; the Four Sons of Horus are placed on the two long sides of the sarcophagi and coffins of this period, but they have changed their positions: Amesti and Duamutef are now on the right side and Hapi and Qebehsenuef are on the left side. Isis and Nephthys would be connected here with the east and west respectively. The lid still refers to the sky covering the coffin and features as the mother and protector of the deceased. The lid of the coffin of Merenptah, for instance, is decorated with the image of the goddess Neith as mother of the deceased, and the Four Sons of Horus are depicted at the four corners of the coffin. They play the roles of protectors, and one of their roles is to pronounce a judgment for the deceased.[51] The Four Sons of Horus during the New Kingdom were also described as the stars protecting Osiris or as birds flying to the four corners of the sky. The sky was envisaged as a vault or as the belly of a cow, which would explain the role of the Four Sons of Horus as supporters of the vault of the sky or the four legs of the heavenly cow, and in this sense they would help the deceased within the coffin to ascend to the sky. They serve here as a bridge between earth and sky.

As mentioned above, the texts and images within and outside the coffin were placed in a position readable to the deceased within the coffin. With the introduction of the anthropoid coffins since the Middle Kingdom, the body of the deceased was situated in the coffin to follow the same principles. The body was placed on its back, with the face directed upward.[52] This position of the body within the coffin has its effect on the distribution and the placement of the texts and images on the coffins. Coffin lids are occupied no longer only by the image of the goddess Nut and offering formulae invoking Osiris and Anubis but also with texts and images that were normally placed on the front and back of the coffin during the

[42] Willems, *Chests of Life*, 135.
[43] Willems, *Chests of Life*, 140.
[44] Willems, *Chests of Life*, 140-1.
[45] Raven, *JEA* 91 (2005), 37-53.
[46] The New Kingdom coffin places Isis at the head and Nephthys at the feet of the deceased. The only difference between the Middle Kingdom decoration schemes is that Amesti and Duamutef are placed on the right while Qebehsenuef and Hapi are placed on the left: Willems, *Chests of Life*, 141; von Falck, *SAK* 34 (2006), 129-30.
[47] PT spell 338=*Pyr*. §552b-d
[48] Raven, *JEA* 91 (2005), 42.
[49] Willems, *Chests of Life*, 202.
[50] Willems, *Chests of Life*, 200.
[51] Assmann, *MDAIK* 28 (1972), 47-73; *MDAIK* 28 (1972), 115-139.
[52] Niwinski states that the mummy inside the coffin was placed in a horizontal way as the coffin was deposited in the same way within the tomb, however during the opening of the mouth ritual the coffin with the mummy was put vertically on the foot board of the coffin and thus the mummy inside the coffin was standing and not lying and this as he argues is 'a crucial moment of animation ritual'; Niwinski, *GM* 109 (1989), 55.

Middle and New Kingdoms.[53] The back of the coffin is the floor board on which the body of the deceased was placed.[54] The exterior long and short sides as well as the inner sides of the case are also inscribed with texts and decorated with images. These images and texts, as will be discussed in this book, mediate the passage of the deceased inside the coffin from death to resurrection.

In Old, Middle and New Kingdom coffins, the texts and images work together to ensure an eternal life for the deceased within the coffin. The emphasis during these periods was on the texts mediating the passage of the deceased from death to resurrection or from death to eternal life in the underworld. These texts comprise liturgies recited on the body of the deceased in the night before burial, in which the deceased Osiris is pictured lying on a bier and attended by Isis, Nephthys and other gods. These recited texts were then placed on the coffin sides to keep the body of the deceased inside the coffin within eternal recitation.[55]

During the Middle and New Kingdoms the coffins carried everything necessary to carry out the ritual for the deceased inside it. The two long sides, the two short sides, the inner walls and the floor board were covered with texts, the aim of which is to mediate the passage of the deceased to become an *ꜣḫ*. To become an *ꜣḫ*, the deceased should undergo the different stages of the rites of passage, to escape death and reintegrate in the world of the hereafter.[56] He has been separated from his old state by death and in order not to stay for long in separation, the deceased's body is first mummified. According to Assmann, there are two types of mummification: the first, the physical one, in which the body of the deceased is taken to the undertaker to embalm it; and the second, a spiritual mummification, which is done by reciting the ritual texts for the deceased. These texts belong to the *sꜣḫw* genre and are aimed at the restoration of the deceased's social and physical aspects.[57] They were recited for the deceased on the night preceding the burial or on the day of the funeral. Placed on the coffin sides, they are what is known as the Coffin Texts.

The question here is: How can the coffin be described as a ritual machine? First it is important to look at how a ritual in ancient Egypt was constructed and how this was applied to the coffin. In the Pyramid Texts, for instance, it is not always explicit how a ritual can be constructed, and sometimes it is impossible to give a specific explanation to texts other than those of the Offering Ritual.[58] Such texts are not provided with vignettes, representations, or ritual directions, except for Spell 355, in the Pyramid of Teti, which is entitled 'Opening of the Doors of Heaven'. The Pyramid Texts preserve only the ritual recitations.[59] Allen argues that the Pyramid Texts that address the deceased in the second person are ritual in nature. They were recited in the rites probably taking place during the funeral or after burial, and they were inscribed on the walls of the chambers of the pyramid to ensure their ongoing effect.[60]

Although the Pyramid Texts are best approached for analysis in three major groups (Offering rituals, Resurrection Ritual and Morning Ritual) it is difficult to give a precise description for the episodes and continuity of each ritual.[61] On the basis of his study of the Cannibal Hymn within the Pyramid Texts, Eyre argues that the reconstruction of a liturgy within the Pyramid Texts should be an 'imaginative exercise,'[62] and needs to connect between the mythological and the ritual context of the spell. In addition, some other elements should be considered, such as where the spell was placed on the walls of the pyramid and its sequence. In fact, each pyramid should be dealt with as a unity and the ordering of the texts on the walls of the pyramids varies from one to another.[63] The Pyramid Texts are arranged mostly in vertical columns on the interior walls of each pyramid. The arrangement and the numbering of the Pyramid Texts since their initial publication by Sethe has caused confusion in referring to the actual orders and functions of these spells on the walls of each pyramid.[64] Sethe arranged the Pyramid Texts starting with the Pyramid of Unas and then Teti, Pepi I, Merenre, and Pepi II, in chronological order, but this arrangement does not reflect the actual order of the spells within each pyramid. This has led modern scholars of Egyptology to study the texts of each pyramid individually.[65]

Many of the Pyramid Texts spells were presented in the first person to be spoken by the deceased himself and thus personalising the text to an individual.[66] The shifting from the first person to the second person within the Pyramid Texts may refer to the fact that the origin of the Pyramid Texts was a papyrus roll, read by a priest and addressed to the deceased, and this shifting of the pronouns refers to the editorial revisions and thus personalising the text in each pyramid. In the pyramids of

[53] Most of the scenes which were even placed on the tomb walls before the 21st Dynasty were also placed on the sides of the coffins of this period; Niwinski, *GM* 49 (1981), 52.

[54] Hornung argues that the upper part of the coffin represents the east side and the lower part is the west, and that is why the scenes of the falcons and sunrise appear on the upper side while the lower side has the depiction of what refers to the west; Hornung, *Innerrhoder Geschichtsfreund* 28 (1984), 8 (quoted from Heyne, in: *Fs Hornung*, 62).

[55] On Middle Kingdom liturgies in the Coffin Texts, see Assmann, *Totenliturgien*. I, for the liturgies in the Book of the Dead and tombs of the New Kingdom, see Assmann, *Totenliturgien*. II; for the Late Period liturgies, see Assmann, *Totenliturgien*, III.

[56] Van Gennep, *The Rites of Passage*.

[57] His physical status will be restored by undergoing the mummification ritual, while his social status will be restored by passing safely through the judgment of the dead: Assmann, *Death and Salvation*, 270-6.

[58] Allen, in: *Hommages Lecalnt* I, 5-28. For the full discussion on the placing of the spell of the Cannibal Hymn on the walls of the pyramid of Unas, see Eyre, *The Cannibal Hymn*, 41-7.

[59] Eyre argues that only the offering rituals in which lists show the items to be offered can be used as evidence of a ritual direction within the Pyramid Texts: Eyre, *The Cannibal Hymn*, 41.

[60] Allen, *The Ancient Egyptian Pyramid Texts*, 5.

[61] Allen, *The Ancient Egyptian Pyramid Texts*, 5-6.

[62] Eyre, *The Cannibal Hymn*, 40.

[63] Leclant, *in: Textes et Langages de l'Égypte pharaonique II*, 37-52.

[64] Sethe, *Die altägyptischen Pyramidentexte*, 22.

[65] Leclant (ed.), *Les Textes de la Pyramide de Pepy I^er^*.

[66] Allen, *The Ancient Egyptian Pyramid Texts*, 6.

Unas and Pepi these editorial corrections are very clear on entire wall sections.[67]

The attempt made by Allen at reconstructing the texts within the pyramid of Unas is unique.[68] Allen tries to treat the material architecture as representation of the passage of the king from the underworld to the sky. Allen's analysis indicates that different spells with different content were placed on purpose in specific areas of the burial chambers of the pyramid, implying that the texts and architecture worked together to ensure an eternal life for the king. The individual spells within the pyramid chambers are grouped together in what he called sequences of the spells. The texts begin from the burial chamber (*dw3t*), and they proceed through the space to the antechamber (*3ḫt*) and then to the corridors and the doorway. The whole architecture of the Pyramid of Unas is simply representing the same theme that is represented on the walls of the New Kingdom tombs, referring to the path of the sun from the west to the east. The sun dies in the west, uniting with Osiris in the Duat and rising in the east.[69] The only difference between the Old Kingdom pyramids and the New Kingdom tombs is that the New Kingdom tombs are illustrated, while the Old Kingdom pyramids present only the texts for recitation.[70]

The same methodology was used by Vischak to argue that the same concordance occurs in the tombs of the elite of the Old Kingdom, exemplified in the case of the decoration of the tomb of Ankhmahor.[71] The only difference between the two methods is the use of mainly pictorial representations rather than texts on the private tomb walls.

In the Coffin Texts, decorations, orientation of the texts, titles, rubrics and glosses are of great importance.[72] They provide evidence of how, when and by whom the ritual might be performed. In the Middle Kingdom coffins, the decoration consists of text bands, and usually goes with the placing of the body of the deceased on its left side and thus facing east.[73] The long back west side is inscribed with texts for Anubis as the patron of the western desert, and thus good burial for the deceased in the west is ensured.[74] On the front (eastern) side, an invocation offering is inscribed for Osiris as provider of offerings and thus connected with the east. The east side of the coffin is the place of communication between the living and the dead. For that reason the offering formulae invoking Osiris as Foremost of the West is inscribed on the east.[75] The place of the offering tables in Old Kingdom tombs was the east. The east was also the place of the sunrise. Osiris was the god of resurrection, and the east was the place where the sun was born every morning.[76]

Gods and goddesses, as shown above, were placed on specific parts of the coffin protecting the deceased with their speeches and also form a constellation around the body of the deceased within the coffin. Their speeches were pronounced by priests participating in the performance of the ritual.

Titles, as Willems argue, 'place the text to which it belongs in ceremonial context.'[77] Unfortunately, de Buck was not interested in the titles of the spells and did not pay full attention to them. In the case of the Shu spells, for instance, he argues, 'the using of titles to a spell is only of a limited interest for a proper assessment',[78] and they are, according to de Buck, later additions, which do not necessarily correspond with the original purpose of the text.[79] The titles and rubric can occur at the beginning or at the end of a spell. For instance CT spell 1082 (*CT* VII 354c) has the label 'Spell for being in Rosetau'.[80] These titles and labels explain what exactly the purpose of a spell is, but there are some explanatory labels that are less than clear. In such cases the ancient editors of the Coffin Texts used some other language construction that helps in explaining the purpose of a spell.[81] To bring attention to something that needs to be stressed, they used, for instance, *jr* + a nominal construction, which puts stress on a particular nominal part of a spell: for instance, in CT 1081, 'As for anyone who is seen there alive, he cannot perish (*skj*)'.[82]

Glosses are no less important than titles, and they can explain what might be obscure for a modern reader. CT 335, which occurs in 33 sources collected from different sites in Egypt, is the best such example. In *CT* IV 188-189a, the text reads 'I am the Great One who came into being himself'. A gloss on coffin B9Ca adds 'Who is he, the Great One who came into being himself? He is Nun, the primeval water'. The explanatory glosses in some spells can take more space than the main text. For instance, CT 339 (*CT* IV 238a-239c) reads, 'I raised the hair from the sacred *wḏ3t* Eyes in the time of the rage'. The glosses in most sources of the spell explain this in more detail: 'What really is the sacred *wḏ3t* Eye in the

---

[67] Allen, *The Ancient Egyptian Pyramid Texts*, 6.
[68] Allen, in: *Hommages Leclant* I, 5-28.
[69] Allen, in: *Hommages Leclant* I, 24.
[70] Allen, in: *Hommages Leclant* I, 24-8.
[71] Vischak, *JARCE* 40 (2003), 133-57.
[72] For the importance of the titles to a ritual, see Willems, in: Willems (ed.), *The World of the Coffin Texts*, 203-7.
[73] Willems, *Chests of Life*, 122-4; *The Coffin of Heqata*, 364.
[74] Willems, *Chests of Life*, 124.
[75] Lapp, *Die Opferformel des Alten Reichs*, 233.
[76] This back (west) and the front (east) sides of the coffin are not arranged in the same way on coffins from Asyut, but they replaced each other: Willems, *Chests of Life*, 118-122. This may have been done because the artists in Asyut noted that the orientation of their necropolis was not ideal, and they have to reverse the two sides of the coffin to go with the orientation of cosmos: Bleiberg, in: *Studies Redford*, 118-9.
[77] Willems, *The Coffin of Heqata*, 276.
[78] Willems, *The Coffin of Heqata*, 197; in: Willems (ed.), *The World of the Coffin Texts*, 272.
[79] Willems, *The Coffin of Heqata*, 273; in: Willems (ed.), *The World of the Coffin Texts*, 198.
[80] Silverman, in: Allen et al., *Religion and Philosophy in Ancient Egypt*, 35.
[81] Silverman, in: Allen et al., *Religion and Philosophy in Ancient Egypt*, 35.
[82] *CT* VII, 354a (spell 1081).

time of the rage?' (and) 'Who actually raised the hair from it?' 'It is the right Eye of Re' is the answer.[83]

Not all Coffin Texts are provided with titles and glosses, and in this case the object frieze can give a clue to the ritual context of a spell. Jéquier's fundamental study focuses on the individual objects rather than presenting the object frieze as a whole.[84] The object frieze is simply a register showing the items and the implements to be offered to the deceased during ritual. The objects within the register are usually depicted standing on a table, and they are accompanied by explanatory labels, which may occur in a register above the objects or distributed among them.[85] The object frieze and the placing of the spell on the coffin can provide information on the performance of certain rituals. It helps explain the religious texts inscribed on the inner and outer parts of Middle Kingdom coffins.[86]

Jéquier argues that the object frieze usually replaces other items that are not among the tomb equipment. Willems rejects this suggestion, arguing that the items represented within the object frieze are those used as funerary equipment of the deceased in his tomb.[87] Willems's argument seems convincing. For instance, the object frieze on the back of the coffin of Mentuhotep (T1Be) shows a headrest, and the spell inscribed below is for offering a headrest (CT spell 823).[88] Among the funerary equipment of the tomb of Mentuhotep, a headrest was found, which in turn can be evidence that the object frieze depicts the ideal tomb inventory. The object frieze is not the same on all coffins, and neither are the items represented. In many cases there is a locational relationship between the frieze objects on the sides of the coffin and the parts of the body buried in it: for instance, representations of a headrest on the head end of coffin B2BO, wigs on the head end of coffin S10C, and masks on coffin AIC.[89] However, this arrangement of the objects is not the same on all coffins. The headrest on the coffin of Mentuhotep (T1Be) is depicted on the back because the back of a coffin, near the back of the head, can be the proper place for the headrest behind the head.

In some other CT spells, where titles and the object frieze do not exist, the stages of a particular ritual can be shown.[90] Spells giving stage directions indicate how a ritual should be performed. For instance, CT spell 925 deals with the offering of seven unguents and reads, '*smr* priest. The chest (*hn*) is opened; oil (*mrḥt*) is brought before this N'. Although the text does not give detailed directions for the performance of the ritual, it can be envisaged that a *smr* priest is the one who will perform this part of the ritual, and that the tools (the chest and the oil) needed for performing the ritual exist.[91]

In his work on Middle Kingdom coffins, Willems argues that reconstructing rituals depending on the coffin decorations is impossible. He argues:

'It is as if we are visiting the backstage storeroom of a theatre, where we may perceive the attributes used by the players without, however, knowing for which play or plays they are intended'.[92]

Willems succeeded in reconstructing rituals on Middle Kingdom coffin using texts and pictorial material elsewhere in pyramid texts and tomb paintings from the New Kingdom, and by comparing these with the ornamental texts, iconography on Middle Kingdom coffins, and coffin texts, he was able to find ritual functions for large portions of these Middle Kingdom Coffin Texts, such the offering of a headrest to the deceased in CT spell 823, mentioned above.

The same traditions survived during the New Kingdom on the anthropoid coffins. Niwinski notes that the scenes of burial and mummy transport, offerings, and mourners occur on the white anthropoid coffins of the 18th Dynasty.[93] The same old traditions of placing ornamental texts as evidence for ritual practice survived on the anthropoid coffins. *ḏd mdw* formulae are the divine speeches by the gods and goddesses on these coffins. These formulae are known from coffins and sarcophagi of all periods. As with most of the coffin decorations, these texts have been understood as divine speeches by gods and goddesses, without ritual functions. However, Assmann,[94] Watikus[95] and then Willems[96] have interpreted them as ritual texts and the divinities who pronounce them as represented by priests during the enactment of the myths in the funerary ritual.[97] Through pronunciation of the texts, the divine world (mythological world of the gods) and the world of the living (where they are recited) are connected together by the power of word. Language plays the role of the actions, and all these actions were performed in the cult of the deceased and at the same time in the realm of the gods. The priest approaches the divine world not as a human but as a member of the divine world itself. Through his recitation of the spell, the communication between this world and the divine world takes place, where the priest is a member of the gods.[98] These speeches were recorded on the coffin sides in words and kept in writing and in turn can be used

---

[83] Silverman, in: Allen et al., *Religion and Philosophy in Ancient Egypt*, 37.
[84] Jequier, *Les frises d'objets des sarcophages du Moyen Empire*.
[85] Willems, *Chests of Life*, 202.
[86] Willems, *Chests of Life*, 200.
[87] Willems, *Chests of Life*, 209-211.
[88] *CT* VII, 23L-24F (spell 823); for the ritual of the offering of a headrest within CT spell 823, see Abbas, 'Coffin Texts Spell 823 and the Rites of Passage: The Archaeological Context of the Coffin of Mentuhotep', In: Kousoulis et al, *Proceedings of the Tenth International Congress of Egyptologists, University of the Aegean, Rhodes, 22-29 May 2008* (forthcoming).
[89] Willems, *Chests of Life*, 209.
[90] Willems, *The Coffin of Heqata*, 151.

[91] Willems, *The Coffin of Heqata*, 151; for more examples of a similar relation between the Coffin Texts and the object frieze, see Willems, *Chests of Life*, 203-6.
[92] Willems, in: *Essays te Velde*, 343.
[93] Niwinski, *21st Dynasty Coffins from Thebes*, 11.
[94] Assmann, *MDAIK* 28.1 (1972), 47-73; *MDAIK* 28.2 (1972), 115-139; Assmann, *Das Grab der Mutirdis*, 92-93.
[95] Waitkus, *GM* 99 (1987), 68-70.
[96] Willems, *Chests of Life*, 141-159.
[97] Willems, *Chests of Life*, 198.
[98] Assmann, *Death and Salvation*, 244-6.

in the cult of the deceased. For instance, in Assmann's words:

> 'As artificial voice, writing was intended to extend cultic recitations beyond the time span of its ritual performance and to keep the deceased forever within the range of the priestly voice. In this function it served to realize permanent recitation'.[99]

This role of the spoken word is made explicit in mortuary liturgies, which were texts intended for recitation in the mortuary cult of the deceased. The recitation of these texts as a rite of passage mediates the passage of the deceased to his new state as an *3ḫ*.[100] The texts and also images on Egyptian coffins were not placed haphazardly: every single image and text would have a function to fulfil.

On the 21st Dynasty coffins, the speeches of the gods, as we will see on the two coffins of *P3-dj-jmn*, continue to be in use. No serious attempt has been taken to interpret the images on these coffins as renderings of certain rituals. I am aware of a single study by Anders Bettum on a coffin dating to the 21st Dynasty at Oslo Museum. In this study, Bettum concluded that the scenes on these coffins (described by him as icons) concentrate only on the mythical aspects of the rituals and it is difficult to reconstruct rituals on these coffins using only icons.[101]

It is my aim in this book to deal with these divine speeches of the gods and goddesses and the different scenes on the coffin sides as renderings of certain rituals, and to show how the images and speeches on the coffins can be envisaged as a single unity.

### *1.3. The 21st Dynasty and the Rise of the Priests of Amun in Thebes*

It is not my aim here to go into the details of the chronology of the 21st Dynasty and its history, but I will give a brief account on the transition from the 20th to the 21st Dynasty. The 21st Dynasty is marked by the end of the glory of the Egyptian empire of the New Kingdom and the beginning of the Third Intermediate Period, when Egypt faced the famine described in historical sources as the Year of the Hyenas. It also marks the severe economic regress in Egypt that followed the collapse of the Egyptian empire. The end of the 20th Dynasty saw civil war in Egypt and the loss of control over Nubia. After the civil war started, Ramesses XI announced the *wḥm mswt* the 'Repetition of Birth'[102] or the renaissance, reflecting the rulers' attempts to ritually re-establish order after a period of chaos.[103] This also means the establishment of *Maat*, the concept of order against the chaos or *jsft* that the country was experiencing.[104] The period of the renaissance lasted from the end of the civil war until the death of Ramesses XI.[105] From the late years of the reign of King Ramesses IX, Egypt experienced bad economic and social conditions, with famine causing an increase in food prices and a lack of respect for the kings who were supposed to be responsible for the maintenance of order or *Maat*. This lack of respect was not only for the living kings, but also for the dead. As a result, private and royal tombs in the Theban necropolis were violently robbed.[106] For that reason, a national program for rescuing the mummies in the Theban necropolis was launched and also sanctioned in the doctrines of the *wḥm nswt*.[107]

After the death of Ramesses XI the country was divided into two provinces, with capitals in Thebes and in Tanis and a vice-regent at the head of each province. These rulers held other titles of power, such as head or chief of the military power, priest of Amun and also vizier.[108] The king kept supremacy over the two vice-regents. Smendes ruled in the north and Herihor in the south. Smendes remained in office for a long time, and he is the one who took over the throne of Egypt after the death of Ramesses XI. Herihor died in Thebes after a short period of vice-regency during the reign of Ramesses XI. Herihor was followed by Piankh, who also died during the reign of Ramesses XI, and after his death Pinudjem 1st followed him in the office of the High Priest of Amun in the south, with the other titles.[109]

With the death of King Ramesses XI, the 20th Dynasty as well as the era of Renaissance ended and a new dating appeared in texts based on the Tanite Kings. At this time, a formal agreement was drawn up between Smendes and Pinudjem 1st, respecting each other's spheres of influence. Smendes and his heirs were to be recognized by Theban priests as the real and legitimate kings of Egypt as long as the priests were recognized by the northern king as military commanders and High Priests of Amun at Thebes. This agreement was confirmed by intermarriages between the northern kings and the upper Egyptian priests of Amun.[110]

The political and major economic and social decisions were taken or reached through the oracle of the triad of Amun-Re, Mut and Khonsu in Thebes. This meant that the King and the High Priest of Amun were the only ones who could interpret these oracles. It also meant that the King and the High Priest became the mediators between the gods and the people, which might explain why the 21st Dynasty has been described as the 'theocracy of Amun'.[111] The great political decisions could only be made through Amun-Re, whose will and oracle could

[99] Assmann, *Death and Salvation*, 249. See also, Assmann, *Totenliturgien* I, 53.
[100] Assmann, *Death and Salvation*, 238, 249; *Totenliturgien* I, 14-5; the same can also be said about the *Verklärungssprüchen*, the aim of which is to mediate the passage of the deceased to his new state of an *3ḫ*. Assmann, *Totenliturgien* III, 26-31.
[101] Bettum, *Death as an Eternal Process.*
[102] van Dijk, in: Shaw (ed.), *The Oxford History of Ancient Egypt*, 309.
[103] Niwinski, in: Uehlinger (ed.), *Image as Media*, 30.
[104] Niwinski, *BSFE* 136 (1996), 18.
[105] Goff, *Symbols of Ancient Egypt in the Late Period*, 51.
[106] Niwinski, *21st Dynasty Coffins from Thebes*, 38.
[107] Niwinski, in: Uehlinger (ed.), *Image as Media*, 30-6.
[108] Niwinski, *21st Dynasty Coffins from Thebes*, 39.
[109] Niwinski, *21st Dynasty Coffins from Thebes*, 39.
[110] Kitchen, *The Third Intermediate Period*, 256.
[111] Bettum, *Death as Eternal Process*, 56-7.

only be interpreted by the King and the High Priest. This elevated the status of Amun-Re as a creator god, now higher than the king himself and any other god. The role of the king was reduced to an oracle reader. This also might explain why Wenamun described in his report how Egypt's trade affairs with the Levant were in disrepute, because the pharaoh was no longer feared and respected as before.[112] Egypt during this Period could be described as being ruled by religion, where every state official held priestly title, as the god was now the head of the state and every member or every servant of the state was a servant of the god or simply a priest.[113]

The relations between the north and south remained peaceful despite the division of the power between the priests in the south and kings in the north. As mentioned before, relations between the north and south were strengthened by intermarriages.[114]

The 21st Dynasty has long been described as a period of decline in both political and cultural aspects, but the evidence is otherwise. Great national and royal building projects were no less than during the Late Ramesside Period.[115] Also, the art of mummification, the production of coffins, and the accompanying theology reached their peak.[116] The Instructions of Amenmope, described as one of the greatest works in the literary genre of instructions, tells of how great to live according to the rules of Maat. The 21st Dynasty has been described as the Late New Kingdom rather than the Third Intermediate Period due to the continuation of artistic trends of the New Kingdom in funerary art.[117] It was not a time of decline, as sometimes described, but instead a dynamic era in which its cultural products, especially mortuary practices, exhibited a creative tension between tradition and innovation.

The 21st Dynasty is also known for introducing new iconographic motifs, which found their way onto the coffin sides. These images and scenes, as will be seen from the coffin of *P3-dj-jmn*, refer to ideas that were expressed in texts in earlier periods. Richly decorated tombs were no longer built during this period and the coffin, as mentioned above, became the tomb itself. Religious scenes referring to certain rituals were placed on the coffin's outer and inner sides instead of on tomb walls. This poses the question why such coffins existed during this period. To answer this question, it is important to discuss briefly the archaeological context of the coffins of *P3-dj-jmn*.

### *1.4. The Archaeological Context of the Coffin Ensemble of P3-dj-jmn*

There are two famous caches for the coffins of the High Priests of Amun from the 21st Dynasty. The first is the Royal cache at Deir el-Bahri or the First Finding of Deir el-Bahri. This was discovered in 1881 in TT 320. The tomb's discovery goes back to the family of Abd el-Rassoul who found the tomb in 1875 and it was plundered by the family for more than five years before the official discovery announced in 1881in the south valley of Deir el-Bahri. This cache had the royal mummies and coffins of the most famous kings of Egypt and fourteen coffins belonging to the elite members of the 21st Dynasty.[118] The Second cache was found in the tomb of Bab el-Gassus. Described as the Second Find of Deir el-Bahri, this has the greatest number of coffins of the High Priests of Amun from the 21st Dynasty. The tomb, discovered by Daressy and Bouriant in 1891, included 153 coffins, including 101 doubles sets of coffins.[119] This is the greatest and the most important discovery of the 21st Dynasty tombs. The coffin of *P3-dj-jmn* was found at the tomb of Bab el-Gassus.

The tomb of Bab el-Gassus is very close in design to TT 320. It seems to have been constructed on two stages, as was TT 320. Niwinksi attributes the two tombs to the same period and also to the 'same authorship'.[120] He argues that the tomb must have finished during the reign of Psusennes II.[121] When discovered, the Bab el-Gassus tomb located at the front of the temple of Hatshepsut seemed to be untouched by the hands of tomb robbers. No other decorated tomb dating to the 21st has been found in Thebes, which poses the question of whether the tomb of Bab el-Gassus was used as a collective tomb or a 'group burials'[122] for the priests of the 21st Dynasty. It is also not clear if the owners of the coffins found within the tomb of Bab el-Gassus had their tombs near Deir el-Bahri or not. Although Niwinski dates the tomb to the reign of Psusennes II, it is hard if not impossible to date undecorated tombs and particularly when they have been reused through the following centuries. There is also evidence that the priests of the 21st Dynasty were buried in the precinct in the temples of Medient Habu, Deir el-Bahri and Ramessum. These temples were in active use during this period with the ancestor worship of Thebes, where deified Kings and private persons were venerated.

---

112 Lichtheim, *Ancient Egyptian literature* II, 224-30.

113 Niwinski, *21st Dynasty Coffins from Thebes*, 15.

114 There was a fortress built by the southern rulers around all Upper Egypt until the borders north of Fayyum. This fortress was not against the northern but to prevent the Libyan Tribes who were attacking the valley. These Libyan Tribes named Meshwesh and Libu were attacking Egypt since the time of Merenptah when they made alliance with the Sea People, but they were defeated. Their influence on Egyptian society did not end with their defeat during the reign of Merenptah. Because of the shortage of food and the pressure they faced by the sea people, they immigrated to Egypt and settled in 12th and 13th Centuries. They then joined the army and some families gained wealth especially during the resign of Ramesses XI until they succeeded later in ruling Egypt; Shaw, in: Shaw (ed.), *The Oxford history of ancient Egypt*, 328; van Dijk, in: Shaw (ed.), *The Oxford history of ancient Egypt*, 306-9; Taylor, in: Shaw (ed.), *The Oxford history of ancient Egypt*, 333-9; Leahy, *Libyan Studies* 16 (1985), 53.

115 Niwinski, in: Hawass et al, *Egyptology at the dawn of the twenty-first century* II, 417.

116 Niwinski , *JEOL* 30 (1989), 89; see also, Taylor, in: Wendrich (ed.), *Egyptian Archaeology*, 230-3.

117 Niwinski, in: Hawass et al, *Egyptology at the dawn of the twenty-first century*, 416-8.

118 Niwinski, *JEA* 70 (1984), 74; *21st Dynasty Coffins from Thebes*, 24-5.

119 Niwinski, *21st Dynasty Coffins from Thebes*, 26.

120 Niwinski, *JEA* 70 (1984), 74.

121 Niwinski, *JEA* 70 (1984), 73-8; *21st Dynasty Coffins from Thebes*, 25-6.

122 Taylor. In: Wendrich (ed.), *Egyptian Arachaeology*, 229.

In the Festival of the Beautiful Valley a procession was led through the necropolis of Thebes venerating the dead ancestors and the final stop was at the temple of Deir el-Bahri with the existence of the temple of Mentuhotep Nebeheptre and the funerary temple of Thuhmosis III, the area was a perfect place for the worship of the ancestors. This might also indicate that there should have been some tombs for the priests around this area that have not been found. Niwinski also argues that the kings' tombs that have not been found in the Valley of the Kings might also be located within this area.[123]

Tomb robbers are known since the Old Kingdom and tomb builders followed different ways to prevent tomb robbery.[124] These attempts continued during successive periods of Egyptian history. For instance, in the New Kingdom, kings had chosen the Valley of the Kings as a place of burial, but this cemetery was violated by tomb robbers, as well attested by several documents handed down to us relating tomb robbery during the Late New Kingdom.[125] This might have been the main reason why the southern rulers of Egypt carried out a project to rescue the royal mummies from the Valley of the Kings, where the tombs of Seti I and Ramesses II were opened according to the orders of Herihor and the kings' mummies moved to the temple of Medinet Habu.[126] It is even recorded that all the tombs in the Valley of the Kings were reopened and the mummies moved to a new tomb, with new wrappings and placed in new coffins. It is still also not clear whether the mummies found in the Royal Cache in TT 320 are all those that were moved or whether there are other caches that have not yet been discovered.

The social and economic situation in Egypt had changed by the end of the 19th Dynasty and the beginning of the 20th. Documents show that building well decorated and furnished tombs had decreased.[127] The poor economic circumstances encouraged many people to enter the tombs for robbery or for using their funerary equipment. During the 20th Dynasty, textual evidence shows that even the Theban elite were not capable of building tomb chapels or burial chambers.[128] The people who were able to commission tombs at this time are those who were actually controlling the west bank economically and politically, the High Priests of Amun,[129] but even their tombs were in most cases reused burial chambers. A graffito found at the Deir El-Medina necropolis, dating to the 21st Dynasty, relates that Butehamun, scribe of the necropolis was buried in a reused 18th Dynasty tomb, that of Nakhtmin (TT 291).[130]

The tomb of Bab el-Gassus and the tomb of the royal caches were made inaccessible and their burial chambers were lowered to keep them safe from tomb robbers. Hiding the burial chamber was not the invention of the 21st Dynasty, but the lowering of the burial chamber and hiding it is first attested in the tomb of Ramesess XI (KV 4), where in the middle of the burial chamber there is a 12 meter shaft dug deep into the ground. The burial chambers in the tombs of Bab el-Gassus and the royal cache were designed in the same way.

The Bab el-Gassus tomb is a group burial[131] and does not have a superstructure for rituals to be carried out for the deceased on the day of burial or festival days. The tomb was normally a place where the contact between the living, dead and also gods took place, and with the absence of tomb superstructure and the inaccessibility of the burial chamber, where might such contact take place?

Takao Kikuchi argues that, due to the change in tomb design and architecture during the late New Kingdom and the 21st Dynasty, the tomb's function as a ritual place where the deceased, gods and the living came into contact disappeared. She also argues that the private houses of this period, as that of Butehamun in Medinet Habu, could function as a space for ritual practice for the dead. She studied the texts and the decoration program in the houses of Butehamun and the six priests' houses in Karnak Temples that date to the same period. She found that these houses could be regarded as places where the contact between the dead, living and the god can take place. They can also be places where the ritual practice for the dead took place on the day of burial and on various festivals.[132]

Niwinski, however, argues convincingly that the precinct of the temple of Hatshepsut and other temples such as Medinet Habu, Mentuhotep Nebheptre and Thuthmosis III, were places where the Opening of the Mouth and other rituals were carried out on the statues of the dead.[133] Families of the dead placed statues and offerings in the precincts of these temples. But does this mean that the tomb of Bab el-Gassus is a group burial that was reused more than once, or were these coffins moved to it at one time and the tomb then sealed? Did the people buried

[123] Niwinski, *21st Dynasty Coffins from Thebes*, 26.
[124] Kanawati, *The Tomb and Its Significance in Ancient Egypt*, 32-7.
[125] Goff, *Symbols of Ancient Egypt in the Late Period*, 46, 54-5.
[126] Goff, *Symbols of Ancient Egypt in the Late Period*, 47; Niwinski, *BSFE* 136 (1996), 16.
[127] Cooney, *JARCE* 47 (2011), 5.
[128] New type of tombs called *st-krs* is found in the documents of the 20th Dynasty which occurs in P. Bulaq X and O Petrie 18 which according to Cooney might refer to a place of burial within a family tomb, a space within exsiting burial and also a place of interment with others in a burial chamber; Cooney, *JARCE* 47 (2011), 9 and the documents listed there.
[129] Cooney, *JARCE* 47 (2011), 16.
[130] Cooney, *JARCE*, 2011, 8-9. The text reads: 'The West is yours. All Praised-Ones are hidden within it, wrongdoing will not enter it, nor any guilty person. The scribe Butehamun has moored there after an old age, his body sound and intact. Made by the scribe of the Necropolis Ankhefenamen'; the translation is after McDowell, *Village life*, 73. For other evidence of reusing ancestors burials, see Cooney, *JARCE* 47 (2011), 9-15.
[131] Taylor uses this term to describe the burials of the Third Intermediate Period; Taylor, in: Wendrich (ed.), *Egyptian Archaeology*, 229; see also Niwinski, *21st Dynasty Coffins from Thebes*, 26-29.
[132] Kikuchi, *MDAIK* 58 (2002), 343-71.
[133] Niwinski, *21st Dynasty Coffins from Thebes*, 29. These statues were most probably mad out of mud and this is why they have not survived; Nelson, in: Strudwick and Taylor (eds), *The Theban Necropolis*, 91.

there have original tombs, and were they at some point moved to the Bab el-Gasus tomb?

We have some evidence for the reburial of the priests within the tomb of Bab el-Gassus. For instance, on the footboard of the 21st Dynasty anthropoid inner coffin of a lady named *di-n-s-jmnt* in the Fine Arts Museum of Budapest, there are two lines of hieratic inscription on the footboard, reading:

The Chantress of Amun *di-n-s-jmnt* the justified, the *rmnw ḫnsw-[m?]*/////// the x+6th year of II *šmw*, day 20, taken to reburial.[134]

The signs are hard to read, but the inscriptions contain important information on reburial taking place on the west of Thebes during the 21st Dynasty. The text, according to Liptay, can be interpreted in the following way: a deceased whose name is *dj-s-jmnt* is reburied by a certain *rmn* called *ḫnsw-m-*[...]. The reburial (*wḥm ḳrst*) took place on the 20th day of the second month of *šmw* and the year is unidentified. The date seems to be close to that of the Beautiful Feast of the Valley, celebrated in the second half of the second month of *šmw*. Other coffins have similiar texts relating the reburial of their owners on the west bank of Thebes, and this might indicate that the priests buried within the Bab el-Gassus tomb had other tombs before being moved there.[135] The dating of the reburial, as shown above, might also reflect the fact the reburial was accompanied by rituals or included in ceremonies for the ancestors buried on the west bank.[136] There is also evidence that the priests of the 21st Dynasty were buried in the precinct in the temples of Deir el-Bahri,[137] Medinet Habu[138] and Ramesseum.[139] These temples were in active use during this period with the ancestor worship of Thebes, where deified Kings and private persons were venerated. Performing such rituals for the dead in temple precincts connected the funeral rituals of the dead with the temple festivals and daily rituals. The lack of security made people depend on temples as community funerary chapels.[140]

The tomb during the New Kingdom has three zones: the superstructure and middle section, including the tombs' open court and the interior tomb chapel, where the cult activity took place; and the lower structure, which includes the burial chamber and the coffin.[141] With these three zones, the tomb served as a place where the deceased's transformation took place. They worked together to ensure the deceased free movement in and out of the underworld and to facilitate his communication with the world of the living and the dead through painting, statue and stelae.[142] This function of the tomb seemed to have disappeared during the 21st Dynasty. Placing or moving the dead in group burials changed the Egyptian concept of the tomb as a dwelling place. Only one zone was left, the burial chamber with the coffin and the mummy.

Building huge and visible burials for the elite with funerary and tomb equipment, as Taylor argues, was abandoned not only because of the poor economic situation during this period but also because of the lack of security in the Theban necropolis of the west bank.[143] The tomb's function as a dwelling place was taken over by the coffin, which served not only as a body container but also as a ritual and resurrecting machine for the deceased placed inside it. With the absence of the tomb's three zones mentioned above, the coffin became the main and central element that named and also pictured the deceased, and it was also the means by which the deceased could have an existence in the world of the living. It served as a place of transformation that should carry everything necessary for the deceased to be transformed into an *3ḫ*. That is why, for instance, in one of the letters to the dead dating to the 21st Dynasty, a husband speaks to the coffin and not to his deceased wife inside it, which gives an indication that the coffin was believed to make contact with the dead and connect her with her living husband.[144] It functioned as a tomb, the sides of which were used as writing surface for texts and images. It also can be said that the coffin served as a tomb chapel for the deceased,[145] where the daily and afterlife scenes that had been on tomb walls were placed instead on the coffin sides during the 21st Dynasty.

### *1.5. The coffin Ensemble of P3-dj-jmn*

The coffin ensemble of *P3-dj-jmn* comes from the tomb of Bab el-Gassus excavated by Daressy and Bouriant in 1891. The tomb contained 153 coffins, including 101 doubles sets of coffins, which were later moved to Giza Museum.[146] These coffins were given A numbers by Daressy while they were still in *situ*, before being moved

[134] The transliteration and the translation are after, Liptay, *Coffins and Coffin Fragments of the Third Intermediate Period*, 10.
[135] Dodson, *JEA* 77 (1991), 181-2; Niwinski, *21st Dynasty Coffins from Thebes*, coffin No. 6 of Antwerp at the Museum Vleeshuis; Taylor, *Death and Afterlife*, 181, fig. 128.
[136] Liptay, *Coffins and Coffin Fragments of the Third Intermediate Period*, 10.
[137] Niwinski, *21st Dynasty Coffins from Thebes*, 26 and 29.
[138] The temple of Medinet Habu was used as a burial place for the 22nd High Priests of Amun and also for the God's Wives of Amun. These burials are located before the entrance of the main temple on the processional way as in the case of the elite tombs at Tanis; Hölscher, *The Excavation of Medinet Habu* V, 8-10, 17-30. The temple was also in use as a burial for the high-status elite of the 25th and 26th Dynasties as also the case with the temple of Deir el-Bahri, Sheikholeslami, in: Strudwick and Taylor (eds), *The Theban Necropolis*, 131-7.
[139] The Ramesseum was a place of burial for the elite during the 22nd Dynasty, Nelson, in: Strudwick and Taylor (eds), *The Theban Necropolis*, 90-92; Quibell, *The Ramesseum*.
[140] Cooney, *JARCE* 47 (2011), 19.

[141] Seyfried, K. J., in: Assmann et al, *Problems and Priorities in Egyptian Archaeology*, 219-53.
[142] Cooney, *JARCE* 47 (2011), 19.
[143] Taylor, in: Wendrich (ed.), *Egyptian Archaeology*, 237.
[144] This letter was written by the scribe of the necropolis Butehamun to his wife. The letter is O.IFAO 689. For the translation and commentary on the letter, see Frandsen, in: Demarèe and Egberts (eds), *Village Voices*, 31-50.
[145] Niwinski, *Studies on Illustrated Theban Papyri*, 34-36; van Valsem, *The Coffin of Djedmonthuiufankh*, 359-61 argues that the coffin's decorations cannot be renderings of the Ramesside tomb decorations, see also Aston, *Burial Assemblages of Dynasty 21-25*, 399, n. 3135.
[146] Niwinski, *The Second Find of Deir El-Bahri*, VII.

to Cairo Museum.[147] The coffin ensemble of *P3-dj-jmn* that concerns us here was numbered A 87[148] and CG 6080 for the lid of the outer coffin, CG 6081 for the case of the same coffin, CG 6082 for the lid of the inner coffin, CG 6079 for the case of the inner coffin and CG 6078 for the mummy cover.

The A numbering system by Daressy was given to locate the place of each individual coffin within the tomb of Bab el-Gassus and was later modified by Niwinski into a detailed map, in which he shows the location of single coffin. According to Niwinski's map the coffin ensemble of *P3-dj-jmn* was found in the lower corridor E.[149]

Not much is known about the priest *P3-dj-jmn*. His titles indicate that he was the God's Father, the Beloved, One Who Knows the Secrets of Amun and his Ennead Designated Priest, Front-bearer of Amun, *P3-dj-jmn* the Justified.[150]

The coffin ensemble of *P3-dj-jmn* is multicoloured, painted in red, green, and dark green on a yellow ground, then varnished. The interior of the both inner and outer cases have a red background and the two principle figures of Osiris on the inner of the outer case and Isis on the interior of the case of the inner coffin are multicoloured and varnished. The rest of the scenes on the interior of both cases are drawn in thin white lines.[151] The coffin ensemble is in a very good state of preservation; there are some spots on the original surface that do not affect the coffins. The beards on the inner lid and mummy cover are missing as well as the amulets once held in the hands of the deceased on the outer lid.[152]

As mentioned above, this study is not a typological one, but it is important to give a brief description for the typology of the coffin ensemble of *P3-dj-jmn*. According to the typological study of Niwinski on these coffins, the lids of the outer and inner coffins and the mummy cover of *P3-dj-imn* belong to the type IVB. In this type of lid the middle part of the collar is replaced by figural representations. This type of lid is also distinguished by its vivid colours, and it is similar in form and composition, especially the upper part, to those of the transitory type II B, with the exception that the middle part of the collar is replaced by figural representations. This type of lid is also characterized by the vertical compositions on its lower part. The side and border inscriptions on the lids are written vertically. The decorations are also distinguished by high degree of density [153]

The outer decorations of the cases of both the inner and outer coffins belong to type B. In this type, the exterior scenes on the case are separated from each other by vertical inscriptions.[154]

The interior decorations of the cases belong to type 2b. In this type the principle figure which occupies the floor board joins the decoration on the bottom with that on both sides, described by Niwinski as *centripetal* composition. The figures on the interior of the cases of the outer and inner coffins are painted on brick-red background, drawn in red lines and then multicoloured. The main central figures on the floor of both cases are represented with outstretched wings, the ends of which end at or touch the side walls of the cases.[155]

---

[147]This recording of coffin ensembles caused some problems later because of the heavy weight of the outer coffins; they were separated from the inner counterparts belonging to the same ensemble and which lasted during the transport of these coffins to Cairo Museum. This is as Niwinski argues has caused some problems when constructing coffin ensembles where the outer coffin got different numbers of the Journal of Entries than the inner coffins. At Cairo Museum, these coffins have been given CG numbers and some others have been given to museums all the over the world; Niwinski, *The Second Find of Deir El-Bahri,* VIII.

[148] Daressy, *ASAE* 1(1900), 141-148.

[149] Niwinski, *21st Dynasty Coffins from Thebes*, table I.

[150] These are the titles of *P3-dj-jmn* and which occur on the lower part of the lid of the outer coffin and the lower part of the lid of the inner coffin.

[151] Niwinski, *The Second Find of Deir El-Bahri*, 21.

[152] Niwinski, *The Second Find of Deir El-Bahri*, 21.

[153] Niwinski, *21st Dynasty Coffins from Thebes*, 79; *The Second Find of Deir El-Bahri*, 21.

[154] Niwinski, *21st Dynasty Coffins from Thebes*, 84-9; *The Second Find of Deir El-Bahri*, 21.

[155] Niwinski, *21st Dynasty Coffins from Thebes*, 90-5; *The Second Find of Deir El-Bahri*, 21.

## Chapter Two

## The Outer Coffin of *P3-dj-jmn* (CG 6080-6081)

### *2.1. The Lid of the Outer Coffin (CG 6080)*

#### *2.1.1. General Description of the Lid (Pl. I)*

The lid of the outer coffin of *P3-dj-jmn* is of the type IVB of Niwinski's typological work on these coffins. In this type of lid the middle part of the collar is replaced by figural representations. So, the sequence of the scenes starts from the part between the two hands of the owner of the coffin. The upper part of the lid of the outer coffin of *P3-dj-jmn* is the head of a man with a tripartite[156] wig and a false beard.[157] The ears and the beard were made separately and then attached to the mask. The wig is decorated with a broad ornamental headband. The breast and arms are covered with a *wsḫ* collar composed of parallel rows of various ornamental motifs.[158] The lowest of these ornamental motifs are lotus flowers. The floral motifs are life-giving emblems, especially the lotus, which is considered a symbol of resurrection.[159] The wide collar ends at the deceased's shoulders with two falcon heads (fig. 2).[160]

#### *2.1.2. The Upper Part of the Lid*

The decoration (images and texts) on the lid under the wide collar is divided into registers and is given numbers as shown below on fig. (1). The parts under the collar in this lid type[161] are divided into a number of horizontal decorative panels with vertical and horizontal stripes of inscriptions and ornaments. These are numbered as follows:

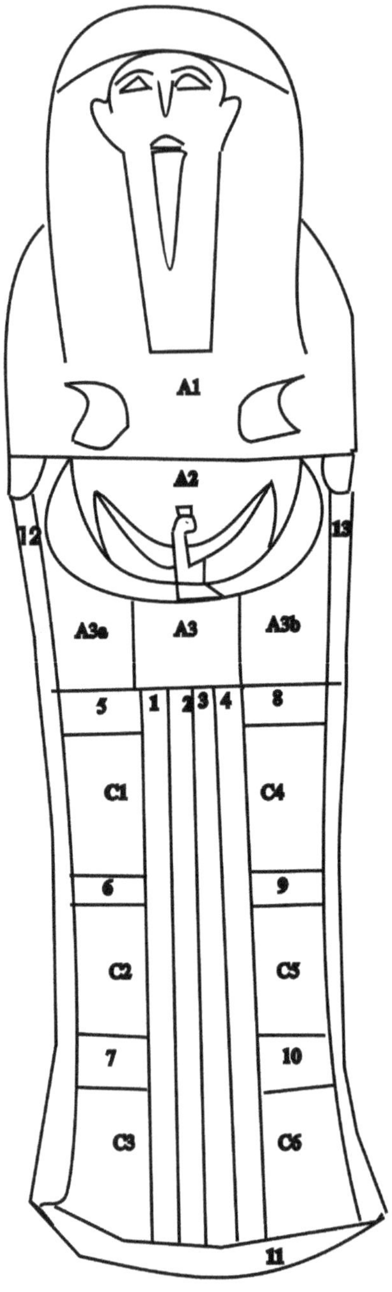


Fig. 1. The lid of the Outer coffin of *P3-dj-jmn*(CG 6080) with the numbers and letters showing the distribution of the texts and scenes (drawing by the author)

(A1) The central part under the collar shows a winged pectoral scarab standing on a *ḏd* 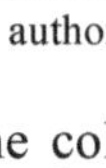 pillar. The scarab is surmounted by a solar disc protected by two cobras  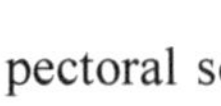  *bḥdtj*. The rectangular pectoral which surrounds the scarab is supported by a row of alternating signs of *ḏd*  and  *tjt* and crowned by a cornice decorated with a winged solar disc. Above the pectoral is a representation of a *sḫm* sign. On the two sides of this sign there are two jackals lying and wearing the double crowns with two *ꜥnḫ* 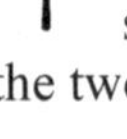 signs between their paws. A text is accompanying the two jackals and reads:

[156] This kind of wigs was typical for woman and male deities and then it was used by private individuals from the 6th Dynasty. During the New Kingdom this type of wigs became typical for both male and female deities and by having them on the coffins of the 21st Dynasty divine attributes to their owner were added; van Walsem, *The Coffin of Djedmonthuiufankh*, 109.

[157] The false beard designates the god Osiris and it is also a characteristic of male coffins and can never be found on female coffins; Bonnet, *RÄRG*, 80; *LÄ* I, 627-8. So, the deceased is here like Osiris. The blue colour of the hair, the beard and the varnish yellow which is a characteristic of all the coffin of the priests of Amun add divine aspects to the owner of the coffin and solar aspects of the sun god Re; van Walsem, *The Coffin of Djedmonthuiufankh*, 110.

[158] The *wsḫ* collar, as Niwinksi argues, might vary from a coffin to another and its size is used as a criterion for the dating of a coffin's lid. These collars might be covered with crossed arms and the forearms may be carved in relief and then painted or only painted. Some other collars might be covering the arms except for the hands and elbows and the carved forearms may be visible under the collar. Some other collars may cover the arms except for the hands and elbows and the carved forearms may be visible under the collar. Some collars may cover the arms without the hands and could reach under the belly. On the collar of *P3-dj-jmn* only the hands are visible and carved in relief; Niwinski, *21st Dynasty Coffins from Thebes*, 67 and 79.

[159] Weidner, *Lotos im alten Ägypten*, 120-9.

[160] Niwinski, *The Second Find of Deir El-Bahri*, 1-2, pl. I.

[161] Niwinski, *21st Dynasty Coffins from Thebes*, 67.

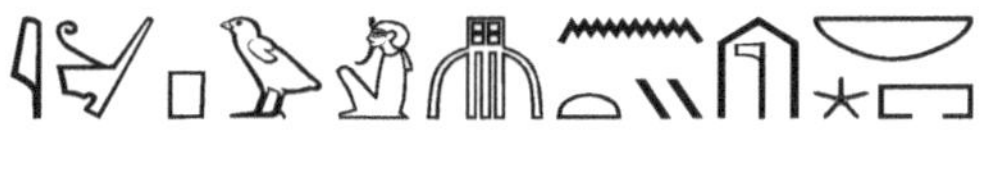

*jnpw ḫntj sḥ-nṯr nb dwꜣt*

Anubis Foremost of the Booth of the God, Lord of the Underworld.

Above the two jackals there are two *wḏꜣt* eyes. On the right and left sides on the jackals, there are two winged cobras protecting two small *wḏꜣt* eyes and *šn* ring. To the right and left of the pectoral are two *bꜣ* birds presenting offerings. The two birds are accompanied by a caption reading, (*ꜥnḫ n wsjr*). The birds are accompanied by two squatting figures in the shape of mummified headed jackals holding the feather of *Mꜣꜥt* and the *wḏꜣt* eyes. The whole scene is topped by the two clenched hands of the deceased, which once held carved amulets now lacking. On both sides below the collar are two painted crossed forearms, which have ornamental decorations. Below the forearms are two elbows decorated with lotus motif. The forearms consist of the motif of a winged cobra with solar disc, and Neith protecting *wḏꜣt* eye (fig. 2). Above the elbows is a Benu-bird with a composite crown accompanied by a lotus bound and a caption that reads:

*bnw nṯr ḫpr ḥꜣt dwꜣt*
The Benu God who exists in front of the Underworld.

Fig. 2. The upper part of the lid

### *2.1.2.1. Commentary and Analysis*

The upper part of the lid of the outer coffin of *Pꜣ-dj-jmn* is occupied by *wḏꜣt* eyes and offering texts related to Osiris and to Anubis. The lid is now divided into registers and refers to the same themes as on Middle Kingdom Coffins. The lid and outer decorations on the front side on Middle Kingdom coffins are reserved for offering formulae invoking Osiris and sometimes Anubis. On the lid of the coffin of *Pꜣ-dj-jmn*, one of the registers is occupied by images and text captions that relate the same themes as Middle Kingdom coffins. Anubis as patron of the necropolis is addressed here. The two *wḏꜣt* eyes were placed on the front side on Middle Kingdom coffins, which is also the east, to enable the deceased to watch the offering presented to him and also to watch the sunrise. On the lid of *Pꜣ-dj-jmn*, the two *wḏꜣt* eyes are placed just under the wig. The Middle Kingdom *wḏꜣt* eyes are replaced by the complete face of the deceased, which forms the upper part of the lid.[162] So, the deceased will be able to watch the offerings presented to him by the aid of his two eyes and the *wḏꜣt* eyes depicted under the collar.

The image of the scarab is a symbol of the newborn sun and the *ḏd* pillar is a reference to Osiris.[163] The deceased within the coffin is identified with both gods, and with the sunrise the deceased, who is Osiris, is born as an image of the scarab. This represents the movement from the underworld to heaven, and it also functions as a symbol of the solar resurrection in which the deceased wishes to participate.[164] The deceased is watching the sunrise, prelude the sun's journey across the sky. The scarab surmounted by a sun disc is a typical reference to the sunrise, and the depiction of the two *bꜣ* birds bringing offerings to the living Osiris is an indication of the identification of the deceased with both gods (Re and Osiris).

### *2.1.3. The Middle Part of the Lid*

(A 2) The middle part of the lid is occupied by the kneeling figure of the goddess Nut turning right. The goddess is depicted with outstretched wings and arms. Both arms hold the *ꜥnḫ* sign. On both sides of the head of the goddess Nut are two winged cobras protecting two *wḏꜣt* eyes with their outstretched arms. Just behind the end of the outstretched wings of Nut there are two standing figures. The figure to the left is a jackal-headed wearing the double crown and is a accompanied by a caption reading:

*jnpw ḫntj jmntt*
Anubis Foremost of the West

[162] Lüscher, *Totenbuch Spruch 151*, 115.
[163] Niwinski, *GM* 109 (1989), 53-66.
[164] Hornung and Staehelin, *Skarabäen und andere Siegelamulette aus Basler Sammlungen*, 14-5; Goff, *Symbols of Ancient Egypt in the Late Period:* 209-20. For a recent discussion on the scarab as personification of the sun god Re and as a symbol of resurrection see, Minas-Nerpel, *Der Gott Chepri.*

The figure on the right is a human-headed wearing the *Atef* crown and is accompanied by a text in which he gives offerings consisting of bulls, wine and bread (fig. 3).

Fig. 3. The middle part of the lid

#### *2.1.3.1. Commentary and Analysis*

On Middle Kingdom coffins the decoration of the lid was very simple. There are basic textual and decorative elements. First, lids were either flat or vaulted as in shrines. The decorative program on these lids consist of a single ornamental column of hieroglyphs running from the head to the feet, but by the end of the Middle Kingdom we can see three or four text registers on the lid instead of one.[165]

The text on these lids is an offering formula in which Anubis features as the Lord of Sepa and Foremost of the God's Booth, but the favours asked for him may vary. For instance, the deceased asks for happy passage to underworld. There are also different formulae following 'an offering which the king and Anbis give......'.[166] In addition to the offering formula to Anubis, some Middle Kingdom coffin lids also have a speech in which the goddess Nut is addressed as the deceased's mother, derived from *Pyr.* 638a and *Pyr.* 1607a-b. In these, the deceased is told, 'your mother Nut spreads herself over you, she causes you to be a god without enemies'.[167]

The lid on Middle and New Kingdom coffins is called mother of the deceased. The goddess Nut was the most prominent figure on the lid and sometimes was replaced by the goddess Neith.[168] Neith also replaced the goddess Nut on 21st Dynasty lids: for instance, on the lid of the outer coffin of Henuttawy, daughter of Pinedjem.[169] The deceased inside the coffin travels through her body as a star.[170] As a mother, the goddess Nut was depicted on the lid protecting the deceased.

On the coffin of *P3-dj-jmn* both Anubis and Nut feature on the lid. Anubis is depicted on the upper register (A 1) and there he is addressed as:

*jnpw ḫntj sḥ-nṯr nb dw3t*

Anubis Foremost of the god's booth, Lord of the Underworld.

Anubis is also addressed on the register at the middle of the lid as:

*jnpw ḫnty imntt*

Anubis Foremost of the West.

The goddess Nut is shown on the lid with outstretched wings. She is flanked by these figures on right and left. On the lower register there is a speech by the deceased addressing the goddess and asking her to spread her wings over him and to cause him to be among the imperishable stars.

#### *2.1.4. The Register under the Figure of the Goddess Nut*

A 3- The third register on the lid under the figure of the goddess Nut is a pectoral with a scarab in the middle and solar disc on the top. The pectoral is surmounted by a frieze of alternating signs of 𓋹 *ʿnḫ* and 𓄤 *nfr*. The solar disc is bordered by figures of falcons wearing the *Atef* crown and winged *wḏ3t* eyes with cobra (fig. 4). The depiction of the image of the falcon Hours with the sun disc and the *wḏ3t* eyes is a clear reference to the sun god Re and his regenerating power. The depiction of these falcons on the lid is significant. As we will see later that the connection between Osiris and Re is clear in the decoration program on the lid of the coffin of *P3-dj-jmn* and this depiction of the falcon as representation of Horus, the son of Re and also Osiris, justifies this identification of the two gods. [171] To the right and left of the pectoral there are two scenes.

---

[165] Willems, *Chests of Life*, 173.
[166] For a survey on the different *Bitten* asked for the deceased in the offering formula for Anubis see, Willems, *Chests of Life*, 173-4.
[167] Willems, *Chests of Life*, 174.
[168] Assmann, *MDAIK* 28.1 (1972), 47-73; *MDAIK* 28.2 (1972), 115-139.
[169] Neith and Nut can be replaced by a winged figure of a vulture as on the lid of the coffin of Maatkare (Daressy 61, 028), a falcon as in the case of the lid of the coffin of Pinedjem II, and a winged solar disc as in the case of the Cairo Museum inner coffin of Dirpu CG 6083; Goff, *Symbols of Ancient Egypt in the Late Period*, 94.
[170] Ikram and Dodson, *The Mummy in Ancient Egypt*, 193-6.
[171] Van Walsem, *The Coffin of Djedmonthuiufankh* , 119-20.

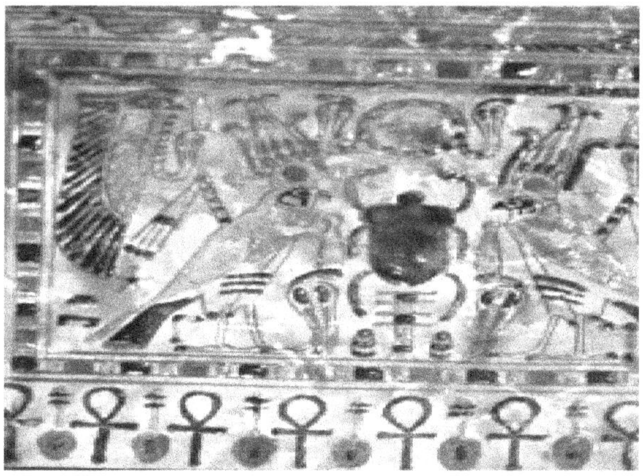

Fig. 4. The third register on the lid

(A3a) To the left the deceased is shown bringing offerings to Osiris who is seated on his throne and in front of him is a label which reads:

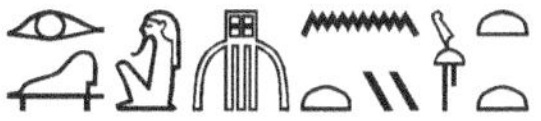

*wsjr ḫnt jmntt*

Osiris Foremost of the West.

The inscription is flanked by the winged *wḏ3t* eyes. Behind the deceased is a personification of *M3ʿt* standing and holds the emblem of the west, protecting the deceased. Above *M3ʿt* is a small squatting figure with the head of a baboon (fig. 5).

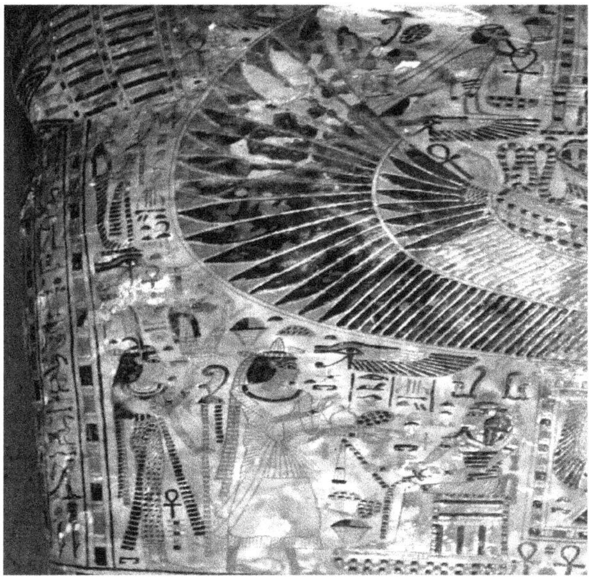

Fig. 5. The deceased brings offerings to Osiris

(A3b) To the right of the pectoral, the deceased is shown bringing offerings to a deity with a head of baboon and wearing the *Atef* crown. Behind the deceased stands lioness headed goddess with a cobra on her head[172] (fig.6).

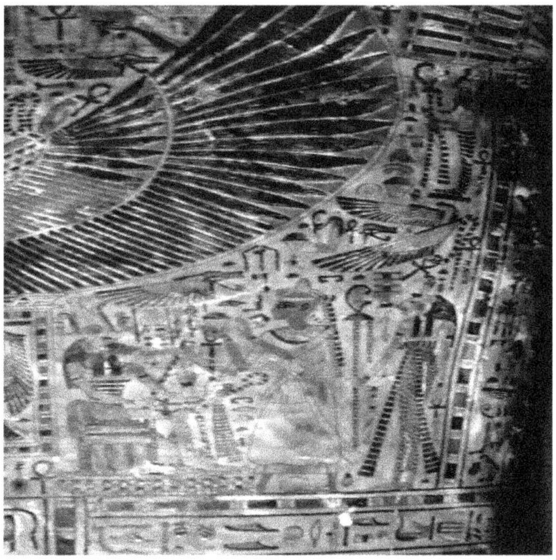

Fig. 6. The deceased brings offerings to a headed baboon deity

### *2.1.4.1. Commentary and Analysis*

On Middle Kingdom coffins, an offering formula for Osiris was placed on the front, facing east. As argued above, this has a connection with the placing of the offering tables during the Old Kingdom, when these tables were set on the east side of the tomb, and also to associate the deceased with the sunrise.[173] Osiris's connection with the sunrise is important here. This side on Middle Kingdom coffins also has the representation of a false door flanked by two *wḏ3t* eyes. The *wḏ3t* eyes and the offering formula were placed on the lid of the coffin of *P3-dj-jmn*. The reason for placing them on this side of the coffin is the changing of the body position within the coffin during this period. The body was placed on its back facing upwards, and the ritual scenes on these coffins go with the placing of the body within the coffin. Osiris's offering formula is now on the lid. The inscriptions in front of the image of Osiris describe him as:

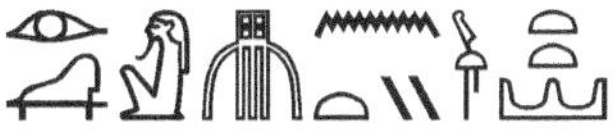

*wsjr ḫnt jmntt*

Osiris Foremost of the West.

The depiction of Osiris and the goddess Nut on this side will enable the deceased to watch the sunrise and to share in the daily cycle of the sun god Re. The deceased will travel in the body of Nut to be like the imperishable stars.

[172] Niwinski, *The Second Find of Deir El-Bahri*, 2.
[173] Willems, *Chests of Life*, 118-9

### *2.1.5. The Lower Part of the Lid*

#### *2.1.5.1. The Middle of the Lower Part of the Lid*

The lower part of the lid is divided into two parts by four columns of hieroglyphic inscriptions reaching to the borders of the feet. Each column begins with the same text giving the name and titles of the deceased and then continues with a different text (fig. 7). The columns of texts from the left to the right run as follows:

1 2 3 4

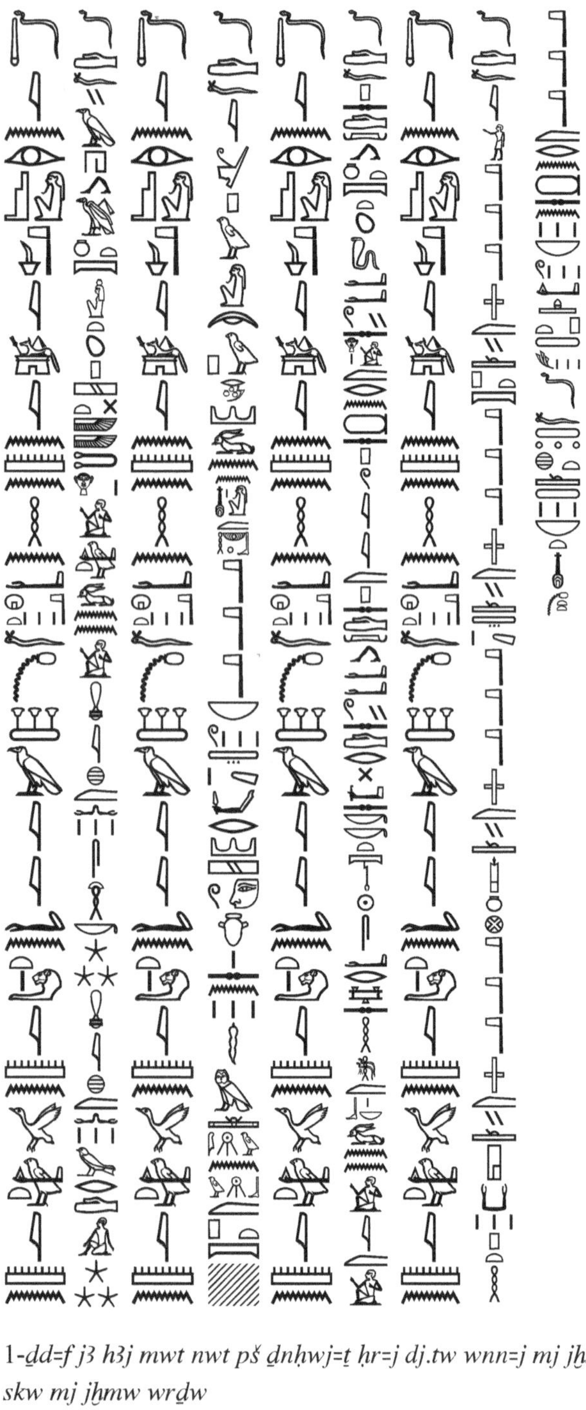

1-*ḏd=f jꜣ hꜣj mwt nwt pš ḏnḥwj=ṯ ḥr=j dj.tw wnn=j mj jḫmw skw mj jḫmw wrḏw*

He says: Oh mother Nut, spread your wings over me, and make me exist like the Imperishable Stars and the Unwearying Stars.

2-*ḏd=f (j) jnpw jʿḥ pw r mꜣnw wnn-nfr m ḥb nṯrw nbw tꜣ ḏsr ršw jb-sn nḏm šw wbn m pt*

He says: (Oh) Anubis, (Oh) moon at Manu, Wenennefer is in festival and all the gods of the necropolis their hearts rejoice and are happy (when) Shu is risen in the sky.

3-*ḏd=f psd (pḏ) nwt ʿwj=s ḥr=j m rn=s pwj m psd ʿwy=s dr=s kkwt sʿr ḥddwt m bw nb wnn=j jm=j*

He says: May Nut stretch her arms over me, in this her name of She who stretches her arms, and may she drive away darkness and bring up light in every place I am in.

4-*ḏd=f j nṯrw jmjw pt nṯrw jmjw tꜣ nṯrw jmjw jwnw nṯrw jmjw ḥwt-kꜣ-ptḥ nṯrw m rn=sn nbw dj ḥtp ḏfꜣw ḫt nbt nfrt wʿbt*

He says: Oh gods who are in the sky, gods who are in earth, gods who are in Heliopolis, gods who are in Memphis, gods in all their names, give offerings and provisions of every good and pure thing.

Fig. 7. Texts on the middle of the lower part of the lid

##### *2.1.5.1.1. Commentary and Analysis*

This part of the lid decoration, where the deceased is addressing several gods, has a ritual background.[174] The deceased's plea to Nut to spread her wings over him and to cause him to ascend to the sky simply refers to the deceased's journey to the sky. Before proceeding to this section it is important first to draw attention to the relation between the deceased inside the coffin and the lid

[174] There are some other examples where the deceased is addressing the lid itself asking her to open the doors of heaven for him so that he could see the god when he appears in the sky, to drink of the flood of the god, to sniff the fresh air and to see his beloved ones; Jansen-Winkeln, *Discussions in Egyptology* 30 (1994), 55-63.

of the coffin as representation of the sky and mother of the deceased. It is known that the divine king was the son of Re, who became Osiris when he died. So, the dead king, or any other deceased, becomes one of the actors in the myth of Osiris and Seth. When Osiris was assassinated by Seth, his integrity and the preservation of his body were the responsibility of both Isis and Nephthys, who played the major role in his survival and assumption of the rulership of the hereafter. Part of the netherworld belongs to the celestial expanses, and the stars, as Willems argues, were the souls of Osiris, and the deceased Osiris was their leader. Like Osiris, the sun god Re was considered as the father of Horus and the son of the sky goddess Nut and also travelled through the sky in her body. Through the daily cycle of the sun, Re was engaged in the process of death and resurrection. The association between Osiris and Re becomes clearer when the deceased as Osiris ascends to heaven to take his place in the solar barque.[175]

So, the deceased's plea to the goddess Nut to spread her wings and to cause him to ascend to the sky to be among the stars is a clear reference to his celestial journey. This journey of the deceased, who is here Osiris, is parallel to his journey to the west, which is evident from his speech to Anubis and the gods who are in festival at his arrival to the west. The appearance of the deceased and his arrival to the west is envisaged as his shining in the sky as Shu. The victory of the deceased over death is complemented by his speech to the goddess Nut as the one who is causing his ascent and the one who drives away darkness. The sign of the deceased's vindication is clear when he directs his speech to the gods who are in the Heliopolis, before whom he received his vindication in the hall of justice. The deceased also directs his speech to the gods of Memphis, which is a place where Horus was restored to the throne of his father Osiris and was justified by the tribunal against Seth in the temple of *ḥwt-ꜥ3t* in Memphis.[176] He also directs his speech to the gods of the sky and asks them to present offerings to him.

### *2.1.5.2. The Scenes on the Left Side*

The lower part of the lid is divided into horizontal registers on both sides, with ornamental scenes and vertical columns of texts in the middle. To the right and left of this part there are three scenes on each side. Each scene is represented inside a naos, the roof of which is supported by *ḏd* pillars composed of a frieze of cobras with solar discs. The scenes on the left side run as follows:

Scene 1 (C1. Text 5). The first scene is topped by a horizontal band of text which is written vertically and reads:

*ḏd mdw jn jm3ḫj ḫr wsjr ḫntj-jmntjw nṯr ꜥ3 nb*

[175] Willems, *Chests of life*, 134-136
[176] Assmann, *Sonnenhymnen in thebanischen Gräbern*, 46, n. g.

A speech by the Revered One before Osiris Foremost of the Westerners, the Great God, Lord of.........

The scene beneath the text shows the deceased wearing a cone and offering a vase before the standing figure of Osiris. Osiris is represented with the head of a falcon, with a cobra hanging from his crown (fig. 8). The cobra is followed by its name:

*njt ḥnwt nṯr*

Neith Chanteuse of the God.

Fig. 8. The deceased offers to Osiris

Scene 2- (C2. Text 6) On the top of the second scene there is a text that reads:

*ḏd mdw jn jm3ḫy ḫr 3st* [*wrt*] *mwt nṯr*

A speech by the Revered One before Isis [the Great] Mother of the God.

The scene shows the deceased offering a vase and lotus flower in front of a sacred falcon standing on a pedestal with winged *wḏ3t* eyes behind (fig. 9)

Fig. 9. The deceased offers to a falcon

Scene 3 (C3. Text 7). Above the scene there is a text that reads:

*ḏd mdw jn jm3ḫj ḫr ḥpj nb/////*

A speech by the Revered One with Hapi Lord of///////

This scene is mostly damaged but once contained the figure of the Weeper-Goddess kneeling in front of the sacred emblem of Abydos protected by the winged cobra.[177]

***2.1.5.3. The Scenes on the Right Side***

The other group of scenes is depicted on the opposite side of the lower part of the lid. These scenes on the right side run as follows:

Scene 1 (C4. Text 8)

Above the scene there is a text that reads:

*ḏd mdw jn jm3ḫy ḫr jnpw ḫntj ḳrst*

A speech by The Revered One with Anubis Foremost of the burial.

The deceased is shown offering a vase before the standing human-headed deity (fig. 10).[178]

Fig. 10. The deceased offers a vase

Scene 2 (C5. Text 9)

The text above the scene reads:

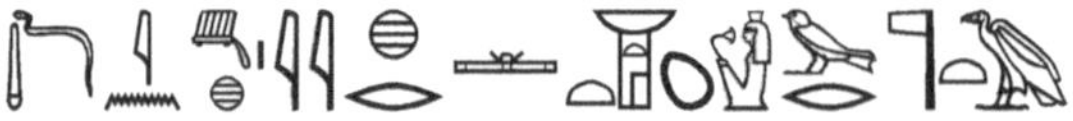

*ḏd mdw jn jm3ḫj ḫr nbt- ḥwt wrt mwt nṯr*

A speech by the Revered One with Nephthys the Great Mother of the God.

The deceased is shown offering incense and a vase to the sacred falcon (fig. 11).

Fig. 11. The deceased makes offering to a falcon

Scene 3 (C6. Text 10)

The text above the scene reads:

*ḏd mdw jn jm3ḫj ḫr dw3-mwt-f//////////*

A speech by the Revered One with [Dua]mutef.

The scene is mostly damaged, but most probably it showed the deceased offering to one of the deities, as on the opposite left side (fig. 12).

Fig. 12. The deceased makes offerings to a deity

The border of the feet was once inscribed, but the inscriptions are now lost and only traces of a text read (fig. 13. Text 11):

[177] Niwinski, *The Second Find of Deir El-Bahri*, 3
[178] Niwinski, *The Second Find of Deir El-Bahri*, 3

*ḏd mdw jn jm3ḫy ḫr*

A speech by the Revered One with

The surface of the lid and the inner lid are not decorated.

Fig. 13. Decorations at the foot end

### *2.1.6. The Borders of the Lid*

The borders on each side of the lid are covered by vertical columns of texts beginning underneath the elbow and run until the borders of the feet. These inscriptions from left to right read:

12 13

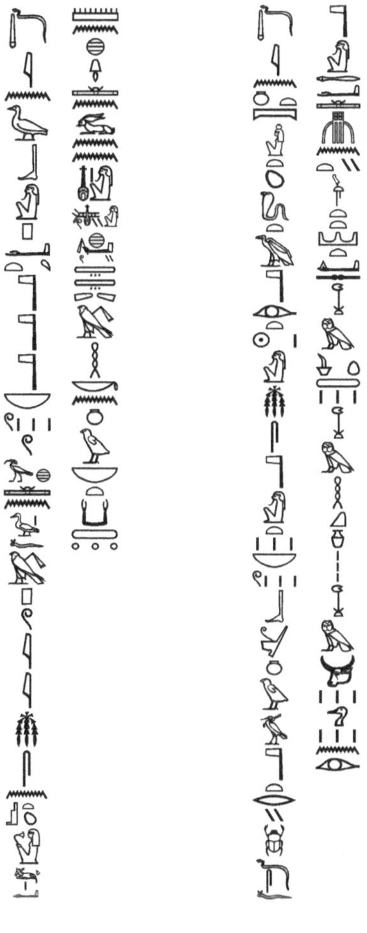

12-*ḏd mdw jn gbb pꜥt nṯrw nb 3ḫ n s3=f ḥr pwj ms.n 3st jwꜥ mnḫ n wnn-nfr nfr-tm ḫwj t3wy ḥr-ḥknw nb k3w*

A speech by Geb, Elite of all the Gods and the Beneficial One to his son, this Horus born of Isis, potent heir of Wenennefer (Osiris) Nefertem, Protector of the Two Lands, Horus Hekenu, Lord of Offerings.

13-*ḏd mdw jn nwt mwt nṯr jrt rꜥ ms nṯrw nbw bjnw nṯr ḫpr ḏs=f nṯr ꜥ3 ḫntj-jmntt dj=s ḫ3 m t ḫ3 m ḥnḳt ḫ3 m k3w 3bdw n wsjr*

A speech by Nut. Mother of the God and the Eye of Re who gave birth to all the Gods, *Benu* who came into existence by himself, the Great God and Foremost of the West: may she give a thousand of bread, thousand of beer, thousand of bulls and birds to Osiris.

The context of these two speeches by Geb and Nut is important here. The god and the goddess are flanking the border of the lid, in which there are also speeches by other gods. In text (2) above, the gods are happy and their hearts rejoice when they see the deceased shining as Shu. So, if the name of Shu reflects the notion of 'erecting oneself',[179] the deceased who is Shu stands erect and is flanked by both Geb and Nut. This also represents one of most common decorative motifs on the 21st Dynasty coffins. It might also refer to the deceased's journey in the spheres of both the sky and the underworld.

### *2.2. The Lid Decorations: Conclusion*

The texts on the two borders of the lid are forms of *Bitten*, in which the deceased is described as a venerated one (*jm3ḫj ḫr*) with a god. These gods are arranged in a particular order on this part of the lid. The texts are also accompanied by scenes in which the deceased is shown holding a vase, presumably containing unguents. Osiris is facing Anubis, Isis is facing Nephthys and finally Hapi is facing Duamutef. The frequent use of unguent vases might be related to the anointing scenes in the ritual of the Opening of the Mouth and connected with the Four Sons of Horus, representing the Canopic jars.[180] The use of vases also might be related to an offering ritual in which these vases were presented. Relevant equipment was found in the tombs containing these coffins. For instance, in the tomb of Deir El-Bahri from which a large cache of the 21st Dynasty coffins was found, garlands, fruit, and also a bronze stand holding four libation vases inscribed with the name of Astemakhbit, daughter of Menkheperre were found. There were also various kinds of offerings found in vases or baskets inscribed with her name. That might also recall the use of these objects in rituals taking place after burial on several occasions. This also means these coffins were not just placed in the tomb without accompanying rituals. The tomb of Psusennes contained ritual objects, including the *pesesh-kef* used in the ceremony of the Opening of the Mouth, a figurine of

[179] For the interpretation of the name of Shu as 'standing erect', see Willems, *The Coffin of Heqata*, 272 and the literature cited there.
[180] Van Walsem, *The Coffin of Djedmonthuiufankh*, 131.

Thoth, and a *ḏd* pillar.[181] The existence of these ritual objects reinforces the suggestion that they were used in rituals on or after the day of burial.[182]

It is clear now that the decoration and texts on the lid focus on three themes: first, the presentation of offerings by the deceased to several deities; second, the deceased's journey across the sky: and third, his protection by the deities on the top and border of the lid. Nut spreads her two arms over him and he is pictured as the Revered One with other gods on the border of the lid.

## 2.3. The Case of the Outer Coffin of *P3-dj-jmn* (CG 6081)

### *2.3.1. Exterior Decorations and Texts (Pl. II.1-2)*

The external decorations on the case of the outer coffin of *P3-di-jmn* start from the part behind the head. In this part there is a standing figure of a goddess with uplifted hands, bordered by two signs of the west, above which are two falcons (fig. 14).[183]

Fig. 14. Decoration behind the head

#### *2.3.1.1. The External Left Side Wall (Pl. II.1)*

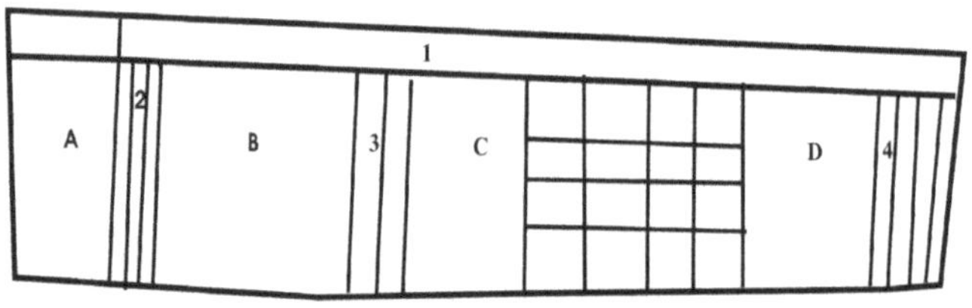


Fig. 15. The External left side wall of the case of the outer coffin of *P3-dj-jmn*(CG 6081) with the numbers and letters showing the distribution of the texts and scenes (drawing by the author)

The upper edge on the left and right sides of the case is ornamented by a single register of inscriptions bordered by two bands of geometrical ornaments. The same geometrical band runs also along the bottom.[184]

(1)The text on the left side wall reads:

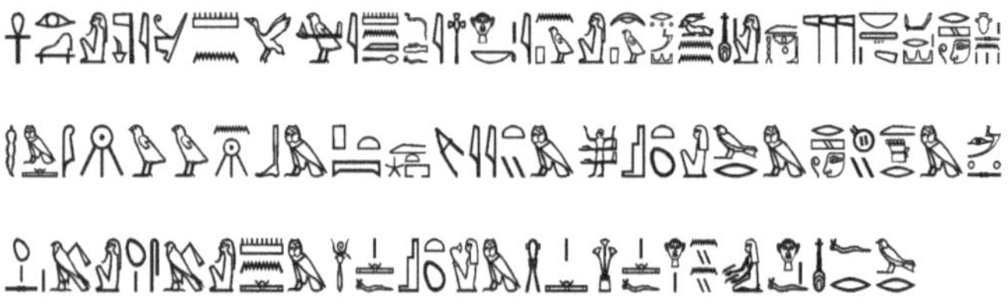

[181] Goff, *Symbols of Ancient Egypt in the Late Period*, 118-9.
[182] Op de Beeck has related some of the pottery vessels in some Middle Kingdom tombs to the rituals taking place on the day of funeral or on different festival occasions when the family visited their dead; Op de Beeck, *ZÄS* 134 (2007), 157-65.

[183] Niwinski, *The Second Find of Deir El-Bahri*, 6.
[184] Niwinski, *The Second Find of Deir El-Bahri*, 6.

*wsjr jt nṯr n jmn pꜣ-dj-jmn mꜣꜥ-ḫrw ḏd=f jnḏ ḥr=k jnpw jꜥḥ pw r mꜣnw wnn-nfr m ḥb nṯrw nb(w) tꜣ ḏsr ršw jb=sn nḏm šw wbn m pt m dwꜣt mrj.tw m ḥꜣj ꜣst wr (t) r ršw m-ḏr mꜣꜣ=s sꜣ=s ḥrw sꜣ=s ḥrw mn m jꜣwt=f ꜣst m sꜣ ḥꜣ=f ḥr njnj ḥꜣ=f nfr wr*

Osiris the God's Father of Amun *Pꜣ-dj-jmn* the Justified says: hail to you Anubis, Oh this Moon at Manu (mountain). Wenennefer is in festival and all the gods of the necropolis, their hearts rejoice and are happy when Shu is arisen in the sky from the netherworld, desired in mourning. Isis will rejoice when she sees her son Horus. Her son Horus is set in his office, with Isis as protection behind him, greeting behind him well and greatly.

The west side of Middle Kingdom coffins represents the back and was usually inscribed with an offering formula for Anubis, the aim of which is to ensure good burial of the deceased in the west.[185] On the west side of the coffin of *Pꜣ-dj-jmn*, the deceased is addressing Anubis, telling him that all the gods are in festival since the deceased has reached the west and shines in the sky from the underworld. The deceased's arrival in the west is envisaged as crossing the sky and reaching the underworld. The deceased's speech also marks his arrival to the west. It has been argued above that the lid decorations refer to the celestial journey of the deceased and, as will be seen later, some of the external decorations on the two long sides refer to the same themes. Isis in the deceased's speech is said to be behind him and greeting him, a reference to her role as one of the two kites who protect the body of Osiris and take care of him.[186] The left side wall is divided into four scenes, each depicting the motif of a gate and separated from the next one by vertical columns of inscriptions.[187]

### *2.3.1.1.1. Scene A (near the head)*

The scene shows a standing figure of the deceased adoring the sacred emblem of Abydos and is accompanied by a caption reading:

*wsjr nb jmntt*

Osiris Lord of the West.

and followed by:

*jmj-wt nṯr ꜥꜣ nb dwꜣt*

(Anubis) in the wrapping, the Great God, Lord of the Underworld.

This scene is also surrounded by three squatting mummiform deities: with human head wearing the Upper Egyptian crown, the head of a baboon and the head of a falcon.[188] These may represent the Four Sons of Horus who were depicted on the edge columns, along the corners of the two long sides of Middle Kingdom coffin, as protector of the deceased.[189] There are also a winged a *wḏꜣt* eye and a falcon perched on the symbol of the west (fig. 16). This scene is separated from the next one by two vertical column of texts that read:

*(2) ḏd mdw jn ḥꜥpj ḫntj sḥ-nṯr ꜥꜣ ḥḳꜣ psḏt wnn-nfr sꜣ wsjr nb ꜣbḏw nswt ntr(w) nb pt tꜣ*

A speech by Hapi Foremost of the Great Divine Booth, the Ruler of the Ennead, Wenennefer, Son of Osiris, Lord of Abydos and King of the Gods, Lord of the sky and earth.

Fig.16. Scene 1 near the head end

### *2.3.1.1.1.1. Commentary and Analysis*

Three of the Four Sons of Horus are depicted on this side of the coffin and Hapi speaks to the deceased as one of the gods in charge of his protection. On Middle Kingdom coffins, Hapi was associated with the head end, where he was one of the four supporters of the sky.[190]

### *2.3.1.1.2. Scene B (near the shoulder)*

The deceased is described as:

*wsjr ḥsj-ꜥꜣ n jt-nṯr imn*

---

[185] Willems, *Chests of Life*, 124.
[186] Willems, *Chests of Life*, 135.
[187] Niwinski, *The Second Find of Deir El-Bahri*, 6.

[188] Niwinski, *The Second Find of Deir El-Bahri* , 6.
[189] Willems, *Chests of Life*, 140.
[190] Willems, *Chests of Life*, 140-1; see above, 3-4.

Osiris the Greatly Praised One of the God's Father of Amun.

He is shown dressed in a festive garment holding a ceremonial staff in his right hand, while with the left hand he is greeting the serpent-headed goddess Hepett-Hor.[191] A caption in front of the goddess reads:

*ḥptt-ḥr ḥnwt jmntt dj=s ḥtp*

Hepet-Hor, Mistress of the West, may she give offering.

The goddess is depicted armed with two knives in her hands, and a table of offering stands between her and the deceased. A winged *wḏ3t* eye flanks the deceased and the goddess. Behind the goddess is a cosmological scene. At the bottom there is a circle inside which are two solar discs joined together by dots. On the two sides of these dots there are two squatting mummy figures, whose heads were replaced by knives. Inside the circle are also two signs of flames and ten small figures holding hoes. At the top, the mummy of the deceased is standing on the circle with the head of a scarab surmounted by a solar barque. Isis and Nephthys are represented standing to the left and right of the mummy. The space between the two goddesses and the mummy was filled was *ʿnḫ* and *ḏd* signs. On the top there is a solar barque with a seated mummy figure with the head of a falcon and a solar disc (fig.17).

Fig. 17. The deceased stands in front of the goddess Hepett-Hor

The whole scene is separated from the next by a text that reads:

*3) ḏd mdw jn gbb pʿt nṯrw nbw 3ḫ n s3=f ḥr pwj ms n 3st jwʿ mnḫ n wsjr*

A speech by Geb, Elite of all the Gods, and the Beneficial One to his son, this Horus born of Isis, potent heir of Osiris.

***2.3.1.1.2.1. Commentary and Analysis***

In this scene the Solar-Osirian unity which is one of the most important principles of this period is clear. The circle with two sun discs inside, two flames and men hoeing the earth refer to the sun coming out from the underworld. While coming out of the underworld to shine in the visible sky, the sun god Re faces enemies. According to the Egyptian vision of cosmos, the act of creation was repeated every day in the appearance of the sun in the eastern horizon. This act was preceded by the conflict with Apep the primeval enemy of the sun god Re. The sun god Re overcame his enemy by the aid of fire which burnt and destroyed Apep. This wall of the case of the outer coffin of *P3-dj-jmn* refers to the journey of the sun god Re from the depth of the underworld until he shines in the sky, but before coming in the visible sky, the sun god Re faces enemies and Apep is one of them. Knives and fire are the tools by which the sun god Re gets rid of his enemies and which are represented here within the circle. The appearnce of the sun in the visible sky is also envaisged as the resurrection of the deceased. For instance in the Book of Overthrowing Apep, the fire of the sun god Re is described:

| | |
|---|---|
| *sḏt jm=k nsrt=s jm=k* | Fire is in you (Apep), its flame is in you. |
| *sḏt jm=tn ḫftjw nw*(sic) *ʿnḫ wḏ3 snb* | Fire is in you, O enemies of the pharaoh, l.p.h, |
| *ʿm=s tn* | And it devours you. |
| *ṯsj tw jr=k rʿ* | Raise yourself Re! |
| *sswn ḫftjw=k* | Destroy your enemies! |
| *rdj sḏt m ʿ3pp* | And fire is set in Apep.[192] |

Fire is envisaged here as a cosmic force which burns and destroys the enemy of Re.[193] The theme of punishment by fire was developed in the Book of the Amduat, where the enemies are cooked by the fire of Re. On the lower register of the Twelfth Hour of the Book of the Amduat, the eye of Re is described as:

| | |
|---|---|
| *ntsn ḫsf ʿ3pp* | They are those who drive off Apep, |
| *m j3bt pt m-ḫt mswt nṯr* | In the eastern sky after the birth of the god. |
| *irrt=sn pw jrjt sṯsw n jtn ʿ3* | What they have done is to elevate the great sun disc, |
| *m 3ḫt j3btt nt pt rʿ-nb* | In the eastern horizon of the sky every day. |
| *jn ns m jrt=f* | It is 'He who burns with his eye', |

[191] Leitz, *Lexikon der Ägyptischen Götter und Götterbezeichnungen* V, 125.

[192] Faulkner, The *Papyrus Bremner-Rhind*, 44, line 22, 14-5; *JEA* 23 (1937), 167.

[193] Goebs, *GM* 194 (2003), 31.

| | |
|---|---|
| *pssw ḫftjw rꜥ m nhpw* | who boils the enemies of Re at sunrise.[194] |

The eastern horizon as Re's birthplace is envisaged to be surrounded by fire. According to the Hermopolitan creation myth, the sun god Re is said to be born on the Island of Fire. This island was on a hill in the midst of the Lake of Knives.[195]

Fire and knives play important roles in the myth of overcoming Apep. The Book of Apep is a magical protection of the sun god Re in his daily journey across the sky. It also includes a description of the process of creation of the sun, and a description of the conflict of Re with the powers of chaos and Apep. A spell in the Book of Overthrowing Apep reads:

| | |
|---|---|
| *nḏr sp2 mnḥj* | Seize! Seize! O butcher. |
| *sḫr ḫftj nw rꜥ m ds=k* | Fell the enemy of Re with your knife! |
| *nḏr sp 2 mnḥj* | Seize! Seize! O butcher. |
| *sḫr ḫftj nw <pr-ꜥꜣ> m ds=k* | Fell the enemy of <Pharaoh> with your knife. |
| *tpw=tn nn sbjw* | These are your heads, O rebels, |
| *ḏꜣḏꜣt=k pfj nn ꜥꜣpp* | This is that head of yours, O Apep, |
| *m šꜥd. n ꜥḥꜣ-ꜥ m ds=f* | Which the warrior has cut up with his knife. |
| *spd spdt* | Be sharp! O *Sothis,* |
| *nsrt ꜣsbjt ḥrj tkꜣ* | Flame of *Asbjt*, who has authority over fire, |
| *sḫr=tn sbj m ds=tn* | You will fell the rebel with your knives, |
| *bḥn=tn wntj m ds=tn* | And you will cut off *Wntj* with your knife, |
| *šꜥd=tn ḥr ḏw=tn* | You are cut off because of your evil,[196] |
| *bḥn=tn ḥr jrjt.n=tn* | You are cut up because of what you have done, |
| *mtrw n jm=tn* | There is a testimony against you, |
| *jrtj=tn ḥr ḏw=tn* | You are dealt with because of your evil. |
| *mꜣꜥ-ḫrw rꜥ r=tn* | Re is triumphant over you, |
| *ḥr bḥn=f tn* | And Horus cuts you up.[197] |

The spell, which is a protection of both the sun god Re and the Pharaoh, relates that Apep will be seized and cut up with the knife of Re. The image is that of the enemy's head chopped off with a knife and then fire set to his body. Here both knife and fire are used as symbolic agents of destruction. All these actions will be done to Apep because of the evil he has done to the sun god Re.[198] The end of the spell relates that Horus as the son of Re will cut up Apep, and Re will be triumphant over his enemy. These spells give explanation to the fire signs and the human beings with two knives. The number of the beings within the circle is twelve, which might allude to the twelve hours of the day or the night.[199]The two small discs refer to the eastern and western extremes of the journey of the sun through the twelve hours of the day or night. The dots may mark the course of the sun from the east to the west. These complicated cosmological thoughts are hinted at in the cicrcle on the external left hand side wall of the case of the coffin of *Pꜣ-dj-jmn*.

The figure of the mummy with the head of a scarab might also refer to Osiris in his solar aspects. The barque with a solar deity with the sun disc on his head above the scarab also refers to the same aspects of the deceased, who is identified with Re and Osiris. The mummy being attended by Isis and Nephthys reflects the two goddesses protecting and attending the deceased Osiris in his solar aspect. The goddesses were placed to the left and right, respectively: Isis facing the mummy and Nephthys protecting him from behind, just as they were depicted on Middle Kingdom coffins.

The whole scene beginning with the circle (which, as argued above, might represent the earth), the dots symbolizing the course of the sun from the depths of the underworld, the overcoming of the enemies by the twelve beings guarding the course of the sun by hoeing the earth and by two beings with their heads as knives, the mummy being protected by Isis and Nephthys, the scarab in the place of the head, the sun barque over the scarab, all work together to ensure the Solar-Osirian unity of the deceased and represent the birth and death cycle in which the deceased participates. The standing mummy figure can represent Shu filling the space between the earth and the sky, and that is reinforced by the fact the deceased in one of the texts on that side of the coffin mentioned above is described as Shu who has reached the west and the gods are happy with his arrival.

#### *2.3.1.1.3. Scene C (near the hips)*

The deceased is dressed in a festive garment and is shown holding a vase  and makes libation before an offering table in front of 16 panels placed in four registers and four vertical columns. The first two columns have the seven reclining cows and their standing bull. Each cow is provided with offerings, *menat* and *flagellum* and is named as follows:

The Mistress of the Two Lands and the Beautiful House,
The Mistress of the West,
The Mistress of the Elevated House,
The Mistress of all the Mountains,

[194] Hornung, *Amduat* I, 203; *Amduat* II, 191-2; *The Ancient Egyptian Amduat*, 375.
[195] For the Island f Fire as a place of creation, see Abbas, *The Lake of Knives and the Lake of Fire*, 50-1.
[196] The suffix *tn* should refer to the evil one and *Wntj* and not to *Sothis* and *ꜣsbjt*: Faulkner, *JEA* 23 (1937), 176.
[197] Faulkner, *Papyrus Bremner-Rhind*, 45, line 22, 21-23; *JEA* 23 (1937), 168.
[198] According to Neith cosmogony in the temple of Esna, Neith was the mother of both Re and Apep, and both of them came out from the same umbilical cord: Quack, *SAK* 34 (2006), 378.
[199] Niwinski, *GM* 109 (1989), 60.

The Mistress of Going out from the Western Mountain,
The Mistress of every Beautiful House in the West,
The Mistress of all the Mountains.[200]

The bull is not named. The third column has oars designated as "beautiful in the southern, northern, western, and eastern sky." The fourth column represents eight figures of mummified deities in four registers with heads of a heron, human, ape, jackal, donkey, falcon, Bes and a human bald head turned back (fig 18). A text before the deceased reads:

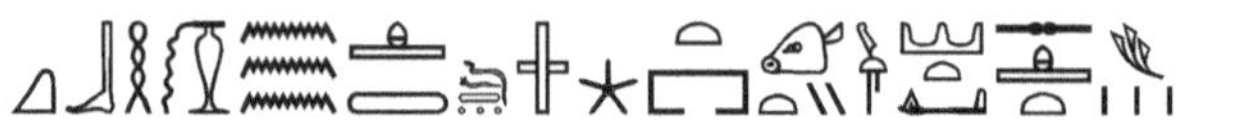

*ḳbḥw ḥtp ḏf3w jmj dw3t ḫntj jmntt dj=s ḥtpw*

Making libation and giving offering (to) those who are in the underworld (by) the Foremost of the West, that she may give offerings.

Fig. 18. The deceased makes offerings to the sacred cows

#### *2.3.1.1.3.1. Commentary and Analysis*

The seven cows are depicted recumbent, which is a standard posture of Mehet-Weret in a cow form.[201] The function of these seven cows, according to Pinch, is to protect and nourish the deceased. That is clear from the accompanying text, which describes the whole scene as making offering to those who are in the underworld by the Foremost of the West, with a reference to Hathor as the connector between the west and the underworld. The seven cows may also refer to the seven forms of the goddess, analogous to her sevenfold human form.[202]

The names of the seven cows associate them with the western mountain. This association may also allude to the cycle of death and rebirth. The cow, particularly in the area of Deir el-Bahri is considered as a mother of the deceased who will receive him and lead him to the underworld.[203] The placing of this scene on the west side of the coffin is significant, since the west side of the coffin is its back and is normally inscribed with texts and decorated with scenes that refer to the west.[204] The placing of the scene close to the feet or legs of the deceased is significant as well. Hornung argues that the foot end of the 21st Dynasty coffin refers to the west and the head end refers to the east. He supports his argument by saying that the scenes dealing with the sunrise, falcons and sun coming out from the underworld, are normally placed at the head end while these dealing with the underworld and the west as the final resting place from which the deceased will start his journey to the underworld are placed at the foot end.[205] The scene of the seven cows and their titles, which all allude to the west, fits well with Hornung's theory, and the scene is set in its proper place.

In her work on the cow scenes on 21st Dynasty coffins, Heyne argues that the scene of the cow emerging from the mountain was derived from 19th Dynasty Theban tombs. In these tombs, the scene was used as vignette to Book of the Dead Chapter 186 and was normally placed at the end of a wall. The cow in these scenes refers to Hathor as Mistress of the West. On the coffin of *P3-dj-jmn*, the scene of the seven cows, which was used as vignette to Book of the Dead chapter 148, can also allude to these cows as representatives of Hathor, Mistress of the West, who was worshipped in the area of Deir el-Bahri where the coffin of *P3-dj-jmn* was found. By comparing the names of the seven cows on the coffin of *P3-dj-jmn* it is clear that these seven cows play the same roles of Hathor as Mistress of the Western Mountain and protector of the deceased.[206]

#### *2.3.1.1.4. Scene D (near the legs)*

The deceased and his *b3* are drinking water poured out for them by the Tree-Goddess Nut, who is depicted coming out from the sycamore tree with a solar disc on her head between two cow horns. The head of the deceased is flanked by a winged cobra  and  *wḏ3t* eye and behind his back there are signs of *ʿnḫ*, *ḥḳ3* and *ḏt* (fig. 19). Behind the goddess are two columns of vertical hieroglyphs that read:

*(4) ḏd mdw jn nwt wrt mwt nṯr ms nṯrw nbw dj=s ḥtpw n wsjr ḫntj jmntt*

A speech by Nut the Great, Mother of the God who gave birth to all the gods, that she may give offerings to Osiris Foremost of the West.

[200] Niwinski, in: *Fs Irmtraut Munro*, 146-7.
[201] Pinch, *Votive Offerings to Hathor*, 147.
[202] El-Sayed, *MDAIK* 36 (1980), 375, 85.
[203] Heyne, in: *Fs Hornung*, 65.
[204] Pinch, *Votive Offerings to Hathor*, 180-1.
[205] Hornung, *Innerrhoder Geschichtsfreund* 28 (1984), 8.
[206] Heyne, in: *Fs Hornung*, 62-3.

Fig.19. The deceased drinks water offered to him by the goddess Nut

### *2.3.1.1.4.1. Commentary and Analysis*

The cult of the Tree-Goddess, as liminal between the world of the living and that of the dead, was widespread in ancient Egypt. Tree-Goddesses would sustain the deceased's thirst and provide him with food and shade to continue his journey toward the underworld. The goddesses who were associated with the tree existed in these marginal areas. They represent the means of communication between this world and the next. For instance, in CT spell 159 the deceased says:

*jw=j rḫ.kw nhty jptw ntj mfkꜣt prrt rꜥ jmtj sny*

I know the two sycamore trees of turquoise from which the sun god Re emerges.[207]

In the Book of the Dead the sycamore is mentioned in connection with the goddess Nut.[208] The deceased says:

*j nht twy nt nwt dj=ṯ n=j ṯꜣw jmj=ṯ*

Oh sycamore tree of Nut, may you give me the air that is in you.[209]

All the dead who are associated or identified with Osiris will be protected by the goddess.

Various goddesses are associated with tree cult in ancient Egypt, including Hathor, Isis, Nephthys, Amentet, Maat, Neith, Naunet and Nut.[210] Hathor and Nut are the most prominent and sometimes appear together in one scene.[211] In the Theban tombs of the New Kingdom, the goddesses Hathor and Nut are depicted as ladies of the sycamore. Nut is shown greeting Hathor, who is coming out from the mountain.[212]

The earliest attestation for the Tree Goddess in royal tombs is in the tomb of Thutmosis III, where she is called Isis; she subsequently appears in the tombs of Amenophis II and Thutmosis IV. In the tomb of Thutmosis III, Isis is shown as the mother of the deceased, supporting him after death as she was doing while he was alive. The king is Horus who is protected and nursed by his mother the Tree Goddess Isis.[213] Such scenes disappear from later royal tombs, to reappear on the private tomb walls of the New Kingdom and on the 21st Dynasty coffins.

On the coffin of *Pꜣ-dj-jmn*, the scene of the goddess Nut comes after that of Hathor. She plays the same role of Hathor as provider of water to the deceased, who has reached the west. Thus, *Pꜣ-dj-jmn* is now under the protection of both goddesses. He is able to enter the netherworld in the company of these goddesses, who provide him with water to continue his journey. The speech of Nut complements the scene of her offering water to the deceased and his *bꜣ*, specifying that she will give the deceased food and drink. The depiction of Nut as coming out of the sycamore with the sun disc between two cow horns on her head alludes also to her role as a sky goddess who will place the god between her horns to start his journey from the west.

In one of the Late Period texts, the water that comes from the sycamore tree is mentioned along with the water which comes from a well and refreshes the deceased. The text reads: *sẖnn.n=k šdt sẖrd ḥꜥw* (you have demolished the well which makes the limbs young) and *sšwr.n=k nht šps* (and you have dried the noble sycamore).[214] Here the water that comes from a well is compared with the fresh water of Osiris poured for the deceased in libation. This water is said to renew the deceased and make him young again. The water poured for the deceased by the goddess Nut from the sycamore seems to play the same role, as it will mediate the passage of the deceased from this life to the next.

The arrangement of the scenes on this side of the coffin, with the scene of the seven cows followed by the scene of the sky goddess Nut offering water to the deceased, is of great interest. All the scenes and speeches on this side deal with the arrival of the deceased to the west and with how he will be sustained with water and food to start his journey to the netherworld. It is also important to note the arrangement of the speeches of the gods and goddesses on this side. Anubis as patron and Foremost of the West is addressed, and Isis is also there as a protector and one who attends the embalming and accompanies the body of Osiris. Hapi, who was attested with protection of the head on Middle Kingdom coffins, is here as well. The program of decoration and the location of the texts on this side of

207 *CT* II, 367a-b (spell 159).
208 Refai, *BIFAO* 100 (2000), 383.
209 Munro, *Das Totenbuch des Nacht-Amun*, pl. 23.
210 Keel, in: Keel (ed.), *Das Recht der Bilder*, 95.
211 There are different interpretations on the identity of the Tree Goddess and what was her function for the deceased. Davies argues that the Tree Goddess is a representation of the sky goddess Nut; Davies, *The Tomb of Nakht*, 46. Hermsen argues that the goddess is Hathor; Hermsen, *Lebensbaumsymbolik im Alten Ägypten*, 72. Assmann considers the Tree-Goddess as another manifestation of the Goddess of the West or a Goddess of the paradise; Assmann, *Das Grab des Amenemope*, 96.

212 The scene is in TT 158 where Nut is shown greeting Hathor with *njnj*; Seele, *The Tomb of Tianefer at Thebes* , pl. 38.
213 Keel, in Keel (ed.): *Das Recht der Bilder*, 92.
214 Altmann, *Die Kultfrevel des Seth*, 80-1.

the coffin work together to ensure a good burial for the deceased in the west and to mark the starting point in his journey into the netherworld.

### *2.3.1.2. The External Right Side Wall (Pl. II-2)*

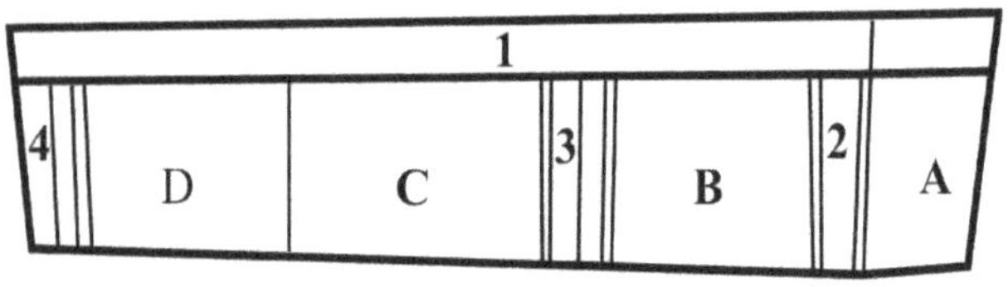


Fig. 20. The external right side wall of the case of the outer coffin of *P3-dj-jmn*(CG 6081) with the numbers and letters showing the distribution of the texts and scenes (drawing by the author)

The arrangement of the scenes and the texts on this side is identical with that on the left side.

(1)The upper horizontal text reads:

*wsjr NN ḏd=f jnḏ ḥr=k wsjr nṯr ꜥ3 nb t3-ḏsr ḥrj-jb 3bḏw jtj nṯr ꜥ3 nb ḫrt-nṯr nswt nṯr ḥk3 ꜥnḫw mrj.tw=f ḥr psḏt nbt ḥḏt iṯi dšrt rnn n3j ḥwt-ꜥ3t wr ḫr m wsḫt m3ꜥt r-gs nb m3ꜥ ḏsr st m jwnw nb ḥtp m jwnw mḥjt nb ḫꜥw m ḥwt-sr*

Osiris NN he says: Hail to you Osiris the Great God, Lord of the Sacred Land who dwells in Abydos, the Sovereign, the Great God, Lord of the Necropolis, the King of the god(s) and Ruler of the Living, who is loved by the Ennead, Mistress of the white Crown, who takes possession of the Red Crown, who has been brought up (nursed) by these of the Great Mansion, Great of Voice in the Hall of Maat beside the Lord of Maat, Sacred of Seat of Heliopolis and the Lord of Offering in northern Heliopolis, Lord of Crowns in the House of the Magistrate (Law court of the gods).

The deceased speaks to Osiris as the Great God, Lord of Abydos and the necropolis. Osiris normally features on the east side of Middle Kingdom coffins, where there was an offering formula invoking him. He is also addressed on that side as Anubis is addressed on the other. Here the deceased directs his speech to Osiris, who has been brought up and vindicated by the gods. In doing so, the deceased wishes to be vindicated as Osiris.

#### *2.3.1.2.1. Scene A (near the head)*

The goddess Nephthys is shown standing with upraised arms. She adores a *ḏd* pillar with two plumes and a solar disc in the middle. Beside the emblem of the west is a table over which there are offerings and a lotus. Above the goddess are two *wḏ3t* eyes, flanking her name with their wings. There is also a vulture standing on the emblem of *jmy-wt*, which is flanked by the two emblems of the west. Behind the goddess and above her are the signs of *ꜥnḫ* and *ḏd* (fig.21). There is a text that separates this scene from the next, written in two vertical columns and reading:

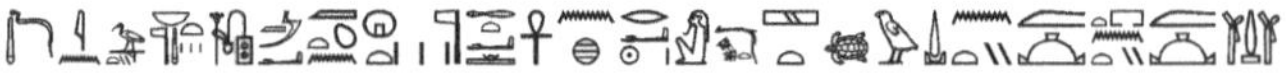

*(2) ḏd mdw jn ḏḥwtj nb mdw-nṯr sš m3ꜥt psḏt ꜥ3t ꜥnḫ rꜥ nsj štjw wḏ3 ntj m j3t ntj m j3t wḏꜥ*[215]

A speech by Thoth Lord of the god's words and the Scribe of Maat, the Great Ennead: Re lives, the turtle burns, sound is the one who is in the Primeval Mound and the one who is in the Mound of the Beheading.

Fig. 21. The goddess Nephthys

#### *2.3.1.2.1.1. Commentary and Analysis*

Nephthys, as one of the two goddesses who protect Osiris, is depicted here adoring his emblem. On Middle Kingdom coffins, Isis and Nephthys were placed at the foot and head of the deceased as kites or mourners. They protect the body of the deceased and complement the role of the sky goddess Nut on the lid of the coffin. Coffin Texts describe the role of the goddesses in collecting the body of Osiris after it has been cut into pieces by Seth.[216] Their position on these two sides has a ritual background: at funerals, two kites or mourners were depicted at the head and foot of the deceased as protectors. Isis and Nephthys also have celestial background, as they are the ones who help Osiris to ascend to the barque of Re and guard the barque from the attacks of Apophis.[217] The celestial role of the goddess Nephthys is reflected in the speech of Thoth, where Re is described as the one who has been saved on the primeval mound, where a slaughter took place between Re and his enemies on the day of beheading. The placing of Nephthys on this side suits the protection of the god.

---

[215] Corteggiani, *BIFAO* 95 (1995), 141-51.
[216] Isis and Nephthys feature in liturgies inscribed on Middle Kingdom coffins and deal with the assembling of the body of Osiris after it had been cut into pieces by his brother Seth, see Assmann, *Totenliturgien* I.
[217] Willems, *Chests of Life*, 133-4.

#### *2.3.1.2.2. Scene B (near the shoulder)*

This part is decorated with the famous cosmological scene of creation. The goddess Nut is depicted naked and supporting herself on her hands and feet. The goddess is bent over the figure of Geb, whose body is naked and covered with reed signs. A caption describes the god as:

*Gbb pꜥt nṯrw nbw*

Geb, elite of all gods

The space between Nut and Geb is divided into two registers. In the lower register Shu is described as:

*šw sꜣ rꜥ nṯr ꜥꜣ nb pt tꜣ dj=f ḥtp*

Shu son of Re the Great God Lord of the sky and earth that he may give offering.

He is supporting the sign of the sky and a kneeling human figure to the left of Shu adores this sign. The scene in the upper register shows a solar barque sailing on the sign of the sky supported by Shu. On the solar barque stands a mummy with the head of a scarab and a solar disc with its rays surmounting the scarab. The solar disc is described as:

*nṯr ꜥꜣ nb pt*

The Great God, Lord of the sky.

A cobra with the white crown descends from the rudder of the barque. Above the barque is a *wḏꜣt* eye with *ꜥnḫ* sign. Behind the rudder is a label reading *jmj dwꜣt* "what is in the underworld." The whole scene is bordered on both sides by the figure of a falcon. The one on the left is called:

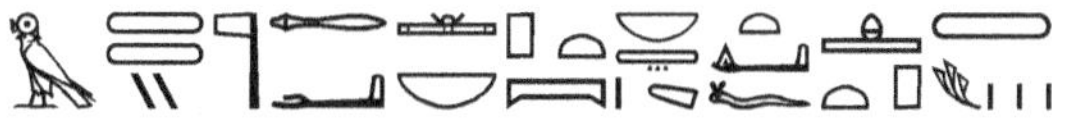

*ḥr tꜣwj nṯr ꜥꜣ nb pt nb tꜣ dj=f ḥtpw*

Horus of the two lands, Great God, Lord of the sky and Lord of the earth that he may give offerings.

The falcon on the left is called *skr-wsjr* (Sokar-Osiris). Beneath the falcon on the right are a standing mummy and the sign of loaf of bread (fig. 22). The text that separates this scene from the next reads:

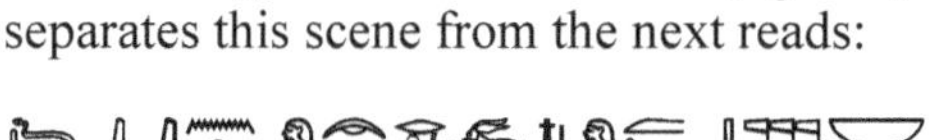

*(3) ḏd mdw jn jnpw jꜥḥ pw r mꜣnw wnn-nfr m ḥb nṯrw nbw tꜣ ḏsr ršw jb=sn nḏm šw wbn m pt*

Speech by Anubis (Oh) this moon at Manu, Wenennefer is in festival and all the gods of the necropolis, their hearts rejoice and are happy when Shu is arisen in the sky.

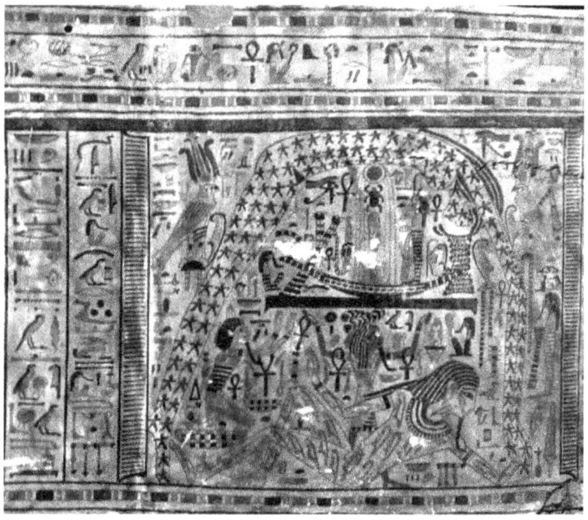

Fig.22. Cosmological scene of creation

#### *2.3.1.2.2.1. Commentary and Analysis*

This scene is not very different from the one on the opposite side. It might refer to the day journey in which the deceased takes part. In the text, the gods are happy when Shu shines in the sky, which might also allude to the deceased standing between earth and sky; thus, he is not only Osiris but Re at the same time. He is Shu filling the space between the two spheres and is thus sharing in the daily cycle of the sun in the day and night skies. The falcons on the right and left, and their titles, refer to the deceased as sharing both aspects of Osiris and Re. Niwniski argues that here:

> "If we imagine the mummy lying in the coffin, embraced and protected by Osiris or Imentet from beneath and Nut from above, thus situated between the earth and the sky, we can understand the mummy, as exactly corresponding to that taken by Shu in the well known cosmological composition of the same period, the so-called scene with Geb and Nut. The deceased is therefore identified with the great god himself in both of his main united aspects; the Osirian one and the Solar one. He is not the only mummy shaped Osiris who becomes king of the dead after his sacred revival, but an incarnation of the sun the deceased travels eternally the space of the visible upper sky during the day and that of the invisible lower sky by night, being at the same time the luminous atmosphere that fills the world and is the source of life".[218]

#### *2.3.1.2.3. Scene C (near the hips)*

The scene shows the deceased in the middle accompanied by Isis and Anubis. He is dressed in a festive garment; his head is bald. He holds a vase in his left hand and signs of

[218] Niwinski, *GM* 109 (1989), 54.

*ḏd, ḥḳ3* and *ʿnḫ* in his right. Behind the deceased stands Anubis, who is shown holding the *ḥḳ3* in his right hand and protecting the deceased with his left hand. Behind Anubis there is an inscription reading:

*s3 ḥ3 =f nb m ʿnḫ ḏd*

All protection behind him in life and stability.

In front of Anubis a caption reads:

*prj m dw3t*

Going to the Duat

Behind the deceased there is a caption reading:

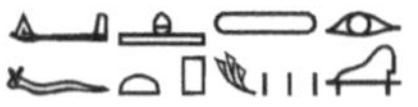

*dj=f ḥtpw(n) wsjr*

He gives offerings (to) Osiris.

The deceased is escorted by Isis, who is depicted with upraised arms in a gesture of adoration; beneath her arms are various kinds of offerings. The text in front of her reads:

*3st dj=s ḥtpw n wsjr nṯr nfr*

Isis may she give offerings to Osiris the Good God.

In front of Isis is the sacred emblem of Anubis, followed by a falcon on a stand. At the top are two *wḏ3t* eyes flanking Anubis, the deceased and Isis (fig. 23).

Fig. 23. The deceased accompanied by Anubis and Isis

***2.3.1.2.3.1. Commentary and Analysis***

Here the deceased, Isis and Anubis are all approaching the sacred emblem of Abydos. The scene refers to presentations of offerings to Osiris, also common in the decoration of this side on Middle Kingdom coffins.

***2.3.1.2.4. Scene D (near the legs)***

The deceased is presenting offerings to the sacred cow emerging from the western mountain. She is described as:

*ḥt-ḥr nbt t3-ḏsr*

Hathor Lady of the Necropolis.

On the slopes of the mountain are a falcon, two signs of the west, four squatting mummiform gods, and a bull at the bottom (fig. 24). Behind the slopes is the depiction of a tomb. The inscriptions after the scene read:

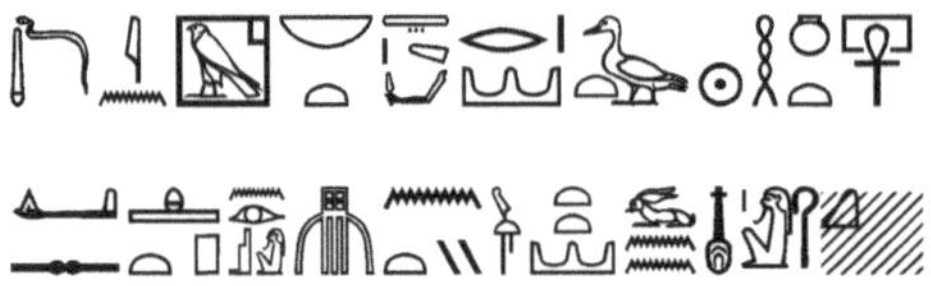

*4) ḏd mdw jn ḥt-ḥr nbt t3-ḏsr s3t rʿ ḥnwt pr-ʿnḫ dj=s ḥtp n wsjr ḫntj-jmntt wnn-nfr ḥḳ3* [*ḏt*]

Speech by Hathor Lady of the Sacred Land (necropolis) daughter of Re and Mistress of House of Life, that she may give offering to Osiris Foremost of the West and Ruler of [eternity]

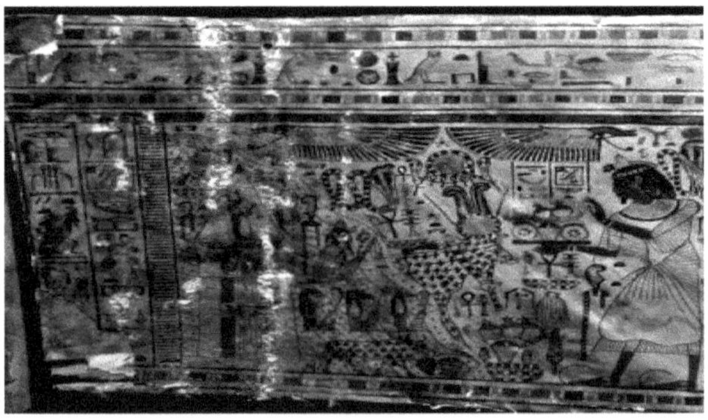

Fig. 24. The deceased presents offering to Hathor

***2.3.1.2.4.1 Commentary and Analysis***

The scene on this side is not very different from the one on the opposite side and is placed at the foot end of the coffin. The location of the scene here marks the deceased's arrival to the west. On the door jambs of the tomb the name of Osiris as Foremost of the West is inscribed. The deceased is presenting offering to the goddess Hathor, who comes out of the mountain with two cow horns, between which rests a sun disc. As argued above, this refers to the cow as the one who will accompany the deceased in his journey to the underworld and the one who will provide him with food and drink. It has been argued that the scene is derived from Book of the Dead Chapter 186.[219]

[219] In the vignettes of this chapter a cow is shown coming out of the mountain and accompanied by another goddess in the shape of a

### *2.4. The Interior Decorations of the Outer Case (Pl. III)*

### *2.4.1. The Decorations on the Floor Board*

The floor board of the outer case of the coffin of *P3-dj-jmn* is occupied by the figure of the *ḏd* pillar with the head of Osiris. The trunk of the *ḏd* pillar and the head of Osiris are filled with water signs.[220] Osiris is shown as a *ḏd* pillar with a head of and arms of a man, and two falcon wings. The head is covered with a striped wig and has the composite *Atef* crown. The arms and the forearms are decorated with bracelets. The forearms are painted on the side walls.

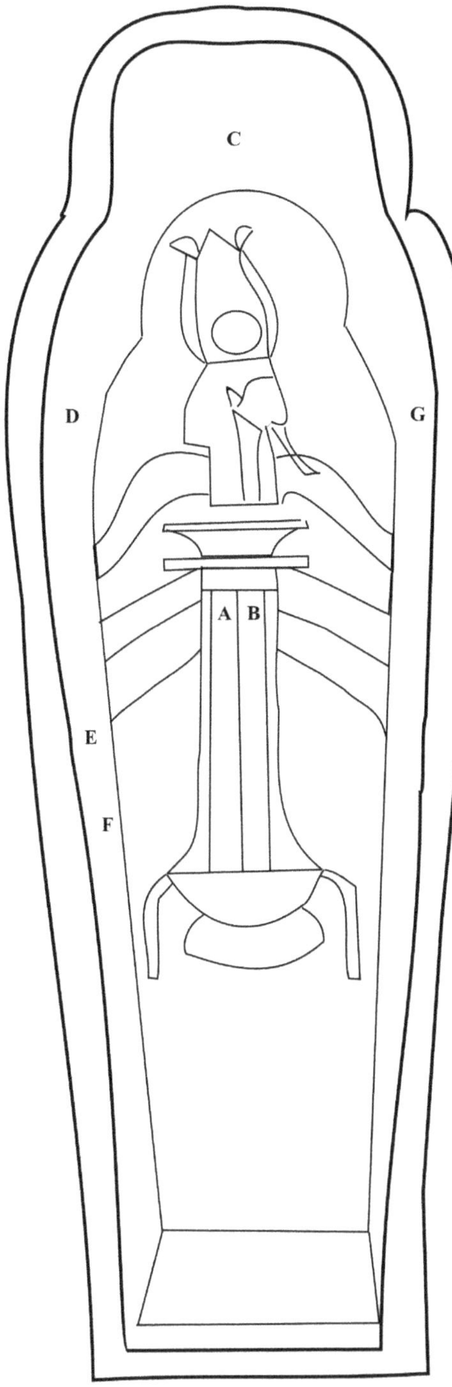


Fig. 25. The interior of the case of the outer coffin of *P3-dj-jmn* (CG 6081) with the letters showing the distribution of the texts and scenes (drawing by the author)

hippopotamus. In Theban private tombs of the 18th and 19th Dynasties, the cow is usually depicted at an end of a wall, but without the hippopotamus goddess. In all the coffins of the 21st Dynasty which have this scene there is no depiction of a goddess in the shape of a hippopotamus, so the scene of the cow on the 21st Dynasties was derived from the tomb decoration and not from the papyri of the Book of the Dead chapter 186; Heyne, in: *Fs Hornung*, 60. The only exception for this is found in the tomb of Neferrenpet TT 178, where the scene of the goddess Hathor coming out of the mountain follows a scene in which a goddess in the shape of Hippopotamus with sun disc and two cow horns precedes; Hofmann, *Das Grab des Neferrenpet*, pl. 32, fig. 41 and pl. 33 fig. 42. The Book of the Dead chapter 186 as a closing chapter on 21st Dynasty Papyri became very popular during this period. For examples on this chapter on the papyri of this period, see Niwinski, *Studies on the Illustrated Theban Funerary Papyri*, pl. 25.

220 There are other cases in which the ritual of presenting the *ḳbḥw* to Osiris is among the decoration of the inner sides of the case and not on the floor board. In such scenes Osiris is depicted sitting on a throne and the deceased offers him *ḳbḥw* water. For instance on the left and right inner walls of the case of the coffin of the high priest *Ns-p3wtj-t3wj* from the 21st Dynasty in Vienna Museum ÄS 6262, Osiris is depicted sitting on a throne and the deceased is offering him *ḥtpw* and *ḳbḥw* and the whole scene is flanked by two *ḏd* Pillars. The same scene is repeated three times on the right and left inner walls of the case; Egner and Haslauer, *Särge dr Dritten Zwischenzeit* I, 9/37-10/37, pl.35/37.

The *ḏd* pillar is [221]filled with water signs in its upper part, and its trunk has two vertical lines of inscriptions that read:

A

B

A-*ḏd mdw jn wsjr nb ḏdw ḥḳ3 ḏt nṯr ʿ3 ḫntj jmntt djt=f ḥtp ḏf3w n wsjr*

A speech by Osiris Lord of Busiris, Ruler of Eternity, the Great God, Foremost of the West that he may give a table of offerings to Osiris.

B-*ḏd mdw jn wsjr nb 3bḏw nswt wr nb m3nw nṯr ʿ3 m ẖrt nṯr dj=f ḳbḥw snṯr n wsjr*

A speech by Osiris Lord of Abydos, the Great King, Lord of the Western Mountain, the Great God in the necropolis, that he may give *ḳbḥw* water and incense to Osiris.

The body of Osiris stands on a large sign of 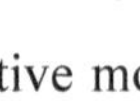 *nbw* and the whole figure is surrounded by decorative motifs. Among these are the winged eyes, the mummy form jackal-headed Hapi and two standing female personifications protecting the deceased, as well as offering motifs.[222] What is important in the scene is the image of Osiris with water signs on his body and the texts inscribed on the trunk of the *ḏd* Pillar.

### *2.4.1.1. Commentary and Analysis*

The water signs on the body of Osiris and the two columns of inscriptions refer to one of the most important rituals in ancient Egypt. In this ritual, water offered to deceased is described as coming out from the body of Osiris. The *ḳbḥw* water which comes from the body of Osiris has a long history going back to the Pyramid Texts. In these texts the deceased is offered a libation of cool water (*ḳbḥw*) or fresh water (*rnpjt*). For instance, Pyramid Texts spell 32 reads:

| | |
|---|---|
| *ḳbḥw=k jpn wsjr* | This is your cool water (libation water), Osiris, |
| *ḳbḥw=k jpn h3 N* | This is your cool water, O N. |
| *prj.w ḫr s3=k* | has come forth with your son, |
| *prj.w ḫr ḥr* | has come forth with Horus. |
| *jw.n(=j) jn.n(=j) n=k jrt-ḥr* | (I) have come and I have brought to you the Eye of Horus, |
| *ḳb jb=k ẖr=s* | that your heart may be calm by means of it. |
| *jn.n(=j) n=k sj ẖr kbwj=k* | (I) have brought it to you under your sandals. |
| *mn n=k rḏw prj jm=k* | Take to yourself the discharge (outflow) that has come out from you. |
| *n wrḏ jb=k ẖr=s* | May your heart not be weary with it.[223] |

In this text, the stress is not on the act of providing the deceased with drinking water that assuages his thirst in the manner of funerary offerings, but on supplying him with the life-giving water that comes from the body of Osiris.[224] Pyramid Texts Spell 32 can be divided into three sections. The first tells that this water is from Horus, son of Osiris; water connects the son and his dead father.[225] The second describes the water as the 'Eye of Horus', which makes the heart of the deceased calm. The Eye of Horus is the cultic expression of every item to be offered. When an item is offered and described as the Eye of Horus, that simply means, in Assmann's words, that 'it will restore something that has been destroyed or used up, put together something that has fallen apart, or replace something that has been lost. It is the symbol of reversibility.'[226] The third section explains that this water is the discharge of Osiris, which comes out from his body. Water flows out from the deceased Osiris and then comes back to him by means of offering the libation. So, the water here symbolises life force, the medium by which life returns to the deceased.[227]

The purpose of the funeral libation in this spell is to revitalize the deceased, and to make him young (*rnp*)

[221] Niwinski, *The Second Find of Deir El-Bahri*, 3-4, pl. II-1.

[222] Niwinski, *The Second Find of Deir El-Bahri*, 3, pl. II- 1-2.

[223] *PT* spell 32=*Pyr.* § 22a-23a, see also *PT* spell 33=*Pyr.* § 24a-25c, and *PT* spell 357=*Pyr.* § 589a reads 'Your name of the fresh water' (*rn=k n mw rnpw*).

[224] Delia, *JARCE* 29 (1992), 183.

[225] Assmann, *Death and Salvation,* 357.

[226] Assmann, *Death and Salvation*, 357; Assmann, in: *Hommages Fayza Haikal*, 8.

[227] Blackman, *ZÄS* 50 (1912), 69-75; *JEOL* 24 (1976), 3; Winkler, *GM* 211 (2006), 129; Willems describes libation offering as a life giving force that enables the deceased to travel to the sky; Willems, *The Coffin of Heqata,* 118.

again. The fresh water is the Nile efflux (*rḏw*),[228] which represents both the seepage of surface water that marks the beginning of the flood and the life force of Osiris as personification of the Nile. The water offered to Osiris is compared with the fluid that comes forth from Horus and the efflux that has gone out from the body of Osiris at the moment of death and returned to him by means of offering libation.[229] In Pyramid Texts Spell 460, the libation offered to the deceased is the water flow that comes from his body.

| | |
|---|---|
| *mw=k ḳbḥ=k bʿḥ wr* | Your water, your cool water is the great water flow, |
| *prj jm=k* | which has come from you.[230] |

In another Pyramid Text spell, the water offered to the deceased is described as:

| | |
|---|---|
| *m-n=k rḏw prj jm=k* | Take to yourself the discharge that has come from you. |
| *rdj.n ḥr ḫmʿ n=k nṯrw ḏr* | Horus has caused that the gods gather for you, |
| *bw nb šm.n=k jm* | In every place from where you have gone. |
| *m-n=k rḏw prj m=k* | Take the discharge that has come from you. |
| *rdj.n ḥr jp n=k msw=f* | Horus has caused that his sons account for you, |
| *ḏr bw mḥ.n=k jm* | In the place where you were drowned. |
| *jp kw ḥr rnpj.tw* | Horus inspects you, you being young, |
| *m rn=k pw n mw rnpj* | In your name of fresh water.[231] |

The spell places the deceased in relation with the gods, and alludes to the myth of Osiris in which he was drowned in the Nile by his brother Seth. Horus, as son of Osiris, gathered the gods and his sons to search for the body of his father in every place where he might have gone.[232] The libation water is called the fresh water, which has come from the body of Osiris. The text ends here with giving this name to the deceased, as Osiris from whose corpse the Nile flows.[233] Even the word for the year in Egypt was *rnp.t*[234] 'the Fresh One'. The fresh water is the Nile efflux (*rḏw*), which designates both the water flow and the life force of the god Osiris. These libations are the actual fluids that have issued from the corpse of Osiris.

The same theme is also repeated in the Coffin Texts. Many Coffin Texts spells show the deceased being offered water that comes from Osiris.

| | |
|---|---|
| *ḳbḥw=k pw nn wsjr N pn* | Here is your cold water O this Osiris N, |
| *prj.w ḫr jt=k* | which has come forth from your father |
| *prj.w ḫr gb* | Which has come forth from Geb, |
| *prj.w ḫr ḥr* | which has come forth from Horus, |
| *prj.w ḫr wsjr* | which has come forth from Osiris, |
| *ḳbḥ jb=k ḫr=s* | May your heart be cool by means of it. |
| *jwj.n=j jn.n=j n=k jrt ḥr* | I have come, and I have brought to you the Eye of Horus, |
| *ḳbḥ jb=k ḫr=s s<ḳ> <jm>=s* | that your heart may be cool by means of it, and be refreshed by it.[235] |
| *m- n=k rḏw prj jm=k* | Take the discharge which has come out from you. |
| *n wrḏ jb=k ḫr=s* | Your heart is not weary by means of it. |
| *mꜣ.t(j) mꜣ.t(j) rnp.t(j) rn.pt(j)* | You being new, you being new, you being young, you being young, |
| *m rn=k pw n jmj ḳbḥ* | In this your name of 'He-who-is-in-the-libation'. |
| *sḫr.n ḥr ḫftjw=k m bꜣḥ=k* | Horus has overthrown your enemies in your presence. |
| *mj prj.t* (sic) *n=k ḫrw* | Come! The invocation comes out for you, |
| *prt-ḫrw n jmꜣḫj N jḳr* | Invocation offerings for the Revered One N, the Excellent.[236] |

The fresh water will revive the heart of the deceased, fresh and cool, because it comes forth from the body of Osiris himself.[237] Horus as the son of Osiris defends his father and overthrows his enemies for him. The offering of libation mediates the passage of the deceased Osiris. When Osiris dies, his body loses it water, and at the same time, the Nile inundates and its water, presented as the libation, flows and covers the whole land, giving all means of life.[238] In this way, Egypt, as Assmann argues, 'constituted the body from which Nile inundation gushed forth like a bodily humor that brought life. We see thus the correspondence of microcosm and macrocosm

[228] Kettel noted the physical appearance of the Nile inundation and compared it with the nature of *rḏw*. He argues that when the Nile flood comes, it carries decomposing plants with special colour and an odour of rotting. *rḏw* as rotting bodily fluids has the same physical resemblance of the Nile during the inundation, green-brownish and carries strong smell: Kettel, in: *Hommages Leclant* III, 323.

[229] Winkler, *GM* 211 (2006), 129.

[230] *PT* spell 460=*Pyr.* § 868b; Allen, *The Ancient Egyptian Pyramid Texts*, 120.

[231] *PT* spell 423=Pyr. § 766a-767a; Allen, *The Inflection of the Verb*, 493; *The Ancient Egyptian Pyramid Texts*, 101.

[232] Assmann, *Death and Salvation*, 357-8.

[233] Assmann, *Totenliturgien II*, 95.

[234] *Wb* II, 429.

[235] Emendments according to the restoration suggested by de Buck 1935-1961, vol. VII, 104, n. 8 and 9 (spell 895).

[236] *CT* VII, 104k-105g (spell 895).

[237] Assmann, *Totenliturgien* II, 342.

[238] Winkler argues that 'the libation is perceived as the microcosmic ritual counterpart of the macrocosmic revivification process, the inundation, a natural event that was ritualized in the resurrection ritual. The connection between the libation and the annual flooding is found in a comparison between the drought of the land and the dehydration of the body': Winkler, *GM* 211 (2006), 132.

underlay the designation of water as the discharge of Osiris.'[239]

To clarify, the human body as a whole consists of parts. The parts may exist without the whole, but the whole cannot exist without the parts. The water or the fluid that issued from the body of Osiris is one of the most important parts of his body, as recorded on the lists of the Graeco-Roman temples, with names of the different parts of the dismembered body of Osiris.[240] For the god to live again, he needs his body to be assembled. So, the water efflux (*rḏw*), or the water flow (*bꜥḥ*), as vital parts of the body of Osiris, symbolise the totality of the body of the god. The water that has come out of his body will return to him by means of libation. When the body dies, it loses its water. The body serves here as a container for the water, which needs to be placed back in the body for it to be whole and sound. The water offered will make the parts a whole, the unsound sound, and will cause the decomposition to stop.[241]

The image of Osiris on the floor board of the 21st Dynasty coffins was a common decorative motif.[242] The presentation of *ḳbḥw* water to the deceased is of great importance, and its placing on the coffin floor board is significant. On Middle Kingdom coffin floors, Willems argues that 'vignettes which surround the body of Osiris on the floor of the coffin can be viewed as abstracted renderings of ritual actions surrounding the presentations of the tomb inventory'.[243] The same can be applied to the 21st Dynasty coffins. The image of the *ḏd* pillar with water signs on the floor board is simply a representation of an offering of *ḳbḥw*. The body, as a container of water, loses it when the body is mummified. For the deceased as incarnation of Osiris to live again in the underworld and to escape death he should get his water back. This is well expressed in the Pyramid and Coffin Texts cited above, where the water that comes from the body of Osiris is the *rḏw* that causes the Nile to flood. The deceased, who shares in this cycle, participates in the water offered to Osiris.

(C) On Cairo Museum Coffin of *P3-dj-jmn* (CG 6081), the *ḏd* pillar with the head of Osiris is surrounded by other decorative motifs that also have to do with the resurrection of the deceased. Over the head of Osiris is the representation of a mummy lying flat at the bottom and a falcon's head emerging from it. Over the falcon's head is a solar circulation composed of a pair of arms between which are two solar discs[244] (fig 26). This motif is a representation of the Solar-Osirian unity, where the body is that of Osiris and the solar circle refers to Re, both gods united in the underworld as a sign for the unification of the body and soul of the deceased.

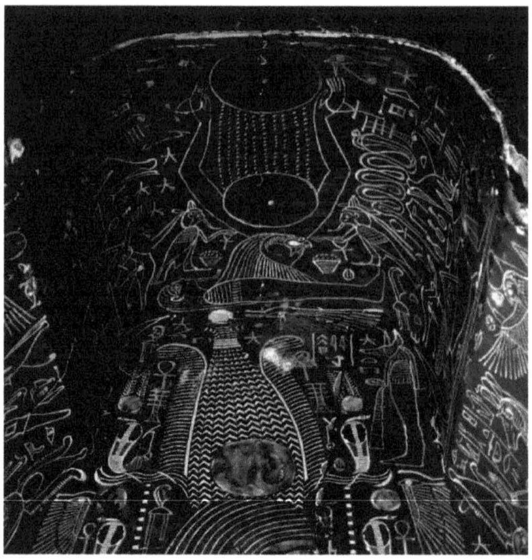

Fig. 26. The decorations over the head of Osiris

### *2.4.2. The Decorations on the Two Inner walls*

(D) On the left wall just on the level of the shoulder, a jackal-headed human Anubis is kneeling and offers a vase in front of a mummy of Osiris with the *Atef* crown. Anubis is protected by a winged cobra with a solar disc over its head. Below this scene is Horus represented in a mummy form with an offering table in front of him (fig. 27).

Fig. 27. Decorations on the left inner wall near the shoulders

(E) Below the wings of the *ḏd* pillar is an image of Osiris in the shape of a sphinx lying on a sky-sign and protected by a winged cobra (fig. 28).

---

[239] Assmann, *Death and Salvation*, 361.
[240] Beinlich, *Die "Osirisreliquien"*, 218.
[241] Winkler, *GM* 211 (2006), 131.
[242] For instance, on the floor of the case of the coffin of the high priest (*wꜥb n ḥ3t n jmn-rꜥ nsw nṯrw jmj-st-ꜥ n pr jmn-rꜥ nsw nṯrwt nsj-jmn-jpt*) in Cairo Museum (CG 6212), Osiris is shown in the shape of a *ḏd* pillar with two wings of a falcon. The head of the Osiris is covered with as stripped wig and a composite *Atef*-Crown. The endings of Osiris' wings and arms are depicted on the side walls as if he is embracing the deceased whose body is placed within the coffin. The *Atef*-crown and the trunk of the *ḏd* pillar are filled with water signs; Niwinski, *The Second Find of Deir El-Bahri,* 51, pl. XXI-1-2
[243] Willems, *Chests of Life*, 203.
[244] Niwinski, *The Second Find of Deir El-Bahri*, 4, fig. 4.

Fig. 28. Osiris as a sphinx

(F) Below this image of Osiris are the three Sons of Horus, Hapi, Duamutef and Qebehsenuef (fig. 29).[245]

Fig. 29. The Sons of Horus

(G) On the right side wall on the level of the shoulder of the *ḏd* pillar with the head of Osiris, a kneeling human figure with a head of a baboon is protected by a falcon Horus of Behdet and adores the figure of  Ptah-Sokar-Osiris (fig. 30). Under the wings of the *ḏd* pillar of Osiris, the same decorative themes are repeated as on the left wall.

[245] Niwinski, *The Second Find of Deir El-Bahri*, 5.

Fig. 30. Decorations on inner the right wall near the shoulder

It is clear now that the offering of the *ḳbḥw* to Osiris forms an episode in a bigger ritual in which water is offered to Osiris. The surrounding scenes on the inner right and left walls of the outer case show that these scenes all have to do with the resurrection of the deceased. The mummy of Osiris with the two hands holding the sun disc clearly refers to resurrection, where the soul and the body of the Re and Osiris are united. This also refers to the resurrection of the deceased, whose soul and body are united as the god.

The image of Osiris as a sphinx standing on the sign of the sky (*pt*) and the Sons of Horus on the left wall are all indications of the rising of the sun in the morning and the resurrection of the deceased. The lid of the same coffin in Cairo Museum (CG 6080)[246] is occupied by the image of the sky goddess Nut protecting the coffin. The image of the sky goddess Nut on the lid with the Sons of Horus on the inner walls of the outer case has a ritual significance. On Middle Kingdom coffins the Four Sons of Horus were depicted on the edge columns along the corners of the two long sides of the coffin as protectors of the deceased.[247] The lid is identified with the sky goddess Nut and the Four Sons of Horus represent the poles that support the sky. This arrangement of the scenes ensures the connection between the body of the deceased and the coffin as his cosmos.[248]

It is now clear that Osiris with signs of waters on his body refers to the resurrection of the deceased, and the *ḳbḥw* water offered to him mediates his passage to this resurrection. It is important to note that the whole idea of Osiris' resurrection expressed in liturgies in Middle Kingdom Coffin Texts has been abbreviated here in just

[246] Niwinski, *The Second Find of Deir El-Bahri*, 1-3, pl. I.
[247] Willems, *Chests of Life*, 140.
[248] The New Kingdom coffin places Isis at the head and Nephthys at the feet of the deceased. The only difference between the Middle Kingdom decoration schemes is that Amesti and Duamutef are placed on the right while Qebehsenuef and Hapi are placed on the left: Willems, *Chests of Life*, 141; Von Falck, *SAK* 34 (2006), 126, 129-30.

two small columns of texts and an image of Osiris with water signs on his body. When the deceased who places his body on this floor board drinks the *ḳbḥw* water offered to Osiris, he drinks the vital fluid of Osiris, and as a result he partakes of the god's immortality.[249] So, the coffin with images and text captions during the 21st Dynasty serves not only as a container for the body of the deceased but also as a ritual machine that constitutes the essential elements for his resurrection and survival in the hereafter.

### *2.5. The Outer Coffin of PA-dj-jmn: Conclusion*

The decorations and the texts on the lid and case of the outer coffin of *P3-dj-jmn* all work together to ensure an eternal life for deceased. The deceased inside the coffin is protected by the sky goddess Nut on the top and is embraced by Osiris, who is depicted on the floor board of the case. He is thus placed between sky and earth, and he is one who shares in the daily cycle of the death and rebirth of the gods. He is Shu who stands between earth and sky, he is Osiris and also he is Re. The coffin here is not only a container for the body, but a 'ritual machine' that ensures the eternal resurrection and protection by the gods and goddess who manifest themselves on its different sides. The coffin is also the tomb itself, which has everything necessary for its inhabitant to start his journey toward the hereafter. Although the posture of the body within the coffin changed during this period, the body no longer placed on its left side facing east but on the floor board facing upward, the location of the scenes and texts goes with the new position of the body inside the coffin. In the coffin of *P3-dj-jmn*, the lid is decorated with the image of the sky goddess Nut, which is not different from what is found on some Middle Kingdom coffins, and her role as the one who covers the body of the deceased is ensured in the deceased's speech asking her to spread her two wings over him. The two long sides are also decorated and inscribed with two formulae which were common on Middle Kingdom coffins, a formula for Osiris on the front (right wall), and the other for Anubis on the left (back wall). This does not mean that the coffin of *P3-dj-jmn* kept on the old tradition of text and vignette distribution of Middle Kingdom coffins without adding new motifs. The new invention of this period is the increase in the use of images instead of texts. New decorative images were added, analogous to those placed on tomb walls.

The images are accompanied by text captions, and in most cases these captions are speeches by gods. So, instead of presenting the rituals in texts for recitation, the rituals are illustrated. The iconographic depiction of the ritual plays the same role as the texts presented for recitation. This suggestion is confirmed by the fact that the illustrations on this coffin are preceded by *ḏd mdw* 'recitation'. This raises the question of whether there were ritual texts recited and performed with the depiction of the ritual, and whether the representation of the ritual in captions on the sides of the coffin can replace the texts intended for recitation.

[249] Delia, *JARCE* 29 (1992), 183; Kettel, In: *Hommages Leclant* III, 318-20; Assmann, *Death and Salvation*, 357-8; *Totenliturgien* II, 96-7; in: *Hommages Fayza Haikal*, 19.

## Chapter Three

## The Inner Coffin of *P3-dj-jmn*

### *3.1. The Lid of the Inner Coffin (CG 6082) Pl. IV*

#### *3.1.1. General Description of the Lid*

The lid of the inner coffin of *P3-dj-jmn* is made of wood covered with plaster. The scenes and images are multicoloured and painted. The lid of the inner coffin looks very similar to the lid of the outer coffin, and the only exception is that the inner lid lacks the beard.[250] The face of the deceased is framed by a striped tripartite wig. Above the head there is a fillet composed of lotus petals. There is a necklace composed of one band around the throat and a collar hangs from the necklace. Below the collar on both sides, the two crossed forearms are painted and the elbows are decorated with lotus flowers.

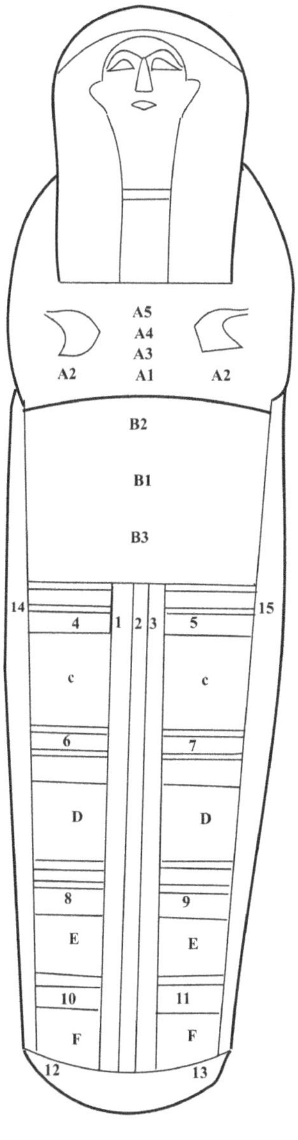


Fig. 31. The lid of the inner coffin of *P3-dj-jmn* (CG 6082) with the numbers and letters showing the distribution of the texts and scenes (drawing by the author)

[250] Niwinski, *The Second Find of Deir El-Bahri*, 9.

#### *3.1.2. The Decorations under the Collar and the Clenched Hands*

The central part of the collar between the clenched hands is filled with figural decorations arranged in four registers (fig.32). These registers from the lowest to the upper most one are as follows:

Fig. 32. Decorations under the clenched hands of the deceased

(A 1) The lowest one shows the resurrected Osiris lying on a funeral bier. The two sisters Nephthys and Isis are represented at the front and back of the bier, respectively. They are shown sitting in a gesture of mourning. Osiris is shown with royal insignia, with a crown, a cobra on the forehead and the *ḥḳ3* emblem in front of him. The bier is designed in a bed form with lion's legs and tail. Above the body of Osiris is his name written as *wsjr*. Beneath the bier there are several crowns and headdresses.

(A2) Below the two crossed forearms and behind the two goddesses there are two small squatting deities with piles of offerings in front of them. The two deities are protected by two falcons with sun discs on their heads and two cobras. The two falcons with a *wḏ3t* eye appear on many cartonnage cases and coffins of the $21^{st}$ Dynasty and also on coffins of the $22^{nd}$ to the $25^{th}$ Dynasties.[251] The identification of these two falcons varies from one coffin to another. They sometimes represent, or are named as, Serqet and Neith, Horus of *Behdet,* or Nephthys and Isis. On the lid of the inner coffin of *P3-dj-jmn,* it is not clear how to read the names of the two falcons. From the speeches of Neith and Serqet on the two borders of the lid, as will be seen below, the two falcons might represent the two goddesses and they complement the roles of Isis and Nephthys, who are there at the bier's head and feet. Their outstretched wings convey the notion of protection as well as wafting air to the deceased Osiris.[252]

Above the elbows on both sides is a heron with a composite crown protected by two winged cobras and

[251] Taylor, in: Sowada and Ockinga (eds), *Egyptian art in the Nicholson Museum*, 274.
[252] Taylor, in: Sowada and Ockinga (eds), *Egyptian art in the Nicholson Museum*, 274.

facing small squatting figures with a feather of *M3ˁt* on their heads (fig. 33).

Fig. 33. A heron with a composite crown

(A 3) The second register is occupied by the image of a falcon protecting the mummy of Osiris by its two outstretched wings. Above the shoulder of the falcon two lions' heads emerge and on the two sides of the falcon's wings there are two *wḏ3t* eyes with a *ˁnḫ* sign attached to its wings. Under the *wḏ3t* eyes on both sides there is a caption reading: *dw3t* (Underworld).

(A 4) The third register shows a solar barque with a seated mummiform figure with the head of a falcon, and a solar disc with cobra on the forehead and two crooks (Gardiner sign list T. 18) in front and behind him. The name of Osiris is written in front of the seated figure and above what seems to be a small shrine. The boat is flanked by two cobras with sun discs on their heads. The two cobras are designated as Neith, on the left, and Serqet, on the right.

(A 5) The fourth register above the solar barque shows a winged scarab, surmounted by a solar disc with two cobras descending from it. The scarab is protected by two winged cobras with two *wḏ3t* eyes between their wings.[253]

### *3.1.2.1. Commentary and Analysis*

Osiris on his bier attended by Isis and Nephthys is a famous ritual scene, in which overcoming death and being king of the underworld are alluded to.[254] The depiction of Osiris and the two goddesses can be compared with the scenes in which the two goddesses assist in the mummification of Osiris. The most famous instance to be cited here is the vignette of Book of the Dead Chapter 151.[255] In this chapter Isis and Nephthys are represented as wailing women at the foot and head of the mummification bed of Osiris. The two goddesses are associated with the coffin ends during the Middle Kingdom. By associating the two goddesses with the coffin ends, the coffin's decorations put the deceased in the place of Osiris, who is mummified and resurrected in the place of embalming.[256]

The role of the two goddesses is played by two priestesses who sit at the head and feet of the deceased, who is lying on his bed. On the coffin of Heqata, for instance, the two goddesses are depicted at the head and foot ends and are accompanied by a text in which they give food for the deceased Heqata. The ornamental text at the head end of this coffin reads:

'An offering which the king and Osiris give: an invocation offering consisting of bread, beer and a thousand of head cattle, birds and textile near Isis and Nephthys for the able Heqata, vindicated'.[257]

The two goddesses play important roles for the deceased Osiris represented on his bed. They assist in his mummification; they also mourn him, and recite glorifications for him.[258] In the ornamental text of Heqata mentioned above, the two goddesses also play important roles in providing the deceased Osiris with offerings. This, as will be explained later, is similar to the scene on the lid of the coffin of *P3-dj-jmn*.

The depiction of Osiris on a bier has also been found in other sources: the Osirion at Abydos Temple, in the burial chambers of a number of royal and private persons dating between the New Kingdom to Saite Period,[259] and in the Hathor Temple at Dendara.[260] The scene on the lid of the inner coffin of *P3-dj-jmn* might be slightly different from the scene occurring on other sources mentioned above but it still alludes to the same idea of the resurrection of Osiris. It is important to look at the exterior decorations of the Middle and New Kingdom coffins, which have to do with the resurrection of Osiris, and at the text corpus on the exterior sides of these coffins.

In his study of Middle Kingdom coffins, Willems argues that their decoration and texts focus on three different aspects; mummification, royalty and offering rituals.[261] The mummification is alluded to in the exterior decoration, where Isis and Nephthys are mentioned on the two short sides as mourners of the deceased. They feature on these two sides as protecting and attending the

[253] Niwinski, *The Second Find of Deir El-Bahri*, 9-10.
[254] The scene is also common on the Theban Papyri of the 11th and 10th centuries; Niwinski, *Studies on the Illustrated Theban Funerary Papyri*, 143-5.

[255] For the spell 151 of the Book of the Dead, see Lüscher, *Totenbuch Spruch 151*.
[256] Willems, in: *Essays te Velde*, 354.
[257] Willems, *The Coffin of Heqata*, 55.
[258] Willems, *The Coffin of Heqata*, 55-6; 89-93
[259] For the New Kingdom tombs see, Waitkus, *GM* 99 (1987), 68-70; on a scene in private tombs see Assmann, *Das Grab der Mutirdis*, 74, scene 31.
[260] Willems, in: *Essays te Velde*, 359.
[261] Willems, in: *Essays te Velde*, 358.

deceased Osiris. The same also can be applied to the mention of the standard gods or column gods on the exterior text columns, with their speeches in which the deceased is described as venerated with a god. Willems analysed the decorations and text columns and reached the conclusion that the gods who are shown at the corner-columns of the coffin must be seen in relation to the protection of the deceased. They protect the deceased and pronounce a judgment.[262] Assmann similarly published the outer coffin of Merenptah and reached the conclusion that the gods at the corners of the coffin play the role of coffin protectors, and one of their roles is to pronounce a judgment for the deceased.[263]

These column gods have been described by Assmann[264] and Willems[265] as gods participating in the night vigil around the bier of the deceased, the purpose of which is to bring a deceased Osiris back to life. This means that the deceased should overcome death. Overcoming death also means overcoming Seth and as a result a deceased Osiris is vindicated by the gods. When Osiris is vindicated, he becomes king of the underworld and Horus, the king of Egypt.[266] That also means that the mummification of the deceased who is lying on his bed should be considered as his coronation. The coronation of Osiris and his vindication have taken place in the judgment of the dead, where he was vindicated against Seth.[267] That is how the ritual might work on Middle Kingdom coffins, but can this be applied to the decorations of the lid of *P3-dj-jmn*?

The deceased on his bier being attended by Isis and Nephthys and also Horus is a common theme in texts entitled as setting up the bier. These texts form a liturgy in the Coffin Texts (spells 1-26),[268] and also in the Book of the Dead (chapters 169 and 170). The images of Isis and Nephthys are also common in the vignettes of the Book of the Dead chapter 151, in which they assist in the resurrection of Osiris, as cited above.[269] I will try to argue here how the images depicted on this part of the lid can refer to the same ritual themes of resurrecting the deceased Osiris.

In the tomb of Sheshenk III at Tanis,[270] Osiris is shown lying on a mummification bed in the shape of a lion. The body of Osiris is covered by a shrine with cavetto cornice. Osiris is shown in the gesture of resurrection. Horus is standing in front of the mummy with a *was* scepter ending in *ꜥnḫ* sign, which reaches the nose of the Osiris as if he is giving him life. There are thirty-six gods attending the bed on both sides. The whole scene has been described by Assmann and Waitkus as referring to the *Stundenwachen* or the hourly vigil in the place of embalming (fig. 34).[271]

Fig. 34. Osiris on the bed of mummification in the tomb of Sheshenk III at Tanis (after Montet, *Les Constructions et le tombeau de Chéchanq III à Tanis*, Pl. 30)

The scene of Osiris on his bier on the lid of the inner coffin of *P3-dj-jmn* is placed under the collar and close to the head end of the coffin. The two goddesses sit on the two sides of the bier wailing the deceased Osiris depicted lying on the bier. What is really fascinating here is that the god is represented with all signs of royalty, wearing a crown and a false beard. There are also other royal headdresses and crowns under the bier, and one wonders why such objects were placed here and why the deceased Osiris is depicted with all these royal signs. These objects under the bier, as Willems argues, are rooted in the Old Kingdom offering lists and also in the object frieze on the Middle Kingdom coffins. It is also important here to note that the aspects of mummifications are associated with royalty.[272]

The scene on the lid of coffin of *P3-dj-jmn* could be considered as a pictorial rendering of that ritual, which was common in Coffin Texts and also in the Book of the Dead. What is really important to note here is the role played by Horus, who is depicted hovering over the mummy of Osiris as if protecting his father. Horus in this scene does not only exist on the top of the bier, but he is also depicted on the two sides of the bier, flanking the two seated figures and the offerings. It seems as if he is flanking and assisting in the resurrection of his father Osiris. The role played by Horus here is not very different

[262] Willems, *Chests of Life*, 141-59.
[263] Assmann. *MDAIK* 28.2 (1973), 127-30
[264] Assmann. *MDAIK* 28.2 (1973), 127-30.
[265] Willems, *Chests of Life*, 141.159.
[266] See also Assmann, *Totenliturgien* I, 163.
[267] Willems, *Chests of Life*, 141-8.
[268] Assmann, *Totenliturgien* I, 54-60.
[269] Lüscher, *Totenbuch Spruch 151*.
[270] The primary publication by Montet, *Les Constructions et le tombeau de Chéchanq III à Tanis*, 67-69, pl. 30; Willems, in: *Essays te Velde*, 359.

[271] Assmann, *Das Grab der Mutirdis*, 92-3; Waitkus, *GM* 99 (1987), 68-70.
[272] Willems, *Chests of Life*, 150ff.

from his role in CT spell 397. This spell, according to Willems in his comment on some decoration motifs during the 17th Dynasty, is a ferryman spell, in which the deceased in the role of Horus is ferrying across the Winding Waterway to an area near the eastern horizon, to enter the abode of Osiris, whom he wants to embalm in order to come to a new life. Horus is thus the right heir and successor of Osiris. This is made clear in the dialogue of the deceased with the ferryman, which reads:

(Deceased) I am one whom his father loves, one whom his father loves greatly! I am one who awakens his father when he is asleep!
(Mahaf) do you say you would navigate to the eastern side of the sky? With what aim will you navigate?
(Deceased) That I may raise his head, that I may lift his brow.[273]

The role played by the son of the deceased who awakens his sleep father places him in the role of the *s3 mrj=f* (the one beloved to his father), which is not very different from the role played by Horus on the lid of the coffin. Horus is represented as hovering over the body of his father and also protecting him. On the top, Horus is sailing in a boat on which there is a small shrine with Osiris's name written above. The scenery in CT spell 397 is not very different from the scene on the lid of the coffin. First, Horus takes care of the body of Osiris and guards him from front and back as if he is awakening him, and then on the top he is depicted sailing in a boat on the top of which there is a small shrine which seems to house Osiris, whose name is written above it. What is really important to note is that there are two cobra heads on the top of the two wings of Horus. This actually alludes to the same themes in CT spell 397: Horus is travelling in a boat and in front of him is the shrine that represents the aim of his journey; he is travelling between two trajectories, which might refer to the west and east. After reaching the abode where his father is, Horus is able to resuscitate his dead father Osiris, who will then shine in the sky as the sun god Re. This is clear in the scene on the lid of the coffin of *P3-dj-jmn*, where Horus attends the body of his father on the bier, who then sails as a resurrected god in a boat, appearing as a scarab with a sun disc. The resurrection of Osiris and escaping death are envisaged as his coronation, in which he assumes the *wrrt* crown and becomes the ruler of the underworld, while Horus becomes the ruler of Egypt.[274] On Middle Kingdom coffins, the mummification of Osiris and escaping the death caused by his brother Seth is also envisaged as a judgment of the dead, in which Osiris is vindicated against Seth.

The judgment of the dead in ancient Egyptian ritual texts seems to be incorporated within the journey to Sais, in which a speech is pronounced by Neith. The great and small Enneads are the judges who participate in this judgment, also described as column gods. The question here is how to consider the inner lid decorations as referring to the journey to Sais and to the judgment of the dead.

The scene of Osiris on his bier has been interpreted on two levels, mythical and ritual. On the mythical level Osiris is depicted on bier attended by Isis and Nephthys and is protected by his son Horus. Horus travels on a waterway to awaken his father and to give him life. Osiris is then resurrected and appears at the eastern horizon of the sky as a scarab. On the ritual level, the son of the deceased is Horus, who approaches the place of embalming of his father to recite texts in order to awaken him. Isis and Nephthys are represented as two kites, whose roles are also played by two priestesses attending the body of Osiris.[275]

### *3.1.3. The Middle Part of the Lid*

This part of the lid is divided into two registers by the figure of the sky goddess Nut. The first register is the section above the goddess and the second is beneath her wings (fig. 35).

Fig.35. The middle part of the lid

(B1) The centre of the middle part of the lid is occupied by the figure of the sky goddess Nut with her outstretched wings and arms in a gesture of protection. The goddess is depicted with a headdress of a vulture. There is also a small figure of a vulture on her head. The head of the goddess is protected by the wings of two cobras. The face of the goddess Nut is turned to the left and goes with the text on the lower part, in which the deceased asks his mother Nut to spread her wings over him. The area between the head of the goddess and the wings of the two cobras is filled by *ꜥnḫ* signs and two *wḏ3t* eyes.

In the first register above the goddess Nut there is a pectoral with a scarab in the middle flanked by two falcons residing on a *ḥb* sign and escorted by a cobra. The scarab and the two falcons have solar discs with cobras. On either side of the falcons are two *wḏ3t* eyes on the *nb* sign, under which there is a *ꜥnḫ* sign between two *ḥḳ3*

[273] *CT* V, 78c-81c (spell 397); the translation is after Willem, in: *Essays te Velde*, 360.
[274] Willems, *Chests of Life*, 150; Roeder, *Mit dem Auge sehen*, 294-7; Goebs, *Crowns in Egyptian Funerary Literature*, 36-7.
[275] For more detail, see chapter Four.

signs on both sides. The pectoral is surmounted by a winged solar disc and at the bottom of the pectoral are signs of *ḏd* and *tjt*.

On both sides of the pectoral are three sacred emblems depicted; an emblem with a head of a jackal on the top, another similar one with the falcon and a third that is the emblem of Abydos.

Behind the wings of the sky goddess Nut there is a scene on each side in three registers (fig. 36). The scene on the left side shows three registers; in the upper one there is a personification of the horizon kneeling and making adoration gesture before the squatting mummiform figure of Osiris. The space between the two figures is filled with the name of Osiris and a depiction of offerings and *ʿnḫ* signs. The second register shows a *b3* standing in a gesture of adoration and the name of Osiris is written in front. In front of the *b3* is a pile of offerings and behind there is a *wḏ3t* eye. The third register shows three of the Four Sons of Horus squatting mummiform; these are Qebehsenuef, Hapi and Duamutef. The scene on the right side is the same with the exception of the third register where only Duamutef is depicted.

Fig. 36. The figures behind the wings of the goddess on both sides

(B 3) The second register beneath the figure of the goddess Nut is divided into three scenes. The scene in the middle shows a barque with a shrine on the top of it. In front of the barque is a net with a bird on the top of it. There are two apes in the gesture of adoration sitting on either side of the shrine, with name of Osiris written in a small caption as *ʿnḫ wsjr ḫntj* on both sides. Above the shrine there is an image of a scarab with a sun disc with two cobras on the top. The solar disc is bordered by two small squatting figures in a gesture of adoration. In front of these figures are two *wḏ3t* eyes on *nb* signs. The scarab and the two squatting figures are bordered and protected by two winged cobras (fig. 36).

On each side of the middle scene are two symmetrical scenes in which the deceased is making libation in front of a seated figure of Osiris Foremost of the Underworld (*wsjr ḫntj dw3t*). Osiris is depicted seated on a throne atop a platform with two steps, accompanied by the *imy-wt*. In front of Osiris is an offering table with a *b3* bird flying over it. *P3-dj-jmn* is shown making libation in front of the seated figure of Osiris, with water coming out from the vessel on the offering table in front of Osiris. Above *P3-dj-jmn* is a small text that accompanies him while he pours the water from the vessel, reading:

*wsjr jt nṯr jn jmn-rʿ nswt nṯrw p3-dj-tw-jmn m3ʿ-ḫrw ḏd=f*

Osiris God's Father of Amun-Re King of the Gods *P3-dj-jmn* the Justified, he says....

Behind him is a *wḏ3t* eye and a small figure of a squatting deity with the head of a donkey.

### *3.1.3.1. Commentary and Analysis*

As on the lid of the outer coffin of *P3-dj-jmn*, the main central part is occupied by the sky goddess Nut, who spreads her two wings over the lid as protecting and also embracing the deceased within the coffin. The sky goddess Nut spreading her wings over the deceased is a famous theme in Old Kingdom Pyramid Texts, Middle Kingdom lid decorations, New Kingdom Book of the Dead and also on New Kingdom coffins. The goddess is depicted as a young lady clad in a long, close-fitting garment that reaches to her feet. She is depicted kneeling, with outstretched arms and wings. The goddess here plays the role of the mother of the deceased who protects and elevates him to the sky to be among the Imperishable Stars. She plays the same role of the goddess Neith on the outer coffin of Merenptah published by Assmann,[276] in which Neith speaks to the king as his mother and the embodiment of the coffin. The surrounding scenes are also important. Above Nut, to the right and left of her wings, Horus and Anubis stand and face each other, while in the middle the scarab and the sun disc are protected by two standing falcons and two cobras. This combination of symbols indicates that the god, after being received by Nut, shines in the sky and starts his heavenly journey in the shape of a scarab. This scene is also complemented by the Sons of Horus under the two sides of the goddess, as if they are supporting the sky and helping in the ascent of the god to the sky.

In this part of the lid, the shrine that houses the body of the god is shown sailing in a solar barque. The name of Osiris, who is within the shrine, is written *ʿnḫ wsjr*. On the two sides of this shrine are two apes raising their hands in a gesture of adoration to the god within the shrine. These apes are normally shown with the barque of the sun god Re, and also known for rejoicing when they see the sun coming in the sky as a sign of the newborn day. Here they adore the shrine of the god, not Re but Osiris the living. In front of the boat is a net above which there is a small bird. The net and the bird might refer to the chaotic powers and enemies that threaten the god in his journey on the barque.

[276] Assmann, *MDAIK* 28.1 (1972), 47-73; *MDAIK* 28.2 (1972), 115-39.

The deceased is shown offering water to the seated figure of Osiris. Offering water or pouring libation as a ritual is well known since the Old Kingdom Pyramid Texts, but the texts for recitation are absent. The act of pouring the water is shown with *P3-dj-jmn* holding a vase and pouring the water in front of Osiris, but what he recites is missing. The evidence that there should have been a text recited during the act of pouring the water is explicit in the text that accompanies the scene. After the introduction, with the name and titles of the deceased, comes *ḏd=f* "he says." This means here that the iconic depiction of the ritual plays the same role as the ritual text. Instead of presenting the ritual in texts for recitation, the ritual is illustrated and presented in images.

It is also important to note the positions of the Four Sons of Horus on the sides of the lid. Three of them are placed on the left and one is placed on the right. The Four Sons of Horus and the sky goddess Nut are assisting in the ascent of the god, and the deceased with whom he is identified, to the sky. The Sons of Horus will later appear again on the lower part of the lid and also on the interior of the case of the inner coffin of *P3-dj-jmn*. On the Middle Kingdom coffins they appear in vertical columns on the two long sides of the coffin, protecting the deceased; they also participate in the hourly vigil around the bed of Osiris, known as the *Stundenwachen*. They also appear on the New Kingdom coffins with the sky goddess Nut. They appear not only on the long sides as on Middle Kingdom coffins, but are split in columns running along the lid and the two long sides of the coffin, but they still play the same role as on Middle and New Kingdoms coffins.[277] On the coffin of *P3-dj-jmn*, they appear on the lid in images and not accompanied by texts. Their speeches occur on the lower part of the lid.

### *3.1.4. The Lower Part of the Lid*

#### *3.1.4.1. The Speeches of the Gods and Goddess on the Middle Part of the Lower Lid*

The lower part of the lid is divided into two symmetrical parts by three columns of inscriptions running to the feet (fig. 37). These columns of text, from left to right, read:

1 2 3

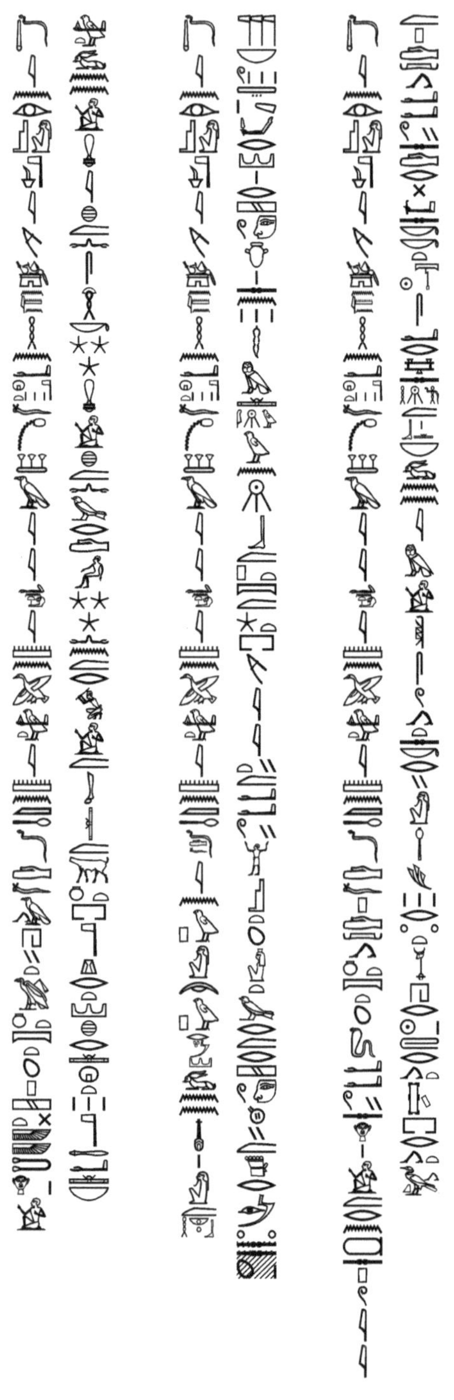

[277] Hayes, *Royal Sarcophagi of the XVIII Dynasty*, 80.

(1) The left column:

*ḏd mdw jn wsjr-jt-nṯr-mrj-ḥry-sštꜣ-n-jmn-ḥnꜥ-psḏt-f-wꜥb-šꜣj-rmn-ḥꜣt-jmn-pꜣ-dj-tw-jmn mꜣꜥ-ḫrw ḏd=f hꜣj mwt nwt pš dnḥwj=ṯ ḥr=j dj.tw wnn=j mj jḫmw skw mj jḫmw wrdw nn mwt=j m wḥm m-ẖnw ẖrt-nṯr ḫr psḏt ꜥꜣ nb*

Speech by Osiris, the God's Father, the Beloved, One Who Knows the Secrets of Amun and his Ennead, Designated Priest, Front-bearer of Amun, *Pꜣ-dj-jmn* the Justified, he says: (Oh) mother Nut, spread your wings over me, and make me exist like the Imperishable Stars and the Unwearying Stars, so that I will not die again in the necropolis near the Great Ennead, Lord of......

(2) The middle column reads:

*ḏd mdw jn wsjr-jt-nṯr-mrj-ḥry-sštꜣ-n-jmn-ḥnꜥ-psḏt-f-wꜥb-šꜣj-rmn-ḥꜣt-jmn-pꜣ-dj-tw-jmn mꜣꜥ-ḫrw ḏd=f (j) jnpw jꜥḥ pw r mꜣnw wnn-nfr m ḥb nṯrw nbw tꜣ ḏsr ršw jb-sn nḏm šw wbn m pt m dwꜣt mrytj m (ḥ)ꜥꜥwj ꜣst wr(t) m ršw m-ḏr mꜣꜣ=sn sꜣ////////////*

Speech by Osiris, the God's Father, the Beloved, One Who Knows the Secrets of Amun and his Ennead, Designated Priest, Front-bearer of Amun, *Pꜣ-dj-jmn* the Justified, he says: Anubis, you Moon at Manu (mountain), Wenennefer is in festival, all the gods of the necropolis rejoice and their hearts are happy, Shu who shines in the sky and in the Netherworld, the beloved, is in joy, and great Isis is in joy, when they see the son/////

(3) The right column reads:

*ḏd mdw jn wsjr-jt-nṯr-mrj-ḥry-sštꜣ-n-jmn-ḥnꜥ-psḏt-f-wꜥb-šꜣj-n-ḥꜣt-jmn-pꜣ-dj-tw-jmn mꜣꜥ-ḫrw ḏd=f pd nwt ꜥwj=s ḥr=j m rn=s pwy m pd ꜥwy=s dr=s kkw sꜥr.s ḥddwt m bw nb wnn.j jm (m) šms skrj ḥḏ jrtj(?) hrw pẖr jnb prt ꜥḳ*

Speech by Osiris, the God's Father, the Beloved, One Who Knows the Secrets of Amun and his Ennead, Designated Priest, Front-bearer of Amun, *Pꜣ-dj-jmn* the Justified, he says: May Nut spread her arms over me in this her name of She Who Spreads Her Arms. May she drive away darkness and brings up light in every place I am in, (in) the following of Sokar, Bright of Eyes, on the Day of Going Around the Wall, emerging and entering …

Fig. 37. Three columns of inscriptions

### *3.1.4.1.1. Commentary and Analysis*

This part has three vertical columns in which the deceased addresses the goddess Nut and Anubis. These two deities appear on Middle Kingdom coffins and they appear here on the lid. Anubis is the patron of the necropolis and also the one who assists in the god's resurrection. The two speeches can also be interpreted in the context of the resurrection of Osiris, who is depicted on his bier attended by Isis and Nephthys. After being resurrected the god ascends to the sky, where he is received by the sky goddess Nut. He will not die again in the necropolis, whose lord is Anubis. The deceased will appear like Shu, which means that he belongs to both earth and the sky. He will ascend to the sky in the shape of a scarab, which is here depicted on a *ḏd* pillar.

The depiction of the scarab on a *ḏd* pillar may represent the sun god at morning, emerging from the realm of Osiris here represented by the *ḏd* pillar, and bringing about regeneration. The juxtaposition also refers to the union of the two divinities, which was crucial for the nocturnal passage through the underworld.[278]

The image of the scarab is a symbol of the newborn sun and the *ḏd* pillar is a reference to Osiris. The deceased within the coffin is identified with both gods and with the sunrise; the deceased, who is Osiris, is born in an image of a scarab.[279] The scarab is a representation of Khepri 'The Becoming One', which is the form adopted by the sun god Re at dawn, when he emerges from the eastern horizon. It also represents the new life that the sun's appearance makes possible.[280] The depiction of the scarab here also refers to the deceased as watching the sunrise,

[278] Taylor, in: Strudwick and Taylor (eds), *The Theban Necropolis*, 106.
[279] Hornung and Staehelin, *Skarabäen und andere Siegelamulette aus Basler Sammlungen*, 14-5; Goff, *Symbols of Ancient Egypt in the Late Period:* 209-20.
[280] Taylor, in: Sowada and Ockinga (eds), *Egyptian art in the Nicholson Museum*, 266.

which reflects the sun's journey across the sky. The scarab surmounted by a sun disc is a typical reference to the sunrise, and the depiction of the two *bꜣ* birds bringing offerings to the living Osiris is an indication of the identification of the deceased with both gods (Re and Osiris). The scarab and Osiris as a combination of Osiris and Re evokes the passage of the sun god Re through gates and paths of the realm of the dead during the twelve hours of the night, a well-known theme in the Books of the Netherworld of the New Kingdom. The god dies with the sunset every day and then starts his journey from the west to the east, to be reborn at dawn. The passage of the god was an important symbol of the continuity of the whole cosmos.

The *ḏd* pillar is a symbol of the god Osiris, and like the emblem of Abydos, the symbol at the beginning had no connection with the god, but with time it was gradually incorporated in Osirian rituals and iconography.[281] From the New Kingdom, the association between the god and the pillar became implicit in texts and also in images. The *ḏd* pillar with the sunrise images of Khepri or the scarab represented Osiris in his netherworld kingdom. The *ḏd* pillar and the scarab refer to the unification of the god's soul and corpse. The god's *ba* as the sun god Re is united with the god's corpse as Osiris, and with this unification the sun god Re is rejuvenated and comes at dawn as the sun spreading his rays, the source of life to all beings.

The deceased's arrival in the necropolis, where the gods rejoice when they see him, is envisaged as the sun god Re appearing in the sky. On a ritualistic level, the deceased's procession to his tomb is here envisaged as his journey across the sky. This might explain why the sky goddess Nut is addressed here by the deceased, who asks her to spread her wings over him. The course of the deceased's journey from his house until he reaches the necropolis is envisaged as the journey of the sun god Re in the body of the sky goddess Nut. This journey of Re takes place in a barque, which is also depicted on the lid of the inner coffin of *Pꜣ-dj-jmn*. The barque on the lid has a shrine, but here it houses Osiris and not Re. After being received by Nut the god travels through her body until he comes in the morning in the shape of a scarab, though still with Osirian features. After he reaches his final resting place the gods are happy, as Shu shines in the sky and also in the netherworld. As a reference to the sky, the deceased directs his speech to Nut and to Anubis as a patron of the west. This might explain why Anubis and Nut are addressed here by the deceased.

### *3.1.4.2. The Decorations and Texts on the Lower Part of the Lid*

The decorations on both sides of the lower part of the lid are composed of four registers of scenes. The first three scenes are depicted in a frame-like naos and preceded by a horizontal band of inscriptions written vertically. These scenes on the left and right sides are identical and composed in two levels. The scenes run as follows.

#### *3.1.4.2.1. The First Register*

The upper level of this register has three seated figures of the Sons of Horus Qebehsenuef, Hapi and Duamutef. They are seated on a chair with low back and hold Heqa, crook and flail in their hands. In front of them there are offerings and a *ḏd* pillar and behind them is a *ḏd* pillar. On the lower level there is a squatting image of Osiris on a raised platform with his name in front of him. He wears a composite crown and a feather of Maat on his knee and behind him is the emblem of Abydos. In front of Osiris are two men kneeling and holding ceremonial staff in their hands (fig. 38). The horizontal inscriptions written vertically above the first register read:

(4) On the left the text reads:

*ḏd mdw in jmꜣḫj ḫr wsjr ḫntj-jmntt nṯr ꜥꜣ nb*

A speech by the Revered One with Osiris Foremost of the West, the Great God, Lord.......

(5) On the right the text reads:

*ḏd mdw jn jmꜣḫj ḫr ptḥ-skr nb ꜣbḏw nṯr*

A speech by the Revered One with Ptah-Sokar, Lord of Abydos, god...

Fig. 38. The first register

#### *3.1.4.2.2. The Second Register*

(D) The upper section of this register has the image of a sphinx wearing the double crown and protected by the outstretched wings of a falcon from behind. Behind the falcon, called *bḥdtj*, there is a *ḏd* pillar. In front of the sphinx is squatting image of Maat in a mummiform. The space between Maat and the sphinx is filled with the name of the sphinx, which reads  *wsjr ḫntj jmntt* "Osiris Foremost of the West." Behind Maat is a *ḏd* pillar and above her is a *wḏꜣt* eye. The lower register shows a seated figure of a goddess between the two emblems of the west. She is depicted with upraised

[281] Altenmüller, *LÄ* I, 48.

and outstretched arms holding *ꜥnḫ* signs (fig. 39). The texts on the left and right sides read:

(6) On the left the text reads:

*ḏd mdw jn im3ḫj ḫr njt wrt mwt nṯr nbt ḳrst*

A speech by the Revered One with Neith the Great, Mother of the God and Lady of the Tomb.

(7) On the right the text reads:

*ḏd mdw jn jm3ḫj ḫr srḳt mwt nṯr nb(t) j3t*

A speech by the Revered One with Serqet, Mother of the God, Lady of the Mound.

Fig. 39. The second register

### *3.1.4.2.3. The Third Register*

(E) This register has a scene of a sacred bull described as *nṯr ꜥ3 nb pt* "the Great God, Lord of the Sky." In front of the Bull there are offerings and a small squatting figure of Isis. The bull is represented with a solar disc on his head and above the solar disc are two feathers. Above the bull are signs of royalty and behind him is the emblem of the west. Above the bull at the far end is a *wḏ3t* eye with a *ꜥnḫ* sign. There are two *ḏd* pillars at the back and in front of the bull. The scene is surmounted by a vault with two cobras and a falcon's head emerging from it (fig. 40). The texts above this register read:
(8) On the left:

*ḏd mdw jn jm3ḫj ḫr ḥpj ḫntj*

A speech by the Revered One with Hapi, Foremost of...

(9) On the right:

*ḏd mdw jn jm3ḫj ḫr jnpw ḫntj jmntt*

A speech by the Revered One with Anubis, Foremost of the West.

The falcon and the bull with sun discs may have dual meaning; they might represent the sun god at morning, emerging from the underworld or the realm of Osiris and bringing about regeneration. They also might represent the deceased as a bull of the sky, which is a well known theme in the Pyramid Texts, where in one of the spells Unas is described as "Unas is the Bull of the sky, aggressive in his nature,"[282] which also refers to the juxtaposition of the sun god and Osiris and alludes to the union of the two divinities.[283]

Fig. 40. The third register

### *3.1.4.2.4. The Fourth Register*

(F) The scene on this side is inverted and contains the representation of a weeper-goddess kneeling on the sign of *nbw*. She is sitting in front of the emblem of Abydos and an emblem with the sacred falcon, in a gesture of adoration (fig. 41). She holds *ꜥnḫ* signs in her hands. The texts above this register on the left and right sides read:

(10) On the left:

*ḏd mdw jn jm3ḫj ḫr gb nb jmntt*

A speech by the Revered One with Geb, Lord of the West.

(11) On the right side the text reads:

[282] *PT* 273=*Pyr.* § 396a-397c.
[283] Taylor, in: Strudwick and Taylor (eds), *The Theban Necropolis*, 106.

*ḏd mdw jn jmꜣḫj ḫr ꜣst nbt nt rsjt*

A speech by the Revered One with Isis, Lady of the South .

Fig. 41. The fourth register

### *3.1.5. The Decorations and Texts at the Edge of the Feet*

There are two vertical inscriptions running in opposite directions on the edge of the feet.

(12) The inscription on the left side reads:

*ḏd mdw jn njt wrt mwt nṯr jrt Rʿ ḥnwt pr-nfr nbt jmntt*

*dj=s ḥtpw m*

A speech by Neith the Great, Mother of the God, Eye of Re,Mistress of the Beautiful House and Lady of the West, that she may give offerings of ....

(13) The inscription of the right side reads:

*ḏd mdw jn ꜣst wrt mwt nṯr nꜣ pwj Nfr-tm ḫwj tꜣwj jwʿ mnḫ n wnn-nfr nb p(t)*

A speech by Isis the Great, Mother of the God: This is Nefertem who protects the two lands, the potent heir of Wenennefer, Lord of the Sky.

The surface under the feet is decorated with the standing figure of a goddess wearing a headdress which is crowned by a solar disc resting between two cow horns. She holds with her outstretched arms and hands two oval shaped objects. Signs of *ʿnḫ*, *ḏd* and *wꜣs* are hanging from her hands by a chain. There are two standing emblems of the west in front and at the back of the goddess.

### *3.1.6. The Texts on the Borders of the Lid*

On both sides along the edge of the lid there are two vertical columns of text running from under the elbow to the end of the feet.

14 15

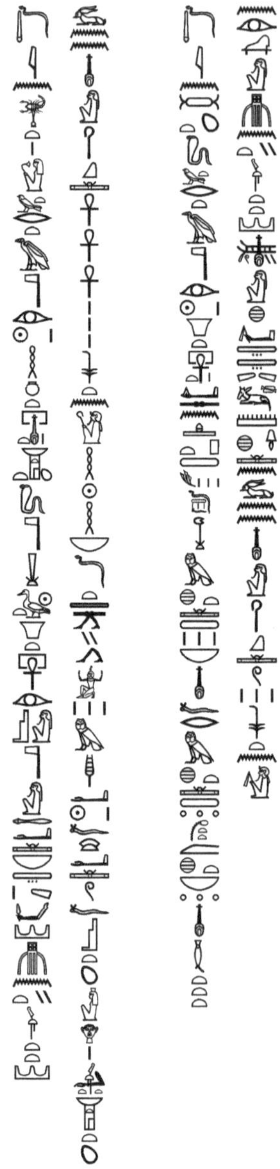

(14) The column on the left reads:

*ḏd mdw jn srḳt wrt mwt nṯr jrt rʿ ḥnwt pr-nfr nbt-ḥwt snt sꜣt rʿ ḥnwt pr-ʿnḫ wsjr nṯr ʿꜣ nb tꜣ-ḏsr ḫntj-jmntt wnn-nfr ḥḳꜣ ʿnḫw nswt nḥḥ nb ḏt sbj ḥḥw m ʿḥʿ.f ḫʿw=f ꜣst ḥr imntt nbt ḥwt*

A speech by Great Serqet, Mother of the God, the Eye of Re, Mistress of the Beautiful House, and Nephthys sister-daughter of Re and Mistress of the House of Life: Osiris the Great God, Lord of the Sacred Land and Foremost of the West, Wenennefer, Ruler of the Living, King of Eternity and Lord of Everlasting, who passes millions with Re in his lifetime, he appears with Isis on the west and Nephthys .......

(15) The column to the right reads:

*ḏd mdw jn njt wrt mwt nṯr jrt Rʿ ḥnwt pr-ʿnḫ dj=s{n} ḥtpw ḏf3w ẖ3 m ḫt nbt nfrt m ḫt wʿbt m ḫt nfrt bnrt n wsjr ḫntj-jmntt nfr-tm ḫwj t3wj jwʿ mnḫ n wnn-nfr ḥḳ3 <ʿnḫw> nswt*

A speech by the Great Neith, Mother of the God, Eye of Re, and Mistress of the House of Life, that she may give offerings and sustenance, a thousand of every good thing and every pure thing, and every good and sweet thing to Osiris, Foremost of the West, Nefertem who protects the Two Lands, the potent heir of Wenennefer, Ruler of the Living and King of .......

### *3.1.6.1. Commentary and Analysis*

The two long sides at the edges of the lid are reserved for the speeches of Serqet and Neith. The speeches of the two goddesses flank the scenes from down below the elbow to the feet of the lid. The main scene in the part under the two clenched fists of the deceased is the scene of Osiris on his bier attended by Isis and Nephthys on the front and back of the bier and Horus above. The two goddesses might also be identified with the two falcons flanking the bier of Osiris. This scene, as argued above, is derived from the Book of the Dead Chapter 151. Serqet and Neith have no part in BD 151 and their roles here are to complement the roles of Isis and Nephthys in the middle. The evidence is the speech of Serqet, when she says that Isis is on the west, which refers to the position of the goddess at the back of the bier of Osiris, here on the west side of the coffin's lid. If we consider how the coffin was placed inside the tombs of this period we will find that the coffin and the body were directed to the north and the feet to the south. This means that the right side of the coffin will face the east and the left will face the west. When we look at the bier of Osiris on the lid, Isis will be on the west and Nephthys on the east, which goes well with positions of the two goddesses on the vignettes of the Book of the Dead Chapter 151.

Serqet played also an important role in the rebirth of the deceased,[284] which is clear from her depiction on canopic chests, where that she protects Qebehsenuef, the son of Horus who is responsible for the protection of the intestines of the deceased. For instance, in an inscription on the canopic chest of Sennedjem in Cairo Museum, the goddess is depicted on the front side of the canopic chest and the accompanying inscriptions read 'Come to me with your body. I have embraced your birthing place'.[285] The same inscriptions are also found on the sledge runners of the outer rectangular coffin of Sennedjem (Cairo JdE 27301). The role of the goddess here can also fit in the context of the ritual images on the lid of *P3-dj-jmn*, where the resurrection of Osiris and his sailing in a boat all refer to the cycle of resurrection and rebirth. On the foot end of some Middle Kingdom coffins, Isis is very rarely flanked by a text mentioning Neith on the right side (south-east) and Serqet on the left side (south-west).[286] As we will see later, the placing of Serqet on that side of the coffin lid draws also on the relation of the goddess with the Four Sons of Horus.

The second speech is by Neith, whose role is not very different from that of Serqet; both of them figure in the scene of the resurrection of Osiris as well as the speeches of the other column gods at the lower part of the lid.

The speeches on the two sides of the lid refer to the role of the goddesses in the protection of the Four Sons of Horus. Serqet and Neith, with Isis and Nephthys, are invoked on the coffin sides since the 12th Dynasty to protect the Four Sons of Horus. During different periods of the Egyptian history, there is some variation and confusion with the placing of these goddesses on the coffin sides and also their relation to the Four Sons of Horus. Isis was connected with Amesti, Nephthys with Hapi, Neith with Duamutef and Serqet with Qebehsenuef. Over the course of time the Egyptians themselves seemed to have been confused at how the four goddesses and also the Four Sons of Horus could be oriented. On the lid of *P3-dj-jmn*, Neith, Serqet, Isis, Nephthys and the Four Sons of Horus are all distributed on different places on the coffin's lid. These goddesses and gods, as will be argued later, have their roles in the judgment of the dead and the justification of the deceased in the hall of the Great Ennead in Heliopolis.

### *3.2. The Lid's Decorations as Representation of the Stundenwachen and the Judgment of the Dead*

There are key words and images on the lid of the inner coffin of *P3-dj-jmn* that refer to the journey to Sais and also to the Judgment of the Dead, which was incorporated in this journey. In his study of the text on the lid of the sarcophagus of Merenptah, Assmann argues that it is a speech by the goddess Neith, who features as the divine embodiment of the coffin. She directs her speech to her son, Merenptah. In the first part of the text, the deceased is pictured inside his mother, the coffin.[287] The rest of the text deals with the actions taking place in the place of embalming, where the rituals are performed by Isis and Nephthys and the Four Sons of Horus. Then the goddess Neith places the gods Shu, Tefnut, Geb and Nut to the left and right of the deceased. These deities proclaim Merenptah to be a king as he appears at the temple of Neith at Sais. All these sequences of events, according to Assmann, take place in the *Stundenwachen*, the nightly wake before burial.[288] The gods of the columns in the inscriptions of Merenptah appear as priests, or as Willems says, 'priests playing divine roles'.[289]

In his study of Middle Kingdom coffin decorations, Willems analysed the the text columns and reached the conclusion that the gods who are shown at the corner-

[284] For the role of the goddess in birth and rebirth see Speiser, *RdE* 52 (2001), 251-64 and also Sabbahy, *RdE* 54 (2003), 286.
[285] Sabbahy, *Egyptian Museum Collections around the W*orld, 1047-1053, pl. II. B.

[286] Willems, *Chests of Life*, 134.
[287] Assmann, *MDAIK* 28. 2 (1973), 127-30.
[288] Assmann, *MDAIK* 28.1 (1973), 47-73.
[289] Willems, *Chests of Life*, 142.

columns of the coffin must be seen in relation to the protection of the deceased. They protect the deceased and pronounce a judgment.[290] Willems also argues that the burial rites included a ceremonial passage of a divine judgment. The journey to Sais was envisaged as the deceased's procession to his tomb, and during this journey the deceased had to stop at certain places symbolizing holy cities in the Delta: Sais, Buto and Hut-ser. While doing so the deceased is admitted to a court, where he undergoes a divine tribunal modelled on the divine tribunal of Seth and Horus. The divine tribunal the deceased has to pass is called as *ḥsbt ꜥ3w* (The calculation of differences).

Willems' interpretation of the term *ḥsb ꜥ3w* is based on two theories; the first is that the calculation of differences is a term designating a tribunal that the deceased has to pass on his way to Sais, which means that the burial rites included a ceremonial passage of divine tribunal.[291] There are two points concerning the judgment of the dead and the divine tribunal. First, it is sometimes represented as a court where the gods determine whether the deceased was guilty of sin or not. The deceased's heart was weighed on a balance against a feather of truth, and he had to pronounce his innocence before Osiris and his forty-two gods. References to this judgment in the Coffin Texts were collected by Grieshammer.[292] The other model of the judgment of the dead was patterned after the mythical tribunal of Horus and Seth. According to the myth, Seth murdered his brother Osiris and took over his kingship. Horus summoned the court in Heliopolis and that court was on his side. Osiris was crowned as king of the netherworld, while Horus was appointed as King of Egypt. The deceased, who was identified with Osiris, is then also one of the actors in the myth. He can win the trial against Seth and be justified in the netherworld as Osiris.[293]

As Willems argues, this complex of thoughts is referred to in the texts and representations of the journey to Sais.[294] According to the inscriptions of Merenptah, after the mummification process, Osiris was justified and crowned as king in the presence of the Enneads and the Two State Chapels. When Osiris reached Sais, his enemies were destroyed. The text columns' gods are mentioned individually, stating their positions to the left and right, head and feet of the deceased. The Ennead features as a court of justice, and they are depicted at the corners of the coffin to protect the deceased. Most probably the role of the gods in the court of justice was played by priests attending the mummy of the deceased. Thus, the journey to Sais seems to incorporate Osiris' victory over his enemies and his coronation as a king in the netherworld.[295]

[290] Willems, *Chests of Life*, 141-59.
[291] Willems, *Chests of Life*, 150-5.
[292] Grieshammer, *Das Jenseitsgericht*.
[293] Grieshammer, *Das Jenseitsgericht*, 111-5
[294] Willems, *Chests of Life*, 148-9.
[295] Willems, *Chests of Life*. 150.

In Middle Kingdom Coffin Texts, there is a liturgy described by Assmann as performed in the *Stundenwachen*.[296] It is his Coffin Texts Liturgy I, which includes CT spells 1-29 and starts with a call upon the deceased to raise himself up:

| | |
|---|---|
| *wsjr N pn* | O Osiris N! |
| *ṯsj ṯw ḥr j3bj=k* | Raise yourself on your left side, |
| *dj ṯw ḥr wnmj=k* | And put yourself on your right side.[297] |

After the deceased Osiris gains his physical power; he goes to a trial, where he is justified against his enemies. In CT spell 15, the judgment is said to be pronounced by the goddess Neith, which, according to Willems, is evidence that the trial takes place near Sais, where Neith appears against the evil word (*ḫꜥj Njt r mdw pf ḏw*) (*CT* I, 45d, 46d).[298] Neith in this text appears as embodiment of the coffin and the protector of the deceased.[299] In the same context in CT Spell 15 (*CT* I, 45c), a god named *bn-k3* is ordered to pull the bonds of a bull (*j bn-k3 jtḥ nṯṯw k3*), which might refer to the slaughter ritual of a bull representing Seth. The Bull as a personification of Seth was killed and his meat was distributed among the participants in the ritual.[300] The victory of Osiris over Seth was completed by the placing of the *wrrt*-crown on Osiris.[301] This is the first viewpoint concerning the occurrence of the *ḥsbt ꜥ3w* in the context of a judgment, which features in the journey to Sais.

Assmann considers the judgment of the dead as an early form of the *Stundenwachen*.[302] The navigation to Sais was incorporated in the *Stundenwachen*; the two might be envisaged as one and cannot be separated. First, in CT spell 335, the names of the members of the divine tribunal are identical with the gods participating in the *Stundenwachen*. For instance, the name of the seventh guardian in CT spell 335 is 'Black-One-Who-is-in-His-Hour',[303] which refers to the hour-service of this god and occurs also in the *Stundenwachen* at Edfu.[304]

If the journey to Sais might represent an early parallel to the *Stundenwachen*, how might the ritual be performed in the place of embalming? The journey to Sais, where the *ḥsbt ꜥ3w* is reached, was in the form of processions, and the *Stundenwachen* was a wake in the place of embalming, which adds more confusion to the notion of the journey to Sais as performed symbolically in the place of embalming. The procession to Sais should have included a procession by boats, which cannot be performed in the place of embalming unless they are in

[296] Assmann, *Totenliturgien* I, 52-60 and 69-103.
[297] *CT* I, 6b-c (spell 1).
[298] Willems, *Chests of Life*, 149.
[299] Assmann, *Totenliturgien* I, 112.
[300] Willems, *Chests of Life*, 149.
[301] Wearing the *wrrt* crown is a sign for the justification of the deceased against his enemies: Assmann, *Totenliturgien* I, 101; Goebs, *Crowns in Egyptian Funerary Literature*, 36.
[302] For the *ḥbs-t3* liturgy as referring to the judgment of the dead, see Assmann, *Totenliturgien* I, 69-103.
[303] *CT* IV, 268d (spell 335).
[304] Willems, *Chests of Life*, 156.

the form of models, or are merely referred to in the recitation.[305] In CT spell 237, which deals with protection of the deceased's mummy during the *Stundenwachen*, the processions to Sais and to Abydos are said to be performed in the place of embalming. In CT spell 237, as in CT spell 335, the deceased reached the *ḥsbt ꜥꜣw* in his way to Sais. CT spell 237 (*CT* III, 311h–315d) reads in part:

| | |
|---|---|
| *jnḏ ḥr=ṯ ḥꜣjt wsjr* | Greetings to you, O (lady) who is behind Osiris, |
| *rmnwtt kꜣ ndjt* | companion of the Bull of Nedit, |
| *snfjt wtw ḥbst bꜣgj* | who makes the wrapped ones breathe, who clothes the weary, |
| *rdjt.n wsjr sꜣ=f r=s* | to whom Osiris turned his back, |
| *ẖrjt-ꜥ wt jnpw* | and assistant of the embalmer Anubis, |
| *m srwḫ ḥꜥw wrḏ-jb* | during the treatment of the body of the One-Whose-Heart-is-Inert, |
| *sꜣḫ wj* | glorify me, |
| *wp=t n=j rꜣ=j* | open my mouth for me, |
| *sšm bꜣ=j r dwꜣwt* | guide my *ba* towards the roads of the netherworld, |
| *dj=ṯ n=j ḥtpwt m-m wrw* | and give me offerings among the Great Ones, |
| *ḥr ẖꜣwwt nt nbw rnw* | on the altars of the possessors of Names. |
| *jnk wsjr jw=j r ꜣbḏw* | (For) I am Osiris and I am on the way to Abydos. |
| *šsp=j ꜣwwt ḥr ḥtp ꜥꜣ* | I receive offerings from the great offering table, |
| *hrw rdjt snmw ḥtpwt n rnw ꜥšꜣw* | on the day of giving food supplies and offerings to numerous names. |
| *dmj.n=j sbḫt ḳꜣt šnwt* | I have reached the High Portal and the entourage, |
| *ḥr ḥsbt ꜥꜣw* | on the day of the calculation of differences. |
| *ꜥḳ=j r ḫm wr ḥnꜥ wrw* | May I enter the Great Shrine together with the Great Ones, |
| *m-m šmsw ꜥꜣ n wsjr* | among the Great Following of Osiris. |
| *jj.n=j ḥꜣp=j bꜣgj n wrḏ-jb* | I have come that I might cover the limpness of the Weary One, |
| *ḥbs.n=j gmt.n=j tšj* | and I have covered up what I have found missing. |
| *wn n=j wꜣt* | Open a path for me! |
| *jnk nb spꜣ* | (For) I am the Lord of Sepa.[306] |

In this spell, there is a description of the activities of the deceased in the workshop of Anubis. The second section of the text is a speech by the deceased to the goddess who is behind Osiris and participates in the treatment of his body. The text also situates the arrival of the deceased at the 'High Portal of the Entourage' on the day of the calculation of differences.[307] Here all the acts in the place of embalming parallel those associated with the journey to Sais and the tribunal that the deceased has to pass in his way, and with the journey to Abydos. So can we conclude that there were processions to Sais and Abydos in the *Stundenwachen*?

CT spell 237 mentions a ritualized tribunal session among elements of the Osiris Festival at Abydos, and pays particular attention to the activities of the deceased in the treatment of Osiris and to the offering rites performed in this connection. Willems argues that:

> There is little room for doubt that the 'Great Ones' mentioned in our texts are none other than the *wrw nw ꜣbḏw*, 'Great Ones of Abydos', who play such prominent part in the Osiris mysteries. On the other hand, we can hardly go amiss in identifying them with the 'Great Ones who are in the Portal' together with whom the deceased eats offering bread on the day of calculation of difference i.e. in connection with a session of the divine tribunal.[308]

It seems that the judgment of the dead, in the form of a divine tribunal, features in the Osirian secret rituals and also in the procession to Sais, and the three appear in the context of the *Stundenwachen*. The nautical element was reduced to allusion in the spells or glorifications recited and the libation offerings.[309] This means that the deceased might symbolically be present on his bier in the place of embalming and all the acts are performed around the bier. Of course, the procession should be performed with boats, and in this case the boat might be represented by a bier, and the water over which the boat sails might be reduced to the form of water poured around the bier. A representation of boats on the bier can also solve this problem. There are some pictorial representations in the New Kingdom temples, where the god on the mummification bed is said to be in his boat.[310] In a similar scene from the Temple of Hibis, one of the gods attending Osiris's bier is called 'Anubis who is in his barque'.[311]

Do the images and texts on the lid of *Pꜣ-dj-jmn* refer to the journey to Sais and to the Judgment of the Dead?

First, it is important to note that the lid is covered by speeches of different deities, who can be described as the column gods, as their speeches occur in columns on different parts of the coffin lid. The scenes and text on the lid are bordered by the two speeches of the goddesses Neith and Serqet, running from down the elbow to the end of the feet. At the feet edges are two texts that mention Isis and Neith. The middle part of the lid is occupied by texts that mention Osiris, Ptah-Sokar, Neith,

305 Willems, *The Coffin of Heqata*, 154-5.
306 *CT* III, 311h-315d (spell 237).

307 Willems, *The Coffin of Heqata*, 132-3.
308 Willems, *The Coffin of Heqata*, 133.
309 Willems, *Chests of Life*, 158; *The Coffin of Heqata*, 133.
310 Willems, *Chests of Life*, 158.
311 Willems, *Chests of Life*, 158.

Serqet, Hapi, Anubis and Geb. The deceased appears on the lid as the Venerated One with different deities. The deceased also asks the goddess Nut to spread her wings over him and to make him like the Imperishable Stars and the Unwearying Stars, so that he will not die again in the necropolis near the Great Ennead. These gods are also not very different from the column gods on the lid of the coffin of Merenptah and also the column gods on Middle Kingdom coffins.

The main scene on the lid of the inner coffin of *P3-dj-jmn*, as argued above, is the bier of Osiris where Isis and Nephthys are represented at the feet and head ends and Horus hovering over the body of his father Osiris. The surrounding scenes complement the roles of the deities around the bier of Osiris. Horus as the son of Osiris is also depicted in a boat upon which there is a shrine housing Osiris, and he is travelling between two trajectories symbolizing the west and east, as represented by the two cobras' heads emerging from the wings of Horus. The two cobras surrounding the boat are named as Neith and Serqet. As argued above, this scene might refer to Horus travelling in a boat towards the abode of his father to resurrect him. This theme of the son who travels in a boat crossing a body of water occurs in the ferryman spells cited above, where the son is asked about the aim of his journey, and he replies that he is in his way to awaken his dead father.

The speeches of the goddess Neith on the different parts of the lid indicate that there might have been a judgment pronounced by the goddess and also might refer at the same time to a journey to Sais. The deceased's arrival in the west is envisaged as his crossing to the sky. The gods of the necropolis are also happy when he reaches the necropolis, where he will not die again with the Ennead. The Ennead here might refer to the gods who are forming protection around the body of the deceased Osiris, who is depicted lying on his bier. The presence of offerings around Osiris and the different kinds of crowns under the bier allude to the fact that the god has been vindicated and has received the *wrrt* crown as a sign of his victory over his brother Seth. This is clear in the speech of Thoth on the case of the inner coffin, as we will see later in this chapter. The image under the collar, of the scarab with a sun disc, is also a reference to the sunrise. Sunrise also means that the god has triumphed over the demons of the night, and for the deceased Osiris means that he has been justified.

Although some might argue that it is really frustrating to 'interpret the scenes sequentially as elements of large scale iconographic program',[312] the texts and the images on the lid of the inner coffin recall both Osirian and solar aspects. The choice of images and also texts or speeches of the gods on the lid function as elements of a unified concept. They draw both on Osirian and Solar unity. The deceased is identified with both Osiris and Re. He is Re travelling in his boat across the sky, and he is also Osiris, whose procession to the tomb is envisaged as the journey of Re crossing the sky. The vindication of the god against his enemies takes place in a tribunal. This vindication is alluded to when the deceased is Re who overcomes darkness and rises in the sky as Khperi, and he is also Osiris who is vindicated against Seth and gains the *wrrt* crown.

It is clear now that the images and texts on the lid of the inner coffin refer to two important themes: the preservation of the body, and the introduction of the deceased into the heavenly sphere.

### 3.3. The Case of the Inner Coffin of *P3-dj-jmn (CG 6079)*

#### *3.3.1. Exterior Decorations and Texts (PL. V. 1-2):*

The exterior of the inner case of the coffin of *P3-dj-jmn* is extensively decorated on all four sides. The top and the bottom sides of the case are bordered by bands of geometrical ornaments. The decorations on the two long sides of the case are composed of four scenes on each side and each scene is separated from the next one by a vertical column of inscriptions that is bordered by a gate motif. Along the upper edge of the case runs a long horizontal inscription that begins behind the head and runs on the external left side wall of the case:

1-

*ḏd mdw jn wsjr-jt-nṯr-mrj-ḥry-sšt3-n-jmn-ḥnᶜ-psḏt-f-wᶜb-š3j-rmn-ḥ3t-jmn-rᶜ-nswt-nṯrw p3-dj-tw-jmn (m3ᶜ)-ḫrw ḏd=f jnpw jᶜḥ pw r m3nw wn-nfr m ḥb nṯrw nbw ršw jb-sn nḏm šw wbn m pt m dw3t mrytj m ḥᶜᶜwj 3st wrt m ršw m-ḏr m33=s s3=s ḥrw mn i3t=f 3st m s3 n ḥᶜw=f dj=s ḥtpw m ḫt nb nfr wᶜb m ḫt nb nfr bnr n wsjr ḫntj jmntt nṯr ᶜ3 ᶜnḫ m m3ᶜ ᶜḥm*

Speech by Osiris, the God's Father, the Beloved, One Who Knows the Secrets of Amun and his Ennead, Designated Priest, Front-bearer of Amun, *P3-dj-jmn* the Justified, he says: Anubis, you Moon at Manu (mountain), Wenennefer is in festival, all the gods of the necropolis rejoice and their hearts are happy, Shu who shines in the sky and in the Netherworld, the Beloved, is in joy, and Great Isis is in joy, when she sees her son

[312] Taylor, in: Strudwick and Taylor (eds), *The Theban Necropolis*, 105.

Horus set in his office. Isis is protecting his limbs, that she may give offerings of every good and pure thing, of every good and sweet thing, to Osiris Foremost of the West the Great God, truly living, Divine Image.

### *3.3.1.1. The Scene behind the Head*

The part behind the head is decorated with a standing figure of a goddess with outstretched and upraised arms. She wears a long green sheath-dress, blue sash, green collar, and bracelets. She has a divine cone surmounted by a cobra with a solar disc on its head. From her arms two *ʿnḫ* and *ḏd* pillar signs hang. There are two emblems of the west in front and at back of the goddess. The space between her and the two emblems of the west is filled by *ʿnḫ* and *w3s* signs. There are also two *wḏ3t* eyes ending with two small hands touching the cone of the goddess (fig. 42). The scene is bordered by two vertical columns of texts on the right and left sides. The text on the left side reads:

*ḏd mdw jn jnpw r m3nw wnn-nfr ḥḳ3*

A speech by Anubis who is on the mountain, Wennenefer the Ruler.

The text on the right reads:

*ḏd mdw jn Gbḫntj jmntt wnn-nfr nb*

A speech by Geb Foremost of the West, Wenennefer the Lord.

Fig.42. The standing goddess behind the head

#### *3.3.1.1.1. Commentary and Analysis:*

The scene of a goddess standing at the head and feet end of a coffin was common during the Middle and New Kingdoms. The head was normally occupied by Isis or Nephthys and sometimes by Neith. The goddess is not named, but she stands in the same position and attitude of the goddesses normally depicted on that side. The two emblems of the west flanking the goddess may give her the characteristics of the Goddesses of the West. The main role of the goddess here is to protect the head of the deceased and also to receive the deceased and nourish him with *ʿnḫ* signs.

### *3.3.1.2. External Left Side Wall (Pl. V-1)*

#### *3.3.1.2.1. Scene A (near the head)*

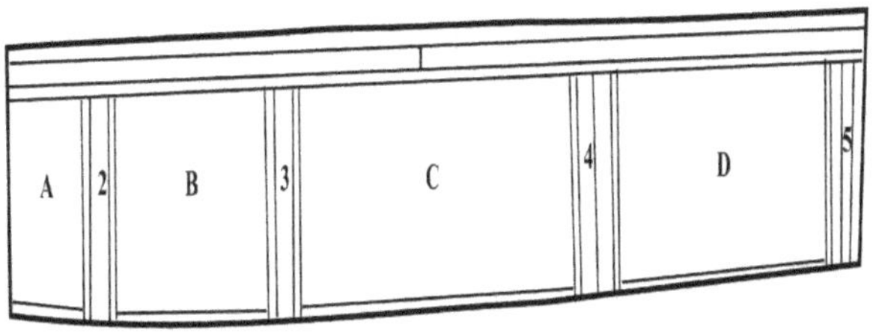


Fig. 43. The external left side wall of the case of the inner coffin of *P3-dj-jmn* with the numbers and letters showing the distribution of the texts and scenes (drawing by the author)

The first scene on the external left side wall at the head end shows on the right side the emblem of Abydos. In front of the emblem an inscription reads:

*wsjr nb jmntt wnn-nfr ḥḳ3*

Osiris Lord of the West, Wenennefer, the Ruler.

The emblem is accompanied by *imj-wt*. In front of these two emblems the deceased stands upon a *ḥb*-sign pedestal. He is stretching his hand towards the two emblems. The scene is surmounted by a winged *wḏ3t* eye. Behind the figure of the standing deceased is a serpent with a beard and human legs standing on a ceremonial support. Behind the bearded serpent is a standing lotus flower with a human head. There are also six squatting figures facing the lotus stem. The two upper figures have jackal heads, the middle one has a baboon head and the lower is donkey-headed and represented frontally (fig. 44). A column of vertical inscriptions separates this scene from the next and reads:

(2) *ḏd mdw jn njt wrt mwt nṯr ḥnwt pr-nfr nbt-ḥwt snt-nṯr ḫnty*

A speech by Neith, the Great, Mother of the God, Mistress of the Beautiful House, and Nephthys, the God's Sister, Foremost of …

Fig. 44. The first scene near the head end

### 3.3.1.2.1. Commentary and Analysis

The emblem or symbol of Abydos is a dome-shape object resting on a pole and is surmounted by a sun disc and double plumes springing from the *ḏw* hieroglyph.[313] The symbol or the emblem of Osiris seems to have originated from the Thinite Nome. At the beginning the symbol has nothing to do with Osiris, but with time, as Osiris rose to prominence at Abydos, the symbol was incorporated into the rituals performed for the god there. From the New Kingdom the symbol was interpreted as a reliquary containing the head of the god Osiris. Later, the emblem was thought to represent the god himself. Like the *ḏd* pillar, it stands in the place of the god in the funerary iconography of the 21st Dynasty and also in later periods.[314]

*jmj-wt* is another name of Anubis as the One-Who-Is-In-His-Bandage and the one who is responsible for the mummification of the deceased. The god is normally mentioned with two titles on the coffin sides; he is described as *jmj-wt* and is usually placed on the west side wall as the god connected with embalming and burial rites. He is also described as the one who is in front of the divine booth which refers to his cult or worship in the world of the living by establishing a cult in a shrine by the living for the god and for that reason he is placed on the east side.[315]

The deceased standing in front of these two emblems holding the *ˁnḫ* sign in one hand and raising it in adoration with the other is then standing before Osiris and Anubis. These two gods were incorporated on Middle and also New Kingdom coffins in offering formulae invoking both of them on the two long sides of the coffin. On the lid of the inner coffin of *P3-dj-jmn* they are depicted only in images.

[313] Beinlich, *Die "Osirisreliquien*, 222-4; Winlock, *Bas-Reliefs*, 15-26; Otto, *LÄ* 1 (1979), 47-8.
[314] Beinlich, *Die "Osirisreliquien*, 222; Winlock, *Bas-Reliefs*, 23-5.
[315] Hayes, *Royal Sarcophagi of the XVIII Dynasty*, 74.

### 3.3.1.2.2. Scene B (near the shoulders)

The scene on this side shows the famous cosmological composition of creation. Geb is shown lying on the earth, his body covered with reeds. He has a bent beard and a feather of Maat on his head. Above Geb is the image of the naked sky goddess Nut supported on the tips of her hands and feet, her body covered by stars. Between Geb and Nut, Shu is standing dressed in a royal garment holding with his upraised arms the solar barque, on which is a small squatting falcon-headed god wearing the *Atef* crown, with a pile of offerings in front of him. Above the barque are two *wḏ3t* eyes. On each sides of Shu is a falcon standing on the emblem of the west. A small squatting figure on a *ḥb* sign with offerings in front fills the space between Geb and Nut (fig. 45). On each side of Shu and in front of the falcon is a text that reads:

*wsjr nb jmntt dw3t nṯr ˁ3 nb pt*

Osiris, Lord of the West and *Duat*, The Great God, Lord of the sky.

Isis and Nephthys are standing on the right and left of the figure of Nut, stretching their hands in a gesture of protection; both stand on a *sm3-t3wj* symbol. The inscription in front of Nephthys reads:

*nbt-ḥwt snt-nṯr ḫntj-jmntt*

Nephthys, the God's Sister (of) Osiris Foremost of the West.

The inscription in front of Isis reads:

*3st nbt jmntt*

Isis Lady of the West.

The scene is separated from the next one by a vertical column of inscription reading:

(3) *ḏd mdw jn ḏḥwtj sš m3ˁt n psḏt ˁ3t n nbw ḥwt-ˁ3*

A speech by Thoth the Maat Scribe of the Great Ennead and of the Lords of the Great Temple (of Heliopolis).

Fig.45. Scene 2 near the shoulders on the left external wall

### *3.3.1.2.2.1. Commentary and Analysis*

The scene here is different from the one on the case of the outer coffin of *Pꜣ-dj-jmn*. This scene seems to be more ritualistic than cosmological. The two goddesses Isis and Nephthys are standing and raising their hands in adoration towards the standing figure of Shu. In this scene Shu is Osiris, who is praised by Isis and Nephthys. The two falcons on the two sides of Shu are identified as Neith and Isis, which fits in the context of the decorations on the inner case, as most of the scenes deal with Osirian aspects. This scene can also be interpreted in the context of the judgment of the dead that follows, where Osiris, after being awakened, will undergo a judgment in which he will be vindicated. This also might be confirmed by the fact that the text that separates this scene from the next is a speech by Thoth, who stands in the hall of the judgment of the Great Ennead and records the events.

But how does Nut spreading herself over the body of the deceased fit in the context of resurrection, and how also does that fit in the context of the deceased's vindication?

On the outer coffin lid of *Pꜣ-dj-jmn*, the goddess Nut is depicted on the middle of the lid with her outstretched wings, and the deceased asks her to spread her wings over him, and to set him among the Imperishable Stars and the Unwearying Stars. Nut is considered as the place that conceals these stars. On a naos from Saft el-Henna in Cairo Museum (JE 70021), which dates to the 30th Dynasty,[316] the Imperishable Stars and the Unwearying Stars are said to come into being in Nut's body. The text reads:

| | |
|---|---|
| *štꜣ pw jmj nwt* | It is a secret which is in Nut. |
| *jḫmw-sk* | The Imperishable Stars, |
| *jḫmw-wrḏ* | and the Unwearying Stars |
| *ḫpr* | Have come into being.[317] |

The deceased's wish on the lid to be covered by the wings of the sky Goddess Nut is complemented by the scene of the sky goddess Nut on the case. When the deceased enters the body of the sky goddess Nut and starts his nocturnal journey in her body, he is then concealed in the body of the goddess. After the journey, the deceased will be born as the sun god Re. According to Billing:

'The night is the time of reconstitution, the mythical time of mummification and the vigil that takes place in the preparation for the burial. It is also during the night that the deceased is vindicated before the divine assembly, a judicial procedure that establishes the legitimacy required for the deceased to come forth at dawn.'[318]

The deceased's birth from Nut is envisaged as his resurrection. In the text cited above the secrecy of the sky goddess is connected to the night sky, and as Billing argues *št pt* is an expression referring to the nocturnal aspects of the sky journey. It is also the period of darkness in which the god, with whom the deceased is identified, is concealed within her generating body.[319]

By spreading her wings over him, the goddess transforms the deceased, her son, into a god and as a result, the god is integrated within the community of gods. This leads to the resurrection of the deceased, which is a central theme of reconstitution,[320] described by the image of the sky goddess Nut and the deceased's nocturnal journey in her body.[321] The reintegration of the god means that he has escaped death, which is characterized by the liminial stage in the rites of passage.

By placing the deceased in her embrace and enclosing him with her body, the deceased is given life and is resurrected. For instance, CT spell 917 reads in part:

| | |
|---|---|
| *[...]ḫrt-nṯr NN pn* | [..] The Necropolis. O this NN! |
| *pḫr.ti n Nwt smꜣ=s tꜣwj Gb tꜣ jmntt=k* | Turn yourself to Nut that she may unite the two lands of Geb and the land of your west. |
| *rdj.n n=k mwt=k ʿwj=s n ʿnḫ nt st [..] NN* | Your mother has given her arms to you for life of the seat [..] O NN! |
| *ṯs (t)w ḥr gs=k jꜣbt* | Raise yourself upon your left side, |
| *rdj.t ḥr gs=k jmntt* | having been placed on your right side.[322] |

When the deceased Osiris is placed within this constellation of Nut and Geb, he then becomes the heir of the space that they embody. This also refers to the deceased as the heir of the above underworld, symbolized by Nut, and the lower underworld, symbolized by Geb. The passage cited above also refers to the connection between placing of the body of the deceased within this space and the resurrection of his body.[323]

---

[316] Naville, *Todtenbuch*, pl. I, lines 1.4.
[317] The translation is after Billing, *Nut*, 93.

[318] Billing, *Nut* 52.
[319] Billing, *Nut*, 52.
[320] Billing, *Nut*, 93.
[321] Assmann, *MDAIK*, 28-2 (1972), 115-139; Assmann, *Liturgische Lieder*, 61. n. 96, 197 n. 31.
[322] *CT* VII, 120i-m (spell 917).
[323] Billing, *Nut*, 107.

Isis and Nephthys are standing at the two sides of the goddess Nut. They act here as the two trajectories of the horizon, between which the deceased Osiris is travelling. For instance, in Pyramid Texts Utterance 269, Isis and Nephthys are described as:

| | |
|---|---|
| *jj prjw jj prjw* | They come, the ones who have risen up, they come, the ones who have risen up; |
| *jj ḥfdjw jj ḥfdjw* | they come, the ones who have climbed, they come the ones who have climbed; |
| *jj šwjw jj šwjw* | they come who have elevated, they come who have elevated. |
| *prj W ḥr mnwtj ꜣst* | Unas ascends on the knees of Isis, |
| *ḥfd W pn ḥr mnwtj nbt-ḥwt* | This Unas ascends on the knees of Nephthys.[324] |

The two goddesses represent the horizon between which the deceased Unas will ascend to the sky. The horizon represents a place standing between two ontological states and it also represents the threshold between the primordial and created sphere.[325] It is also a place where death is transformed into life, and a place representing the borders between existence and non-existence. It is a place where the deceased will come into being and become an *ꜣḫ*.[326] The journey from death to resurrection is envisaged as a journey in the body of Nut and the two goddesses Isis and Nephthys represent the two poles between which the journey of Osiris from death to life takes place.

Nut here represents the *ꜣḫt* itself and Isis and Nephthys are the sides of that *ꜣḫt*, or the two peaks of it. In the Pyramid Texts Nut is described as the Great *ꜣḫt*. For instance, Pyr. 1a reads:

| | |
|---|---|
| *ḏd mdw jn nwt* | Recitation by Nut. |
| *ꜣḫt wrt* | The Great Horizon. |
| *sꜣ=j pw smsw tti* | This is (my) eldest son Teti, |
| *wp ẖt(=j)* | who has split open my womb.[327] |

The deceased is also described as an *ꜣḫ* who has been born by Nut.

| | |
|---|---|
| *n ṯwt js ꜣḫ* | For you are an *ꜣḫ,* |
| *msw nwt snḳw ḥwt-nbt* | whom Nut born and Isis suckled. |
| *dmḏ=sn ṯw* | They assemble you.[328] |

In these two texts Nut represents the *ꜣḫt* in which the deceased will reside in order to be transformed into an *ꜣḫ*.

Nut is also an active participant in the *Stundenwachen* in which the deceased is transformed into an *ꜣḫ*.[329]

| | |
|---|---|
| *wrš=s m hrw ḥr ḫꜣ=k* | She spends the day mourning you, |
| *sḏr=s m grḥ ḥr sꜣḫ=k* | she spends the night transfiguring you.[330] |

In CT spell 61 the goddess is described as one of the gods and goddess who transform the deceased into an *ꜣḫ*:

| | |
|---|---|
| *sꜣḫ ṯw sꜣty Nwt* | The two daughters of Nut glorify you, |
| *sꜣḫ ṯw Gb Nwt* | Geb and Nut glorify you, |
| *nṯrw šnw rḫjt* | the gods who encircle the people.[331] |

Nut here is the one who is glorifying the deceased and the one who also places her two daughters, Isis and Nephthys, at the two sides of the bier. It is also important to note that the deceased Osiris who travels in the body of his mother Nut will become an *ꜣḫ,* which is the aim of all the texts dealing with the rites of passage in Egyptian rituals.

The texts that describe Isis and Nephthys do not give any indication of their roles within the whole composition. The combination of text and image acts as the medium of information. In his work on the image-text relation in the Book of the Dead, Bruner refers to the text as a more or less fixed element whereas the image could be executed in various ways in concordance with the imagination of the artist.[332] That means that the artist saw in the image a medium through which he could enrich the text or give emphasis to more aspects connected to the image, and as Billing argues, 'the images were not only illustrations, they meant something'.[333] Here the elevation of the deceased to the sky is envisaged as his resurrection, and Isis, Nephthys and Neith watch over this resurrection. Nut, Isis, Nephthys, and Geb play a role in the glorification of the deceased, causing him to be an *ꜣḫ*. All these aspects are referred to by the scene on the outer decoration of the case of the inner coffin of *Pꜣ-dj-jmn*.

### *3.3.1.2.3. Scene C (near the hips)*

The deceased is introduced to Osiris. The scene is divided into parts; in the first Osiris is shown seated on a throne placed on a podium decorated with *ḏd* and *tit* signs, standing on a *nb* base. He wears the composite *Atef* crown and holds all the royal signs of *ʿnḫ*, scepter and flagellum. The inscription in front of him reads:

*wsjr ḫntj jmntt nṯr ʿꜣ ʿnḫ*

[324] *Pyr.* 379a-b (spell 269)
[325] Englund, *Boreas* 13 (1984), 47-54.
[326] Jansen-Winkeln, *SAK* 23 (1996), 201-15.
[327] *Pyr.* 1a (spell 1).
[328] *Pyr.* 623a (spell 365).

[329] Assmann, in: Israelit-Groll (ed.), *Studies in Egyptology presented to Miriam Lichtheim*, vol. I, 19; Münster, *Untersuchungen zur Göttin Isis*, 36.
[330] Junker, *Stundenwachen*, 99 [91-92].
[331] *CT* 1, 262d-e.
[332] Bruner,in: Röllig (ed.), *Das hörende Herz*, 365.
[333] Billing, *Nut*, 195.

Osiris, Foremost of the West, The Great God, the living One.

Thoth is shown as the divine scribe with a head of an Ibis holding a palette and a pen in his hand and records the events. In front of him an inscription that reads:

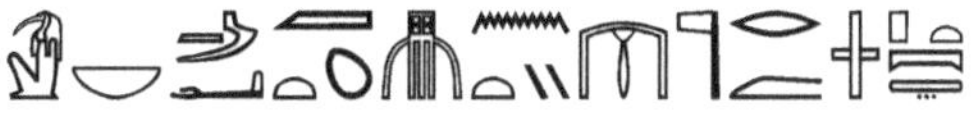

*ḏḥwtj nb mꜣꜥt ḫntj sḥ-nṯr jmj pt tꜣ*

Thoth, Lord of Maat, Foremost of the Divine Booth, which is in sky and earth.

There is a winged *wḏꜣt* eye on the top of the scene and a snake with a beard behind completing the scene. An offering stand with *nmst* jar, lotus and lettuce is in front of Osiris.

The second part of the scene shows the deceased with three deities approaching Osiris. The deceased is escorted by a lion-headed goddess who carries the sign of the West. The caption behind her reads:

*prjt dwꜣt nṯr ꜥꜣ*

She who emerges (from) the Duat of the Great God.

He is dressed in a festive garment and followed by Isis with the head of a cobra. Behind Isis is Hapi with the head of an ape. The lion-headed goddess and Isis hold the hands of the deceased *Pꜣ-dj-jmn* as if they are introducing him to Osiris. Behind Isis stands Duamutef (fig. 46). The vertical column of text that separates this scene from the next is a speech by Duamutef, reading:

*ḏd mdw jn dwꜣ-mwt-f nb pt sꜣ wsjr nṯr ꜥꜣ nb tꜣ ḏsr ḥrj-jb jtrt wnn-nfr nb jmntt dj=f ḥtpw*

A speech by Duamutef, Lord of the Sky, Son of Osiris, the Great God, and Lord of the Sacred Land, Who is in the Middle of the shrine of Wenennefer, Lord of the West, that he may give offerings.

Fig. 46. Scene. 3 near the hips

### *3.3.1.2.3.1. Commentary and Analysis*

In this scene the deceased enters the kingdom of Osiris: the "netherworld of the Great God," as the caption indicates. Niwinski describes the scene as a variant of the judgment of the dead.[334] After the deceased has been resurrected, he then proceeds to the world where Osiris is.

### *3.3.1.2.4. Scene D (near the legs)*

On the left side of this scene behind the deceased there are four recumbent celestial cows and a standing bull, the vignette of Book of the Dead Chapter 148.[335] In the middle the deceased is shown kneeling and drinking from the water poured by the goddess standing in front of him. Behind the deceased stands a falcon on the emblem of the west with a sun disc and two feathers on the head. There is a caption in front of the falcon and above the head of the kneeling deceased, reading:

*wsjr nb jmntt*

Osiris Lord of the West.

The goddess is described with two different epithets:

*nbt ḥwt snt-nṯr ḫntj*

Nephthys Sister of the God, Foremost ...

And behind her there is a caption which reads:

[334] Niwinski, *The Second Find of Deir El-Bahri*, 16.
[335] Niwinski, *The Second Find of Deir El-Bahri*, 17.

*ꜣst ḫntj jmntt*

Isis Foremost of the West.

Behind the goddess is a large sacred sycamore tree under which is a small *bꜣ* bird with human hands holding *ꜥnḫ* signs in a gesture of adoration. There is also a squatting jackal-headed mummiform god on the other side of the tree. Above the deceased is a winged *wḏꜣt* eye and above the tree, two *wḏꜣt* eyes; the one at the front of the tree has an extended human arm with *ꜥnḫ* sign (fig. 47). This scene is separated from the next by two vertical columns of inscriptions that read:

*ḏd mdw jn nwt wrt mwt nṯr ḫntj jmntt jrt rꜥ ḥnwt pr-nfr dj=s ḥtpw n wsjr nb ꜣbḏw nṯr ꜥꜣ*

A speech by Nut, The Great, Mother of the God Foremost of the West, Eye of Re, and Mistress of the Beautiful House, that she may give offerings to Osiris, Lord of Abydos, the Great God.

Fig. 47. Scene 4 near the legs

### *3.3.1.2.4.1. Commentary and Analysis*

The deceased is here received by a goddess who has been described pictorially as Isis and Nephthys and textually as the goddess Nut. On the head of the goddess there are also a sun disc and a feather of Maat. [336] On commenting on this scene on this part of the coffin, it is important to consider several issues. The first is the combination between the vignette of Book of the Dead Chapter 148 and the image of the Tree Goddess Nut and how both can relate to each other, or how the goddess Nut fits in the context of BD 148. The second issue is that goddess is described in two different ways, textually as Nut and pictorially as Nephthys and Isis; is that a kind of syncretism or a matter of ignorance of the artist? It is also important to argue why such a scene has been placed specifically on this part of the coffin.

Book of the Dead Chapter 148 is usually accompanied by vignettes that not only occur on papyri but also on tomb walls, temples, and on coffin sides.[337] What is really important to look at is the placing of the text and vignette of BD 148 on the walls of the New Kingdom tombs. The spell always appears near the stela or the statue of the deceased in the offering place, which was the focal point of the whole tomb.[338] That is how it fits in the context of the decoration on this part of the coffin, where the main aim of having the Tree Goddess here is to provide the deceased with food and drink.[339] The scene is also placed here at the end of the external left wall of the inner coffin of *Pꜣ-dj-jmn*, at the foot end.

The material that deals with the sky goddess Nut in ancient Egypt is often a mix between text and image. As mentioned above, the text has a more or less fixed element, and the image can be interpreted on different levels and can have more than one meaning. The image of the Tree Goddess Nut is here placed at the foot end and marks the entrance of the deceased into the netherworld. The image of the Tree Goddess should not be isolated from the surrounding scenes on this side of the coffin and treated as a separate unit.[340]

It is really important to deal with the image-text here as informative and performative media.[341] First, the scene of the Tree Goddess identified in texts as Nut but in image as another goddess does not only occur on that coffins; there are other instances. For example, on the coffin of Vatican Museum 228 is a scene of a Tree Goddess identified textually as Nut but pictorially, through a hieroglyph on her head, as Neith. Keel argues that this combination illustrates the indifference of the artist with regard to the exact identity of the Tree Goddess.[342] We have seen on different sides of our coffin similar instances: for example, a god pictorially representing Shu identified textually as Osiris. It is not clear why such combinations of names would occur. This should not be considered ignorance of the artist regarding the identity of the goddess. It might represent instead a syncretism of different goddesses through text and image. The standing goddess is identified as Isis, Nephthys and Nut because the three goddesses all have to do with nourishment and the protection of the deceased.

### 2.3.1.2. The External Right Side Wall (Pl. V.2)

The arrangement of the scenes and texts on this side are the same as the ones on the left side wall. The inscription on the upper side reads:

[336] For a brief survey on Nut as a tree goddess, see Billing, *Nut*, 185-92.

[337] For all the sources on which BD 148 occurs, see, Niwinski, In *Fs Irmtraut Munro*, 134.

[338] Niwinski, In; *Fs Irmtraut Munro*, 134-6.

[339] Billing, *Nut*, 185.

[340] Davis argues that images as a unit can form a self sufficient form of knowledge which means that the image can be interpreted as a separated unit from the system with which it forms a part; Davis, *The Canonical Tradition in Ancient Egyptian Art*, 202.

[341] Eschweiler, *Bildzauber im alten Ägypten.*

[342] Keel, in: Keel (ed.), *Das Recht der Bilder*, 64.

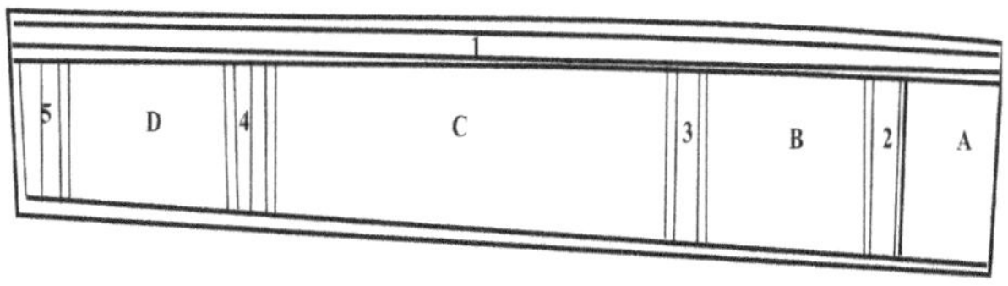


Fig. 48. The external right side wall of the case of the inner coffin of *Pꜣ-dj-jmn* with the numbers and letters showing the distribution of the texts and scenes (drawing by the author).

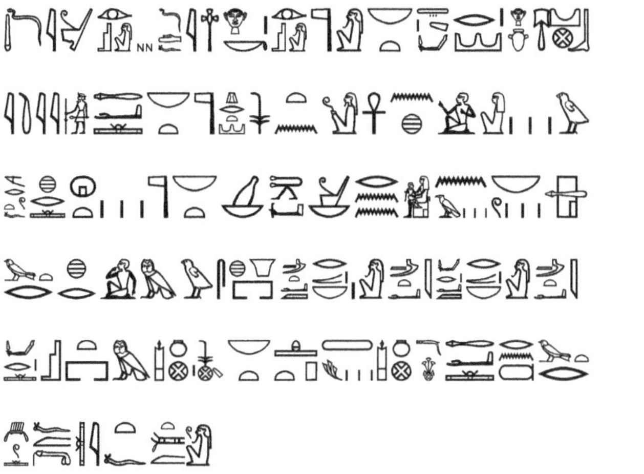

(1) *ḏd mdw jn wsjr NN ḏd=f jnḏ ḥr=k wsjr nṯr nb tꜣ-ḏsr ḥrj-jb ꜣbḏw jṯj ꜥꜣ nb ẖrt-nṯr nswt ꜥnḫw mrj.tw=f ẖr psḏt nbt ḥḏt iṯi dšrt rnn ntjw nbw ḥwt-ꜥꜣt wrt ḫr m wsḫt mꜣꜥt r-gs nb mꜣꜥt ḏsr mꜣꜥ r-gs nb mꜣꜥt ḏsr st m iwnw šmꜥw nbt ḥtpw jwnw mḥj ꜥꜣ rn wrt ꜣw=f m bꜣḥ jt=f jtmw*

A speech by Osiris NN he says: Hail to you Osiris, the God and Lord of the Sacred Land who dwells in Abydos, Great Sovereign, Lord of the Necropolis, the King of the Living who is beloved by the Great Ennead, Lord of the White Crown who takes possession of the Red Crown, who nurses all those of the Great Mansion! He who speaks in the Hall of Maat beside the Lord of Maat, truly sacred beside the Lord of Maat, Sacred of Seat in Southern Heliopolis, Lord of Offering in northern Heliopolis, Great of Name, may his offering be much in the presence of Atum.

### *2.3.1.2.1. Scene A (near the head)*

The deceased is shown wearing a festive garment and giving offerings to the emblem of Abydos. Behind the deceased is a kneeling figure of a goddess in a gesture of adoration; she is described as:

*nbt-ḥwt snt nṯr nb jmntt wsjr nṯr ꜥꜣ nb pt tꜣ*

Nephthys, God's Sister, Lady of the West, Osiris the Great God, Lord of the sky and earth.

She sits on a large *nb* sign beneath which are two *wḏꜣt* eyes. A table of offerings and a small squatting figure with the head of a jackal are depicted in front of the deceased. Above the deceased is a winged *wḏꜣt* eye. The name of Osiris (*wsjr*) fills the space between Osiris and the winged *wḏꜣt* eye (fig. 49). This scene is separated from the next by a vertical column of text that reads:

(2) *ḏd mdw jn ꜣst wrt mwt nṯr nb tꜣ ḏsr dj=s ḥtp*

A speech by Isis the Great, Mother of the God, Lady of the Sacred Land, that she may give offering.

Fig. 49. Scene 1 near the head.

### *2.3.1.2.1.1. Commentary and Analysis*

The first scene on this side is dedicated to the deceased, who stands in front of the emblem of Abydos and presents offerings to it. The eastern side wall of the coffin is reserved for the scenes of Osiris and the introduction of the deceased to Osiris in the hall of the judgment. As argued above, the emblem of Abydos refers to Osiris himself; when the deceased makes offerings to this emblem, he is then making offering to Osiris himself. This scene can also be considered as an introduction to the scenes on this part of the lid.

### *2.3.1.2.2. Scene B (near the shoulder)*

Osiris is shown with all signs of royalty, seated on a throne with two steps resting on a *nb* sign. The steps of the throne are decorated with two mythical animals with the body of a ram and the head of a crocodile, and both of them are protected by a winged cobra. The two mythical beings seem to guard a door. There are two falcons in front and at the back of Osiris standing on a *ḥb* sign and wearing the crowns of Re-Horakhty with cobra. The two falcons are accompanied by a caption that reads:

*wsjr nb jmntt*

Osiris Lord of the West.

Beneath the two falcons are two *bꜣ* birds in a gesture of adoration, holding *ꜥnḫ* signs in their hands and presenting offering to Osiris. A caption behind the bird to the west and in front of the seated figure of a deity with the head of an ape reads:

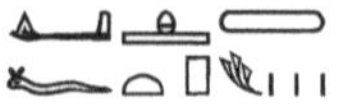

*dj=f ḥtpw*

He may give offerings.

At the top are two winged *wḏꜣt* eyes and beneath them, two cobras. The two sides are bordered by Isis on the right and Maat on the left, both depicted adoring the seated figure of Osiris (fig 50). The scene is separated from the next by a vertical column of inscriptions that reads:

(3) *ḏd mdw jn njt wrt mwt nṯr ḫntj jmntt dj=s ḥtpw*

A speech by Neith the Great Mother of the God Foremost of the West that she may give offerings.

Fig. 50. Scene 2 near the shoulder.

### *3.3.1.2.2.1. Commentary and Analysis*

Here Osiris as Lord of the West is represented seated on a throne flanked by Isis and Maat. The scene is a variant of the judgment scene, where Osiris as Lord of the judgment of the dead is represented with all divine signs. The two mythical beings at the base of the throne guard the entrance of a gate that might represent the gate of the netherworld. This scene precedes the one in which the deceased approaches the hall of the judgment of the dead, where his heart is weighed against the feather of Maat.

### *3.3.1.2.3. Scene C (near the hips)*

The scene shows the judgment of the dead. Osiris is shown sitting on a throne with all signs of royalty; in front of him there is a text that reads:

*ḏd mdw jn wsjr nṯr ꜥꜣ ḫntj jmntt nfr-tm ḫwj tꜣwj iwꜥ mnḫ n wnn-nfr*

A speech by Osiris, the Great God, Foremost of the West, Nefertem, Protector of the Two Lands and Potent Heir of Wenennefer.

In front of Osiris, Thoth stands wearing the *Atef* crown and extending his hands as he speaks to Osiris. He has the symbols of *ḏd*, *wꜣs* and *ꜥnḫ* and in front of him are the symbols of *jmj-wt* and offerings. There is a speech in front of Thoth reading:

*ḏd mdw jn ḏḥwtj sš mꜣꜥt n psḏt ꜥꜣ n nbw dwꜣt*

A speech by Thoth, Scribe of Maat of the Great Ennead of the Lords of the Underworld.

Behind Thoth a caption reads:

*sꜣ ḥꜣ=f nb m ꜥnḫ ḏd wꜣs nb s(n)b*

Protection behind him with all life, stability, dominion and health.

Behind Osiris stands Isis in a gesture of adoration; above her is a winged *wḏꜣt* eye. Behind her a caption reads *sꜣ ḥꜣ.s nb* "All protection behind her." In the centre the balance and the weighing of the heart are represented. Anubis is shown with a wide open mouth and behind him is a coiled snake. Anubis is followed by two small squatting figures. The other side of the balance has a scene in three registers. The first shows a seated lion with two serpents in his mouth and a cobra on its forehead. The second register shows three squatting figures, the first on right jackal-headed, the one in the middle human-headed and the third with the head of a falcon. The third register shows a vulture and a cobra standing on a *ḥb* sign and facing each other. On the right side of the balance the deceased is represented standing with upraised arms. His head is bald with a headband and adorned by an unguent cone[343] and two lotus buds. There are two cobras and winged *wḏꜣt* eyes over the two cobras. There is also a *wḏꜣt* eye above the head of the deceased. At the back and front of the deceased are two falcons standing on the emblem of the west and two cobras in front of the

[343] A typology of these cones has been published by Maraite, in: Obsomer et al, *Amosiadès: Mélanges offerts au Professeur Claude Vandersleyen par ses anciens ètudiants*, 1992, 213-9; see also Taylor, in: Strudwick and Taylor (eds), *The Theban Necropolis*, 101-3. There are also different interpretations applied to the cone and its function for the deceased. It has been argued that it might represent an unguent placed at the head of the deceased to moisturise his hair and body. Another interpretation is that the cone is a symbolic and not 'an actual lump of unguent'. For more interpretations on the cone and its use in ritual, in particularly the Opening of the Mouth ritual, see most recently, Padgham, *A New Interpretation of the Cone on the Head in the New Kingdom Egyptian Tomb Scenes*.

falcons. The falcon on the left is named *ꜣst* "Isis." The space between the deceased and the falcons is filled by *ꜥnḫ* and *wḏꜣt* eyes (fig. 51). The scene is separated from the next one by a vertical column of inscriptions that reads:

(4) *ḏd mdw jn jmꜣḫj ḫr jnpw ḫntj jmntt wnn-nfr ḥḳꜣ ꜥnḫw nswt nb*

A speech by the Revered One with Anubis, Foremost of the West, Wenennefer Ruler of the Living, King and Lord.

Fig. 51. Scene 3 near the hips

### *3.3.1.2.3.1. Commentary and Analysis*

The scene of the judgment of the dead on the inner case of the coffin of *Pꜣ-dj-jmn* cannot be isolated from the whole decorative program of the coffin. Here on the right side the deceased, dressed in a festive garment, approaches the hall of the judgment of the dead. He is standing between two falcons and in front of him is the famous scene of the balance. This vignette might be different from the other vignettes in the Book of the Dead chapters that deal with the judgment of the dead, but it still alludes to the same idea of the vindication of the deceased in front of Osiris, Lord of the underworld. The main deities participating in the judgment of the dead, Anubis, Maat, Osiris and the devourer of the sinners are depicted here in this scene. Anubis is represented twice as standing near the balance with a wide open mouth, and his emblem (*jmj-wt*) is in front of Osiris. Thoth as a scribe of the Ennead is presenting the deceased to Osiris, who is shown seated on his throne and protected by Isis from behind. According to Niwinski, a series of new iconographic compositions was created during the 21st Dynasty, including representations of new complicated ideas of cosmogony and cosmology.[344] From among these, in this vignette are the unusual representations of the grinning Anubis and the lion with the two serpents in his mouth and two cobras on his head.[345]

### *3.3.1.2.4. Scene D (near the Leg and the Part under the Leg)*

The deceased is shown kneeling and presenting offerings to the cow goddess Hathor, who is shown emerging from the western mountains. In front of the deceased there is a pile of offerings and an inscription that gives the titles of the deceased; then follows:

*ḥt-ḥr nbt tꜣ-ḏsr jrt Rꜥ ḥnwt jmntt dj=s ḥtpw*

Hathor Lady of the Sacred Land (Necropolis), the Eye of Re and Mistress of the West, that she may give offerings.

Above the inscription are seven squatting figures with different heads: from right to left, (cobra, ram, donkey, human, jackal, falcon and ape). Behind the cow is a representation of a tomb carved in the mountain from which Hathor emerges. On the tomb entrance the name of *Wsjr* is written, and above it is a winged solar disc (fig. 52). At the summit is a small pyramid with an inscription reading:

*ḥtp dj nsw n wsjr ḫntj jmntt*

An offering that the King gives to Osiris Foremost of the West.

The inscription written in vertical columns reads:

(5) *ḏd mdw jn ḥt-ḥr nb ḏsr st m jwnw šmꜥw nb ḥtp m jwnw mḥw dj=s ḥtpw n wsjr nb ꜣbḏw*

A speech by Hathor, Lady of Sacred of Seat in Southern Helipolis and Lady of Offering in Northern Heliopolis, that she may give offerings to Osiris, Lord of Abydos.

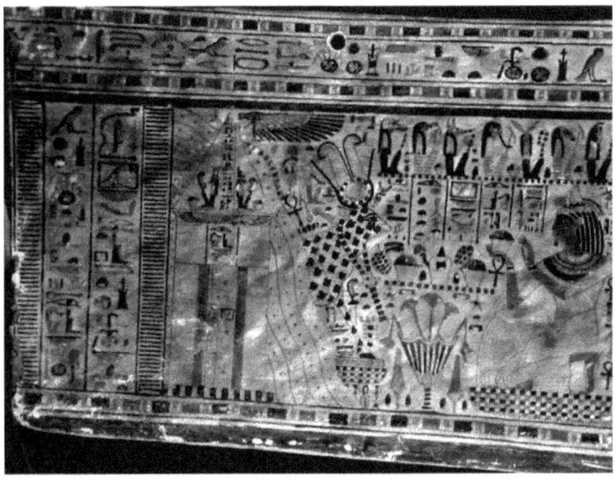

Fig. 52. Scene 4 near the leg

[344] Niwinski, *Illustrated Theban Funerary Papyri*, 38-40.

[345] For a brief survey on the occurrence of the judgment of dead on the tomb walls, coffins and Papyri of the 21st Dynasty, see, Lull, *JEA* 87 (2001), 180-86.

The part under the feet is decorated with the kneeling figure of a goddess between two emblems of the west. She wears a crown with a solar disc between two cow horns. She supports two *wḏꜣt* eyes with her hands, and from her arms hang the signs of *ꜥnḫ* and *ḏd* (fig. 53)

Fig. 53. The part under the feet

### *3.3.1.2.4.1. Commentary and Analysis*

The scene of the deceased as making offering to the cow goddess coming out from the mountain is not different from the same scene that occurs on the case of the outer coffin of *Pꜣ-dj-jmn*. The only difference is that there are seven beings at the top of the scene. The scene is depicted at the foot end of the coffin and marks the deceased's arrival in the west. The identity of the goddess in the scene under the feet is not known.

### *3.3.2. The Inner Decorations of the Inner Case (Pl. VI)*

### *3.3.2.1. The Decorations on the Floor Board*

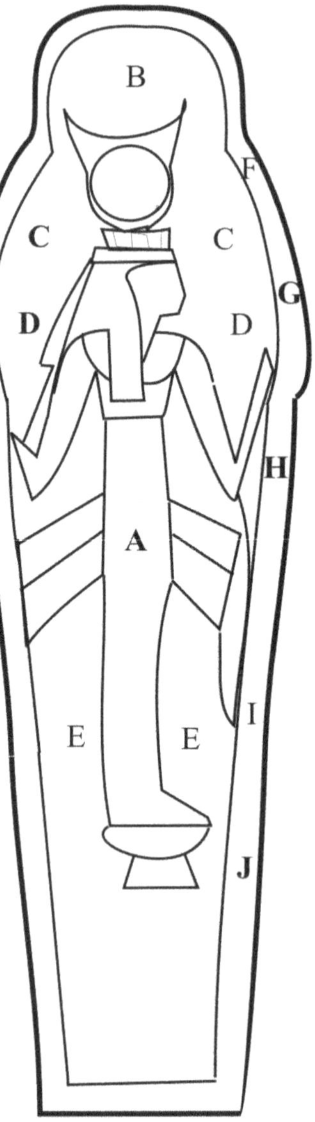


Fig. 54. The interior of the case of the inner coffin of *Pꜣ-dj-jmn* with the letters showing the distribution of the texts and scenes (drawing by the author)

(A) The Bottom of the inner case is occupied by the figure of the winged goddess Isis, who is described as:

*ꜣst nbt jmntt*

Isis, Lady of the West

The goddess is crowned with the solar disc between two cow's horns. She stands on the *nbw* sign. The forearms and hands of the goddess as well as the ends of her wings are represented on the side walls. The main figure of the goddess Isis is surrounded by other decorative and symbolic motifs.

(B) At the back of the head of the goddess Isis is a scarab resting on a *šn* ring and a sun disc with four cobras hanging from it (fig. 55).

Fig. 55. scenes at the back of the goddess

(C) Near the head on the right and left are two winged cobras on a *ḥb* sign flanking the head of the goddess (fig. 56).

Fig. 56. Scenes near the head and shoulder of the goddess

(D) Near the shoulders on the right and left of the goddess are two seated figures, the one on the left with the head of a jackal and the one on the right is a human-headed figure (fig. 56). Under the goddess's wings are two mummiform standing figures of the Sons of Horus Duamutef and Hapi. Hapi is described as:

*ḥʿpj ḫntj štȝjt nb nḥḥ*

Hapi, Foremost of Secrets, Lord of Eternity.

There are also squatting deities near the feet of the goddess; the one to the left is called:

*wsjr nb nḥḥ ḥḳȝ ḏt*

Osiris, Lord of Eternity and Ruler of Everlasting.

### *3.3.2.1.1. Commentary and Analysis*

The central part of the floor board of the case of the inner coffin is occupied by the figure of the goddess Isis. She stands on a large *nbw* sign. The goddess has the emblem of Hathor on her head. Isis is depicted on the floor board of the coffin as embracing the deceased who is placed on the board of the inner coffin. She features here as the Goddess of the West. She welcomes the deceased, who will be placed in the embrace of her two arms, and will also provide him with the food and drink that are necessary for his safe passage in the hereafter. Providing food and drink for the deceased was a role attributed to vasrious goddesses, such as Nut, Hathor and the Goddess of the West. Here Isis, as the Goddess of the West, plays this role.[346]

The goddess on the floor board is here identified pictorially as Hathor but textually as Isis. As argued above, this is not due to ignorance of the artist who painted the scene, but a kind of syncretism. The two goddesses, Isis and Hathor, can play the same role for the deceased here. Isis, as the one who is protecting the deceased from behind on Middle and New Kingdom coffins, fulfils the same role on the floor board of the coffin's case. The sun disc with two cow horns identifies the goddess with Hathor, who welcomes the deceased in the hereafter, provides him with what is necessary for his journey and elevates him to the sky between her two horns.

The placing of the goddess on the floor board provides also several symbolic interpretations on the coffin as microcosms for the deceased, in which the mummy was the central focal point. As described above, the lid of the coffin is occupied by the figure of the goddess Nut as heaven, and by placing the goddess Isis, as representation of Hathor, on the floor she here represents the terrestrial sphere for the deceased, in which he dwells. This makes the coffin the earthly realm of the deceased, where his rebirth and resurrection will take place.

Isis is depicted with outstretched arms and full image occupying the middle of the floor board, like Nut on the lid, and thus she is acting here as the mother of the deceased.[347] As mentioned above, the deceased asks the goddess Nut to spread her wings over him and to allow him to be among the Imperishable and the Unwearying Stars; on the floor board, Isis plays the same role for the deceased.

It is important to note here that the goddess is standing on a *nbw* sign, which also might link her with the title of the Mistress of the House of Gold (*ḫntj ḥnwt nbw*). Taylor argues that this title was an attribute derived from the coffin decorations during the 22nd Dynasty, in which the goddess stands on a *nbw* sign with a plinth, is represented

[346] Taylor, in: Sowada and Ockinga (eds), *Egyptian art in the Nicholson Museum*, 267.
[347] Assmann, *Tod und Jenseits im Alten Ägypten*, 172-9, 225-30.

with a frontal face and is identified with Nut.[348] He also argues that *ḥwt nbw* (House of Gold) was a phrase with a wide range of meanings. It can refer to the burial chamber in a tomb, royal palace, and temples of various deities such as Hathor.[349] The title is linked with Hathor, but here on this coffin, there is no title for the goddess and what we have is a pictorial representation of the gold sign. This occurrence of the title, or its avatar, emphasises the interlinking of attributes that Hathor, Nut and Isis can have.[350]

### *3.3.2.2. The Right Side Inner Wall*

(F) The scene on the upper register shows a recumbent jackal surmounted by winged eyes (fig. 57).

Fig. 57. Upper register on the right inner wall

(G) There is also a kneeling figure of a falcon-headed deity who makes offering in front of the emblem of Abydos (fig. 58).

Fig. 58. A kneeling falcon

(H) There is a small standing deity in front of him with a head of an ape. Beneath are a vulture and a cobra facing each other, and behind the vulture is a pile of offerings. The next register shows the seated figure of a goddess raising her arms in a gesture of adoration. Offerings and a small seated figure of a deity with a beard are placed in front of the seated goddess.

(I) Under the figure of the goddess there is a vulture with a sun disc on her head. (fig. 59).

Fig. 59. Seated goddess and a vulture

(J) The last register shows the Four Sons of Horus (fig. 60). They appear here at the edge of the inner sides of the inner case of the coffin of *P3-dj-jmn*.

Fig. 60. Sons of Horus

### *3.3.2.3. The Left Side Inner Wall*

The same scenes on the right hand side wall are repeated on the left wall. The only exception is with the scene on the level of the shoulder. Instead of the kneeling headed falcon deity on the right shoulder, the deity is represented with the head of an ibis, making offerings to the emblem of Osiris (fig. 61)

348 Taylor, in: Sowada and Ockinga (eds), *Egyptian art in the Nicholson Museum*, 267; Schneider, *Life and Death under the Pharaohs*, 132-3, no. 199.
349 Schot, *LÄ* II (1977), 739-740.
350 Taylor, in: Sowada and Ockinga (eds), *Egyptian art in the Nicholson Museum*, 267

Fig. 61. The right hand side inner wall

### *3.3.2.3.1. Commentary and Analysis*

The inner side walls of the inner case of the coffin of *P3-dj-jmn* are decorated with the Four Sons of Horus at the bottom. These were represented at the four corners on Middle and New Kingdoms Coffins and play a role in the ascent of the king to the sky.[351] Near the head on both sides, Anubis is depicted and beneath are two deities with the heads of a falcon and an ibis flanking the deceased on both sides. It seems as if the deceased, whose body is placed on the floor board, will be embraced by Isis from the bottom and surrounded by several deities on two sides. He is then under the protection of gods.

It is also important to note the image of the scarab on the head of the goddess Isis as coming out of the underworld protected by four cobras. The coffin here serves as 'a ritual machine', through which the deceased will be resurrected. The images on this part of the coffin are not meant to be merely decorative images but also ritual images. The passage from death to resurrection of Osiris, who is placed within the coffin and who is described here as "Osiris Lord of Eternity and Ruler of Everlasting," will be mediated by the aid of these images.

[351] Willems, *Chests of Life*, 136.

## *3.4. The Inner Coffin's Case Decorations and the Hall of the Judgment of the Dead*

The decorations on the case of the inner coffin of *P3-dj-jmn* focus on more than one theme. The most important of these themes are the resurrection of the deceased and his arrival in the heavenly sphere of Re and the earthly sphere of Osiris. This resurrection of the deceased was crucial for his survival in the world beyond.

The underworld, to the Ancient Egyptians, belongs to the ordered cosmos, and it is also separated from this world. This may explain why the otherworld is seen on one side as day and night, and as the necropolis and the tomb on the other side. This means that the underworld, to the Ancient Egyptians, has a part belonging to the sky, and the other part is represented in both the tomb and the necropolis. The resurrection of the deceased, who is here depicted embraced by the sky goddess Nut on the top and by the goddess Isis on the floor board, takes place in his coffin. The coffin is here the tomb itself, which carries all that is necessary for the deceased to be resurrected.

The resurrection of the deceased means also that he is escaping death and is received by the gods and goddesses of the underworld. We have seen on the lid how the decoration program and placement of the speeches of the gods and goddess can be related to the *Stundewachen* or the night of the vigil, in which the deceased Osiris gains his physical and spiritual abilities to move and escape death. The gods and goddesses on the lid, with their speeches, are personified by priests and priestesses playing their roles. These concepts are referred to on the lid decoration in images and text captions.

We have also seen on the lid that the judgment of the dead as a ritual was incorporated in the journey to Sais, which is clear on the lid in the speeches of the goddess Neith on the long side of the coffin and also on the middle of the lid. The other gods participating in the judgment of the dead are those column gods who are represented by the Four Sons of Horus and by other divinities such as Serqet, Geb, Nut, Isis and Neith. On the lower part of the lid the deceased says that he will not die again in the necropolis near the Great Ennead. The Ennead can be represented by the gods and goddesses distributed on the coffin's lid. They feature as a court of justice, and they are depicted at the corners of the coffin to protect the deceased. Most probably the role of the gods in the court of justice was played by priests attending the mummy of the deceased. Thus the journey to Sais seems to incorporate Osiris' victory over his enemies and his coronation as a king in the netherworld.[352]

The exterior decorations on the case of the inner coffin of *P3-dj-jmn* focus on the arrival of the deceased in the hereafter and his attendance in the hall of the judgment of the dead. The scenes on the two external side walls of the inner case focus on the deceased presenting offerings to

[352] Willems, *Chests of Life*. 150.

Osiris or his emblem, his arrival in the hall of Osiris and finally his reception by the Goddess of the West. The main concern is the presence of the deceased in the hall of the judgment of the dead, where he makes offerings to the emblem of Abydos and then is introduced to Osiris and received by the goddess of the West, who pours water for him. On other side the deceased is also shown making offerings to the emblem of Abydos and Osiris is shown sitting on a throne attended by Isis and Maat. Then the deceased, dressed in a festive garment, is taken to the hall of the judgment, where the scale is shown and Anubis escorts him. After the deceased gains his vindication he is then welcomed by Hathor, who is shown coming out of the mountain.[353]

[353] See Chapter Four below for more details on the case's decorations as representation of the hall of the judgment of the dead.

## 3.5. The Mummy Cover of *Pꜣ-dj-jmn (CG 6078)* (PL. VII)

### *3.5.1. General Description*

The mummy cover of *Pꜣ-dj-jmn* is made of wood covered with plaster. The decorations on the mummy cover are multicoloured, painted and varnished. It looks very similar to the outer and inner lids of the coffins of *Pꜣ-dj-jmn*. The mummy cover was placed directly over the mummy and could serve as a second lid for the innermost coffin.[354] The beard of the mummy cover is missing and the wig is striped and decorated with an ornamental headband.

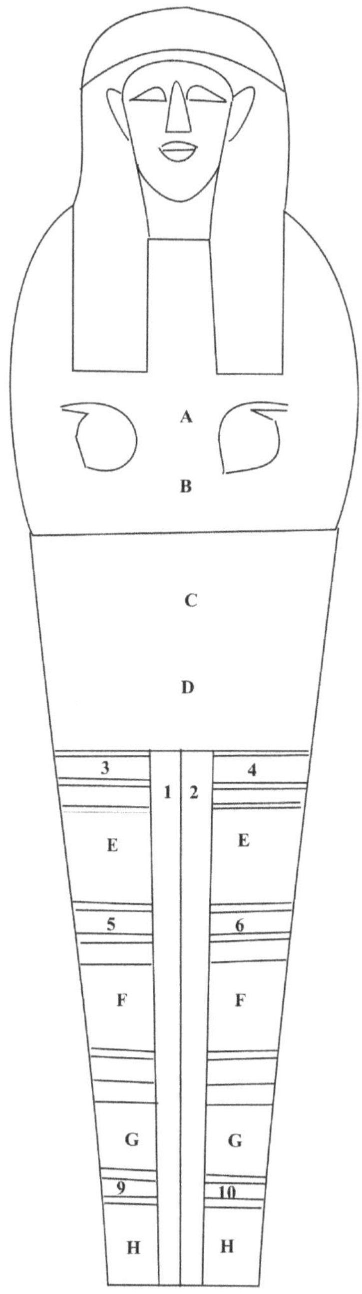


Fig. 62. The mummy cover of *Pꜣ-dj-jmn* with numbers and letters for the texts and images (drawing by the author)

### *3.5.1.1. The Upper Part of the Mummy Cover*

The decorations on this part of the mummy cover start from the part beneath the central collar between the clenched fists.

(A) The first decorative motif on this part is a winged scarab with a heart-shaped amulet hanging from the two wings of the scarab. On each side of the heart amulet is a *Benu*-bird preceded by a small scarab; above each bird is a *wḏꜣt* eye. Above the central scarab is a small sun disc above which is a composite *Atef* crown. On each side of the scarab's wings and above the clenched fists of the deceased are two recumbent jackals of Anubis designated as *jnpw* and *jmj-wt*. Two small squatting figures fill the space between the scarab and the heart amulet (fig. 63).

Fig. 63. The decorations on the upper part of the lid

### *3.5.1.1.1. Commentary and Analysis*

As noted in the previous two chapters above, the scarab is the symbol of the sun god Re when he comes into being in the morning. Here it has the *Atef* crown, which is a characteristic of Osiris. The scarab is also flanked on both sides by Anubis, identified once as *jnpw* and once as *jmj-wt*. The scene shows the Osirian-Solar unity, which is the aim of the whole decorative motif on coffins of *Pꜣ-dj-jmn*. The scarab is a symbol of resurrection connected with the sun god Re at dawn, but here it has the *Atef* crown, which means that the scarab refers to the resurrection of the deceased in the identity of both Re and Osiris.[355] It is also important to note that the scarab has been placed on the upper part of the mummy cover very close to the chest, which might also refer to the deceased in his final stage of resurrection.

---

[354] Niwinski, *21st Dynasty Coffins from Thebes,* 12; Janssen, *Commodity prices from the Ramessid Period*, 209-12.

[355] Goff, *Symbols of Ancient Egypt in the Late Period*, 207-20; Piankoff and Rambova, *Mythological Papyri*, 34.

### *3.5.1.2. The Middle Part of the Mummy Cover*

#### *3.5.1.2.1. The First Register*

(B) The first register shows in the centre a pectoral with the emblem of Nefertem in the middle flanked by two falcons with two small figures of Maat, and two winged *wḏꜣt* eyes. The pectoral is in the shape of a gate with a facade decorated with the winged sun disc. To the right and left of the pectoral are two emblems of Abydos, above which the name of Osiris is written. There are two small figures of Anubis beneath the two emblems of Abydos. The two emblems of Abydos are adored by kneeling figures of Isis on the left and Nephthys on the right. Behind the two goddesses are two winged cobras. There are two falcons at the elbows with small figures of Maat and *wḏꜣt* eyes (fig. 63). The two falcons are accompanied by the following inscription:

*ptḥ-skr-wsjr ḥrj-jb dwꜣt nṯr ꜥꜣ nb dwꜣt*

Ptah-Sokar-Osiris who dwells in the underworld, the Great God, Lord of the Underworld.

#### *3.5.1.2.2. The Second Register*

(C) The second register is occupied by the large figure of the sky goddess Nut with her outstretched wings and holding *ꜥnḫ* sign and *ḥkꜣ* sceptre in her hands. Above the head of the goddess are two cow horns with a sun disc between them, emblem of the goddess Hathor. Above the two shoulders of the goddess are two winged cobras designated as Neith (fig. 64). At the ends of the wings of the Nut there are two vertical inscriptions that read:

*dj=s ḥtpwt ḏfꜣw n wsjr ḫntj jmtt nb ꜣbḏw nṯr ꜥꜣ*

May she give offerings and provisions to Osiris, Foremost of the West, Lord of Abydos, the Great God.

Fig. 64. The second and third register on the middle of the mummy cover

#### *3.5.1.2.3. The Third Register*

(D) This part is occupied by a pectoral with a scarab in the middle. The scarab is placed on a *ḏd* pillar sign and surrounded by a solar disc on the top and a cobra on each side. On each side of the scarab are two squatting figures of Osiris and Nephthys. On each side of the pectoral is a small figure of Osiris seated on a throne and protected by the outstretched wings of a goddess; these wear the crowns of Upper and Lower Egypt (fig. 64).

#### *3.5.1.2.4. Commentary and Analysis*

In the three registers, there are emblems and speeches of gods that can give us some information regarding the decorations on this part of the coffin and how they could be interpreted. In the first register, the emblem of Nefertem and Osiris is flanked by a falcon on each side and Isis and Nephthys are represented flanking the whole scene. Nefertem as a god was associated with the lotus, and its emblem is a replacement for the god himself. The emblem of Nefertem refers to the rebirth of the deceased like the god. The emblem of Abydos is a reference to Osiris; by its presence here with the emblem of Nefertem, the unity of Re and Osiris becomes clear. The two emblems were not placed arbitrarily on this part of the mummy cover. The scenes on the cartonnage represent the deceased in his final state, which means that all the decorations on this part of the coffin refer to the final stage of the solar and Osirian unity, which in turn refer to the deceased as the Revered One who has already escaped death. The resurrection of the deceased Osiris, who is replaced by the emblem of Abydos, is envisaged as the birth of the new sun in the shape of Nefertem. The two emblems are flanked by Isis and Nephthys, which is also an allusion to the scene of the resurrection of Osiris, in which the two goddesses sit on either side of the bier of the god, bewailing him. These complicated thoughts of death and resurrection are referred to in the images of this part of the coffin.

The cycle of death and resurrection is complemented by the image of the sky goddess Nut, who is asked by the deceased to receive him and to make him like the Imperishable and Unwearying Stars. The deceased, who is shown once as Osiris and once as Re, will be received by the sky goddess Nut as a sign of his ascent to the heavenly sphere, to reappear as a scarab, which is evident in the image of the winged scarab beneath the collar.

As argued above, the figure of Nut with her outstretched wings refers to the goddess as the mother of the deceased. Nut here serves as the cosmic womb in which the reconstitution process takes place after burial. When the goddess stretches her wings over him, he is then received by the goddess in order to be reborn again as a new and eternal being. When he enters the body of the goddess, the deceased becomes a different being, the son of the goddess, Re and Osiris. That is made explicit when the deceased is shown as Osiris on his bier attended by Isis and Nephthys or as scarab with the sun disc. Nut, as mother of the deceased, is the one who will provide him with offerings, which is made explicit in the second register, where the goddess is described as giving offerings to the deceased.

### *3.5.1.3. The Lower Part of the Mummy Cover*

The lower part of the mummy cover is divided into two symmetrical parts by two vertical columns of text bordered by geometrical ornaments. The two columns start with the names and titles of *Pꜣ-dj-jmn* and conclude with a speech by the deceased (fig. 65). These texts read, from left to right:

1 2

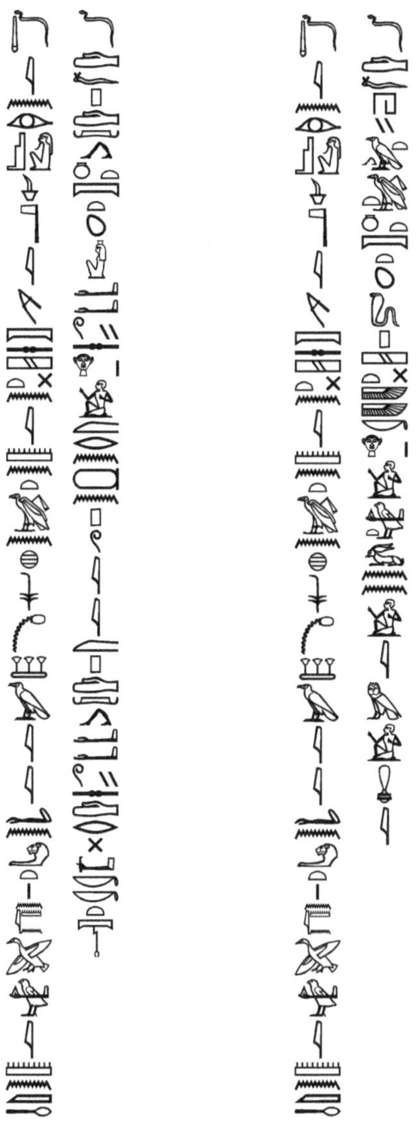

(1) The left column:

*ḏd mdw jn wsjr NN ḏd=f pd nwt ꜥwj=s ḥr=j m rn=s pwj m pd ꜥwy=s dr kkwt*

A speech by Osiris NN, he says: May Nut spread her arms over me, in this her name of She who spreads her arms and drives away darkness.

(2) The right column:

*ḏd mdw jn wsjr NN ḏd=f hꜣj mwt nwt pš dnḥwj=k(!) ḥr=j dj.tw wnn=j jm=j mj*

A speech by Osiris NN, he says: Oh mother Nut, spread your wings over me, and make me exist in me like …

On each side of the two vertical columns of text are four registers of figural representations inside a naos, separated from each other by a single horizontal line of inscriptions written vertically.

Fig. 65. The two vertical columns at the middle of the lower part of the mummy cover

#### *3.5.1.3.1. The First Register*

(E) The first register shows Osiris seated on a throne and flanked by winged *wḏꜣt* eyes and protected from behind by the wings of a falcon. The falcon has the solar sun disc on his head. Offerings are represented in front of Osiris. Beneath the throne of Osiris are the Four Sons of Horus sitting on a *nb* sign (fig. 66). The inscription above the first register on the left and right read:

(3) On the left:

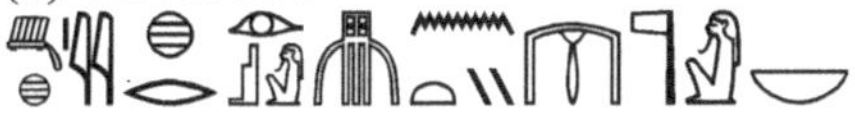

*jmꜣḫj ḫr wsjr ḫntj sḥ-nṯr nb*

The Revered One with Osiris, Foremost of the Divine Booth, Lord...

(4) On the right:

*jmꜣḫj ḫr wsjr ḫntj jmntt*

The Revered One with Osiris, Foremost of the West.

Fig. 66. The first register on the lower part of the mummy cover

#### *3.5.1.3.2. The Second Register*

(F) This register shows Osiris in the form of a recumbent sphinx wearing the Double Crown of Egypt. In front of the sphinx is a small figure of Maat and above is a winged cobra wearing the *Atef* Crown and stretching her wings over the recumbent sphinx. Beneath the recumbent sphinx are the mummiform standing figures of Hapi and Qebehsenuef (fig. 67). The inscriptions above the second register on the left and right read:

(5) On the left:

*jm3ḫj ḫr 3st nb(t) jmntt*

The Revered One with Isis, Lady of the West.

(6) On the right:

*jm3ḫj ḫr 3st wrt*

The Revered One with Isis the Great

Fig. 67. The second register on the lower part of the mummy cover

#### *3.5.1.3.3. The Third Register*

(G) Isis (to the left) and Nephthys (to the right) are shown kneeling on a decorative support of a *nb* sign mounted on *ḏd* and *ṯjt* signs. The two goddesses are clad in long fitted robes and raise their hands. The signs of *ʿnḫ* hang from the arms of the two goddesses (fig.68) The inscriptions above the third register on the left and right read:

(7) On the left:

*jm3ḫj ḫr ḥʿpj*

The Revered One with Hapi.

(8) On the right:

*jm3ḫj ḫr njt*

The Revered One with Neith.

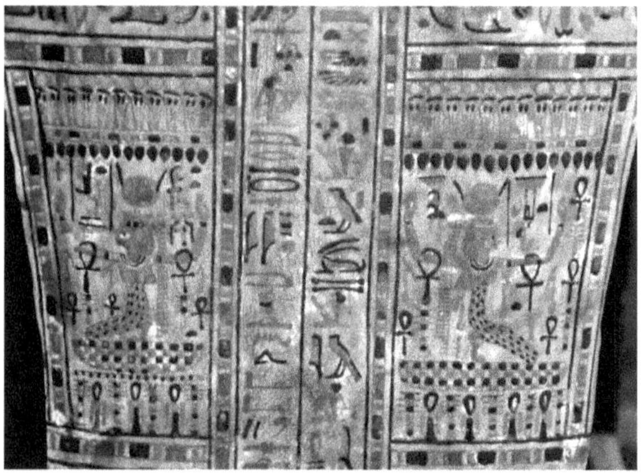

Fig. 68. The third register on the lower part of the mummy cover

#### *3.5.1.3.4. The Fourth Register*

(H) In this register there is a recumbent cow on each side, described as Neith. Above the cow is a vault guarded by two cobras (fig 69). The inscriptions above the fourth register on the left and right read:

(9) On the left:

*jm3ḫj ḫr njt*

The Revered One with Neith

(10) On the right

*jm3ḫj ḫr nbt-ḥwt*

The Revered One before Nephthys

Fig. 69. The fourth register on the lower part of the mummy cover

### *3.5.1.3.5. Commentary and Analysis*

The lower part of the mummy cover has the speeches of the goddesses and gods with whom the deceased is said to be a Revered One. In the middle of the lower part of the lid, the deceased asks the sky goddess Nut to spread her wings over him. As argued above, the coffin, which is the intimate space surrounding the deceased after burial, was identified with the sky goddess as mother of the deceased. Billing argues that, in the Pyramid Texts, the sarcophagus or the sarcophagus chamber is one of the manifestations of the sky goddess Nut.[356] The deceased's wish to be received by the sky goddess Nut refers also to his wish to live eternally in the hereafter.

The deceased in this part is also described as the Revered One with several gods. These, as Willems argues, are divine speeches recited by priests playing the roles of deities in the enactment of certain rituals.[357] The lack of contemporary material for comparison, however, makes it sometimes difficult to envisage the context of such divine speeches on the coffins of the 21st Dynasty.

The various decorations on the different registers at the lower part of the mummy cover show Osiris wearing all royal insignia. The decorative motifs on this part of the mummy cover show the deceased surrounded by the speeches of the gods and goddesses with whom he is a Revered One.

[356] Billing, *Nut*, 2002; Willems, *Chests of life*, 134; Taylor, *Death and After life in Ancient Egypt*, 215.
[357] Willems, *Chests of Life*, 142ff.

## Chapter Four

## Conclusion

### *4.1. Coffin Texts and Coffin Images: Towards a better Understanding of the Ritual Images on the 21st Dynasty Coffins of P3-dj-jmn*

In the two coffins studied so far, the images and texts are densely interrelated, and each complements the other. Although the texts are not as prominent as the images, they give information that can be used for reconstructing rituals during this period.

The study of Harco Willems[358] on Middle Kingdom coffins shows how the object frieze and the spells inscribed on the inner and outer sides of these coffins help in understanding how rituals were carried out on the coffin and the mummy inside it during that period. The object frieze shows the items of the tomb inventory that were used in the performance of such rituals on Middle Kingdom coffins. These rituals were preserved in words of the Coffin Texts on the outer and inner sides of the coffins. These spells form what is known as liturgies, ritual texts recited for the deceased on different occasions.[359] Placing them on the sides of the coffin would keep the deceased surrounded by their eternal recitation. The performance of such rituals is enactment of the myth of Osiris, murdered by his brother Seth and cut into pieces, and the roles of Isis and Nephthys in collecting the dismembered body of the god. The myth also goes on to show how Osiris was vindicated in front of the tribunal of the gods in Heliopolis. In ritual, the resurrection of Osiris is envisaged as the night and day journeys of the sun god Re from the depth of the underworld until he rises in the morning. A part of these rituals, known as the *Stundenwachen*, was carried out on the deceased in the place of embalming at the night preceding the burial.[360] It is a core ritual of the funeral, where the dead god passes through the hours of the night and day to his resurrection.

These rituals are preserved in texts and images from the Old Kingdom until the end of the Egyptian history. The different episodes of the myth are not preserved in one single manuscript or on a single monument, but are collected from different resources. As with the myth, the rituals that relate the myth are also not collected from one single coherent source, but are also distributed on different ritual sets and occasions. It is a striking feature of the Egyptian ritual texts that they are not exclusive or unique compositions attributed to one particular ritual, but composite and formulaic rituals, recycled in different contexts. It is also 'plagiarizing'.[361] So it is not surprising to find a large ritual characteristically made up of lots of fragments.[362] It is even not easy to separate mortuary and temple ritual in practice from a larger and common ritual corpus.[363] Trying to find a coherent and consistent narrative in rituals is not an easy task; these rituals are fragmentary and draw on different metaphors.

The myth enacted in ritual is written or pictured on pyramid walls, coffin sides, and tomb walls. To distinguish between myth and ritual in Egyptian texts is difficult, if not impossible.[364] It is also not clear which one has primacy over the other. The images and texts on the coffins of *P3-dj-jmn* focus on both. Although we do not have object friezes on the sides of the coffin as on Middle Kingdom coffins, or texts showing ritual directions, we will see that the depictions of the unguents, vases, bread, lotus and different other items on the sides of the coffins could be another form, or variation, of the object frieze. The two coffins and the mummy cover are all covered by divine speeches as in the Middle Kingdom coffins. These are present on the coffin sides, evident from use of the formula *ḏd mdw*. These are divine speeches of the gods and goddesses featuring on the coffin sides. They were first understood as purely mythological speeches, but Willems and Assmann describe them as divine speeches recited by priests during the enactment of rituals.[365] The interpretation of these speeches on the coffin of *P3-dj-jmn* adds a new dimension to our understanding of how such rituals might have been placed on the coffins of this period. There is no one comprehensive study that draws on the link between the coffin decorations and rituals during this period, but the existence of such speeches on the coffins establishes a link between them and rituals of this period.

In his study of a 21st Dynasty coffin in Oslo Museum, Bettum argues that certain images on the coffin can refer to 'vague hints' of a funerary ritual or stages in the ritual. These icons have a mix of solar and Osirian aspects. Bettum argues that here:

> 'Certain icons on the coffin may provide vague hints to certain stages of the funerary ritual, but usually not without equally significant references to the Solar-Osirian cycle with which the journey of the deceased, and possibly also the ritual, was paired. For instance may the necropolis scene (icon 26a) be a reference to the burial, but the icon also holds strong solar connotations. Quite a few 21st dynasty coffins have scenes from the *funerary procession* included in the repertoire of icons, sometimes in connection with the necropolis scene (icon 26a). However, these scenes display features from the 19th dynasty burial and funerary equipment, such as the obelisk shaped superstructure of the tomb in icon 26a. They are clearly not renderings of the 21st

---

358 Willems, *Chests of Life*.

359 Assmann, *Death and Salvation*, 238, 249; *Totenliturgien* I, 14-5.

360 Pries, *Die Stundenwachen in Osiriskuklt*, 10-26.

361 Koenig, in P. Kousoulis (ed.), *Ancient Egyptian Demonology*, 126-8.

362 Eyre, 'Funeral, Initiations and Ritual of Life in Pharaonic Egypt', in: M. Alice and J. Patrier (eds), *Life, Death, and Coming of Age in Antiquity: Individual Rites of Passage in the Ancient Near East and its Surroundings/ Vivre, grandir et mourir dans l'antiquité: rites de passage individuels au Proche-Orient ancien et ses environs* (forthcoming).

363 Von Leiven, *JEA* 98 (2012), 249-69; see also Smith, *Papyrus Harkness,* 33-41, for an early Roman Period papyrus having different rituals by a afther to his dead daughter and which also include different sets of rituals more than being just a simple burial ritual.

364 On the relation between myth and ritual, see Baines, *JNES* 50 (1991), 81-105.

365 Assmann, *MDAIK* 28.1 (1972), 47-73; *MDAIK* 28.2 (1972), 115-139; Willems, *Chests of Life*, 141-159.

dynasty funerary procession, since the latter must have taken place within the precincts of temples'.[366]

He also argues that the object frieze does not exist on such coffin, which makes it hard to envisage the images on the coffin sides alluding to rituals. The absence of the object frieze on the 21st Dynasty coffins does not mean that it is impossible to reconstruct rituals from the images and text on the coffin. The Pyramid Texts are not illustrated, and for the most part they are not even provided with ritual directions.[367] They only preserve the ritual recitations.[368] The Middle Kingdom coffins kept the recitations of the texts but are also illustrated with the object frieze and the ornamental texts.

During the 21st Dynasty, new iconographic ideas came into existence. The coffin was not only a body container for the deceased, it also served as a tomb. When we look at the images on the coffins, it is important to remember that the priests placed within these coffins should have rituals carried out on their mummies and also on their coffins. As argued in the introduction, the absence of decorated tombs and the superstructure of the Bab el-Gassus tomb and the inaccessible nature of its burial chamber do not mean that the ancient Egyptian religious system had collapsed or the idea of equipping the deceased with rituals for the afterlife had completely changed during the 21st Dynasty. What is important to consider here is how would we envisage the depiction of such rituals on the coffins without considering their performance on the mummy first? Would it be possible to say that *P3-dj-jmn* was buried at the tomb of Bab el-Gassus without having rituals carried out on his mummy?

In order to answer these questions it is important first to argue about the performance of rituals and how such performance was preserved and handed down to us. To have a better understanding of the performance of the Egyptian ritual texts, it is important to note that wording and content are not enough to have a clear picture of how the Egyptian ritual texts were performed. As Eyre argues:

'The essence of the ritual lies in the integration between words and actions performed in a highly charged context. Words without actions, like actions without words would fail to achieve an effective ritual.'[369]

Both words and actions in ritual go together and neither has primacy over the other; each reflects and moves forward the other.[370] It is hard to envisage a ritual performance without actions, since the rituals commonly involve participants in physical movement or action.[371] Uttering the word can also be described as an action, and that is made explicit from the fact that speaking and naming things are central themes in the mythical actions of the creator. For instance, Ptah is said to create the universe by the power of the word in the Memphite theology, in which he plays the role of the creator.[372] Other instances can be found in the Old Kingdom tombs where the passerby is implored to recite the *ḥtp-dj-nsw* for the owner of the tomb in lieu of presenting solid offerings. Words can also be preserved in writing, and in turn can be used in the cult of the deceased. For instance, in Assmann's words:

'As artificial voice, writing was intended to extend cultic recitations beyond the time span of its ritual performance and to keep the deceased forever within the range of the priestly voice. In this function it served to realize permanent recitation'.[373]

This role of the spoken word is made explicit in mortuary liturgies, which were texts intended for recitation in the mortuary cult of the deceased. The recitation of these texts as a rite of passage mediates the passage of the deceased to his new state as an *3ḫ*.[374]

Egyptian ritual texts survive as a mixture of texts inscribed on pyramid walls, coffin sides, papyri and also as vignettes drawn on papyrus and temple and tomb walls.[375] The relation between the written texts, the drawn vignettes, and the ritual action is also highly complicated. For that reason, the construction of a ritual can be described as 'imaginative exercise',[376] and the relation between the inscriptions and the representations should be considered.

It is true that the ritual performance is preserved in the mixture of vignettes and texts, which can give full record of the words and actions and thus can ease the construction of a ritual.[377] The ritual can be preserved in texts intended for recitation,[378] or in captions in the form of scenes, which can replace or play the same role as the written text. For instance, offering rituals are well preserved in the Pyramid Texts, and they are also depicted in captions on the private tomb walls of the Old Kingdom. Representations of ritual actions are mainly found as components of ritual scenes, and the other components of the ritual scene is its text.[379] Ritual texts

[366] Bettum, *Death as an eternal Process,* 122.
[367] Eyre, *The Cannibal Hymn*, 41. An exception is Spell 355 in the Pyramid of Teti, entitled 'Opening of the Doors of Heaven'.
[368] Eyre, *The Cannibal Hymn*, 41.
[369] Eyre, *The Cannibal Hymn*, 25; speaking the words, as Eyre argues, can also have the power of action.
[370] The first spell in the *Ritual of Letting Seth and His Gang Fall* is to be recited over a figurine of Seth, and the actions taken are: spitting upon, trampling, spearing, and burning the figurine of Seth. These acts, as Egberts argues, 'may be said to visualise the contents of the spells': Egberts, in: Eyre (ed.), *Proceedings of the Seventh International Congress of Egyptologists*, 358.
[371] This is not only strict to the Egyptian ritual texts, but all the religious rituals can be defined as set of texts and actions that are well organized: Bell, *Ritual: Perspectives and Dimensions*, 136-61.
[372] On the role of the word in the creation of the universe see, Assmann, *Theologie und Weisheit im alten Ägypten*, 24-30; Eyre, *The Cannibal Hymn*, 28.
[373] Assmann, *Death and Salvation*, 249. See also, *Totenliturgien* I, 53.
[374] Assmann, *Death and Salvation,* 238, 249; *Totenliturgien* I, 14-5; the same can also be said about the *Verklärungssprüchen,* the aim of which is to mediate the passage of the deceased to his new state of an *3ḫ*. Assmann, *Totenliturgien* III, 26-31.
[375] For the performative approach to the rituals in the Coffin Texts, see Willems, *The Coffin of Heqata*, 9-10.
[376] Eyre, *The Cannibal Hymn*, 41.
[377] Eyre, *The Cannibal Hymn*, 26.
[378] Assmann, *Totenliturgien* I, 15-7; *Totenliturgien* III, 26-31.
[379] Egberts, in: Eyre (ed.), *Proceedings of the Seventh International Congress of Egyptologists*, 359.

belonging to ritual scenes may be termed liturgical. The representations of the laments of Isis and Nephthys may belong to this context, and their performance of the laments can refer to the actual performance of the ritual as it is recorded in the Coffin Texts, in the laments of Isis and Nephthys in P. Bremner-Rhind, [380] and P. Berlin 3008.[381]

Ritual texts intended for recitation are designated by the formulaic heading *ḏd mdw* "saying of words," which is also present on the coffins of *P3-dj-jmn*. The transcription of these spoken words as texts on papyrus, temple or tomb walls, in the format that is equivalent to a service book, is not enough for assuming a performance of a ritual.[382] Ritual performance sometimes is indicated by the formula written on a service-book of the ritualist *ẖry-ḥbt*, whose name at the beginning of a text indicates that the text is for recitation. Several examples are found in the Old Kingdom private tombs at Saqqara. For instance, the deceased says: 'The ritualist (*ẖr*j-*ḥbt*) who will enact for me beneficial rituals...according to the craft of the ritualist.'[383]

The service-book used by the ritualist in the course of performing a ritual does not contain a coherent set of ritual but discrete units of ritual wording rather than continuous ritual narratives. The service-book also contains fragments of material of a diverse nature, used for different occasions and purposes, which gives the ritual its flexibility to be extended or abbreviated or even varied for the individual performance.[384] It is not plausible to look for a great narrative and continuity in the Old Kingdom Pyramid Texts, any more than in the New Kingdom Book of the Dead. Lapp argues that it is even impossible to have continuous ritual narrative within a single spell in the Book of the Dead.[385]

Different definitions of ritual texts have been proposed. Assmann distinguishes between two sets of texts, mortuary and funerary. Mortuary texts or liturgies, according to Assmann, are sets of ritual performed for the benefit of the deceased. In other words, mortuary liturgies are texts used in the context of the cult of the deceased, recited by the mortuary priest in the tomb, and the place where they were performed is the world of the living. Funerary liturgies (called mortuary literature by Assmann) serve as texts to be used in the Hereafter.[386] Mortuary liturgies, according to Assmann, were performed in the place of embalming and in the accessible cult chambers of the tomb; however, they were recorded or placed in the inaccessible sarcophagus chamber.[387] The mortuary literature was recorded on the sarcophagus chamber walls (as the Pyramid Texts), on coffin sides (Coffin Texts), or on papyri (Book of the Dead). Mortuary liturgies were performed on the behalf of the deceased, while mortuary literature was intended to equip him magically.[388]

This classification by Assmann raises different issues. The most important ritual texts used in temple daily cult were also used in funeral contexts. For instance, the New Kingdom Sun hymns were actually derived from a temple cult context, but they were inscribed on the private tomb walls in the New Kingdom to ensure their ongoing effect for the benefit of the deceased in the hereafter.[389]

On the coffins of *P3-dj-jmn*, we have both captions that can allude to a recitation of ritual texts, as in *ḏd mdw* formulae, and the *im3ḫj-ḫr*; both were prominent in ritual texts since the Old Kingdom. The images on the coffins sides do not form a coherent set from which we can reach to a single specific reconstruction of a ritual; instead, they draw on different metaphors as in the case of the ritual texts. For instance, in the Old Kingdom tombs, the funerary procession of the deceased in most cases is illustrated and accompanied by ritual captions, which, as mentioned above, could be designated as liturgical. The emphasis in these funerary scenes is on the image more than it is on the text. It is the same on the coffin of *P3-dj-jmn*. The absence of the ritual texts and ritual directions on the coffin sides does not mean that the images on the coffin sides do not refer or represent rituals. As in ritual texts, it is impossible to see a continuous narration or a set of images that refer to one specific ritual, but, as we will see, the images draw on different metaphors and also refer to different themes. Bettum's argument that the images on these coffins are mythical in nature and only give hints to rituals is open to debate. However, he argues that the icons still refer to rituals.

Reconstructing a ritual from a single image without considering its context is a problematic. In the Old Kingdom Pyramid Texts and in the Middle Kingdom Coffin Texts, it is not always explicit how a ritual can be constructed, and sometimes it is impossible to give a specific explanation to a ritual text.[390] It is also difficult to

---

380 Published by Faulkner, *JEA* 22 (1936), 121-40.

381 Faulkner published also the lamentations of Isis and Nephthys in P. Berlin 3008, which is not very different from the lamentations of the two goddesses in P. Bremner-Rhind: Faulkner, *Mélange Maspero* I. 1, 337-48. For the lamentations of Isis and Nephthys in British Museum EA 10332, see Coenen and Kucharek, *GM* 193 (2003), 45-50.

382 Eyre, *The Cannibal Hymn*, 27.

383 Eyre, *The Cannibal Hymn*, 26.

384 Smith, *The Liturgy of Opening the Mouth for Breathing*, 6-18; Eyre, *Cannibal Hymn*, 26-7.

385 Lapp, *Papyrus of Nu*, 42-9; for the problem of the construction of a single ritual within a spell, see Lüscher, *Totenbuch Spruch 151*, 12-17, 74-77.

386 Assmann, *Totenlitrugien* I, 13; *Death and Salvation*, 238; in: Israelit-Groll, S. (ed.), *Studies in Egyptology presented to Miriam Lichtheim*, vol. I, 2.

387 Assmann, *Totenliturgien* I, 13-14.

388 Assmann, *Death and Salvation*, 238.

389 The use of funerary literature by the living has been discussed by several Egyptology scholars. Among them is Junker who noted that many Pyramid Texts and chapters of the Book of the Dead (Ch. 26, 69, 125, 148, 172, 178 and 180) were used in the *Stundenwachen*, which is well known and depicted on the temples of Dendara, Edfu, and Philae: Junker, *Die Stundenwachen*, 23, 110, 120. Walter Federn also noted the use of the so called Transformation spells in the Coffin Texts and their later extensions in the Book of the Dead in the initiation practices by the living: Federn, *JNES* 19 (1960), 241-257. For an expanded argument on this topic, see Gee, in: Backes et al, *Totenbuch-forschungen*, 73-6. For the most recent discussion, see Von Leiven, *JEA* 98 (2012), 249-269

390 Allen, in: *Hommages Leclant* I, 5-28. For the full discussion of the placing of the spell of the Cannibal Hymn, see Eyre, *The Cannibal Hymn*, 41-47.

reconstruct a ritual from a single text. In order to reconstruct the ritual in Middle Kingdom coffins or in the Old Kingdom Pyramid Texts, it is crucial to study the ritual context of the spells. The same problem occurs on the 21st Dynasty coffins. It is also not explicit how to study a single image without considering its context. So, the image will be dealt with here as a text and the study of its context is important.

The attitude towards the coffin, object frieze and coffin inscriptions changed during the 21st Dynasty. Pictorial and iconic representations of rituals were dominant during this period more than presentation of the rituals in written texts. The texts on these coffins were reduced to captions. The habit of preserving ritual performance in images rather than presenting them in texts is well known since the Old Kingdom.

During the Old Kingdom, captions accompanying boat and ship journeys in private tombs refer to some complicated set of rituals performed for the deceased on the day of funeral. The journey of the deceased from his house to his burial place was envisaged as a journey from this world to the next. The deceased was depicted within a shrine in a boat and crosses a body of water. In his journey over water, the deceased was accompanied by a lector priest who reads from a papyrus roll, and by kites and an embalmer. This ritual was called the "crossing of the lake" *nmjt š*.[391] The ritual was accompanied by the recitation of *s3ḫw* texts, a well known genre of ritual texts.

An example of this ritual is found in the mastaba of In-Snefru-Ishetef (fig. 70). A scene in the upper register shows a boat with a shrine being towed across the water. The shrine most probably houses a statue of the deceased. At the prow of the boat sits a kite (*ḏrt*), two undesignated men, and a lector priest with containers holding his equipment. There is a woman sitting at the back of the boat near the helmsman. At the bottom, a boat seems to sail or rest on sand. Above the boat there is a label reading:

| | |
|---|---|
| *ḏ3jt wrt* | Crossing of the *Wrt*-boat |

A kite is represented facing a priest, who stands in a canopy and reads from a papyrus roll. There is also a kite sitting at the back of the boat with a man designated as an embalmer (*wt*). The text accompanying the scene reads:

| | |
|---|---|
| *sšm ḥb m mw* | Conducting a ritual in water, |
| *jn ḫrj-ḥbt jjmḥ* | By the lector priest Iimeh. |

The rest of the scene shows three men towing a boat, offerings being presented and figures of men slaughtering an ox.[392]

[391] Abbas, in: Corbelli et al, *Current Research in Egyptology* 2009, 1-14.
[392] Wilson, *JNES* 3 (1944), 208.

Fig.70. The funeral procession of In-Snefru-Ishetef at Dahshour, (after Wilson, *JNES* 3 (1944), pl. XIV).

The scene depicts a series of ritual sets, including presentations of offerings, slaughtering bulls, and reciting texts. All these are just hinted at with the captions accompanying the scene. The emphasis here is on the scenes and not on the ritual texts — on the image that is prominent here.[393]

This practice of depicting rituals in images instead of presenting them in texts for recitation became dominant on the sides of the coffins during the 21st Dynasty. During the 21st Dynasty, new iconographic representations were introduced, expressing complicated cosmological and eschatological concepts focusing on the Osiris-Solar unity by means of a number of figural symbols. These images and symbols on the coffins are the Solar-Osirian aspects of the great god with whom the deceased was identified. As a follower and incarnation of the solar god Re, the deceased was believed to travel on the day and night skies, and that is why we see a number of scenes representing the solar journey of Re. These solar aspects of the deceased were understood as multiple creations of Osiris.[394]

### *4.2. The Outer Coffin of P3-dj-jmn*

#### *4.2.1. TheLlid of the Outer Coffin as Representation of the Funeral Pprocession*

In his work on Middle Kingdom coffins, Willems argues that the lid decorations represent the funeral procession,[395] and the exterior decorations on Middle Kingdom coffins focus on burial rites.[396] These rites involve sets of different rituals starting in the place of embalmment during the night preceding the burial; at dawn the procession leaves this place to the tomb of the deceased. These rites also include the presentation of offerings followed by proper burial rites. The Opening of the Mouth as a ritual was included in these rites. Willems also argues that the exterior decorations on these coffins are reserved for the offering rituals that took place outside

[393] Ritual scenes accompanied by captions are well known in ancient Egypt. For Old Kingdom examples, see, Harpur, *JEA* 73 (1987), 197-200; for New Kingdom, see, Hartwig, *Tomb Painting and Identity in Ancient Thebes*.
[394] Niwinski, *Studies on the Illustrated Theban Funerary Papyri*, 15-6.
[395] Willems, *Chests of Life*, 171-4, 240.
[396] Willems, *Chests of Life*, 239; *The Coffin of Heqata*, 46.

the tomb. The different speeches of the column gods on the exterior sides of the coffin are divine speeches of the gods who participated in the night of the *Stundenwachen* around the bier of the deceased. The roles of these gods are played by priests. The enactment of such rituals lasted until sunrise. Their main concern was to protect the body of the deceased and to enable him to gain his victory over death. The texts that deal with this theme are elaborated on two levels. The first is represented in the mythical victory of Osiris and Horus over Seth and the coronation of Osiris as king of the underworld and Horus as king of Egypt. The defeat of Seth and the coronation of Osiris have been decided by a court of justice as part of the ritual of the judgment of the dead.[397] These ideas were incorporated in the rituals taking place in the place of embalmment in the night before burial. At the end of the night wake in the place of embalmment, the coffin was transported on a sledge to the tomb. The transportation of the coffin from the place of embalmment to a sledge in order to be taken to the tomb is envisaged as the sunrise. The funeral procession and the journey of the coffin to the burial place were envisaged as the journey of Re from the east to the west of the sky.[398] These ritual acts, which were incorporated in the night before the burial and in the procession to the tomb, are hinted at on the decorations of the outer coffin of *P3-dj-jmn* as well.

The images on the lid and case of the outer coffin, like the ritual texts, do not allude to a coherent set of rituals. They are bits and pieces referring to different ritual actions at the same time. The images will be arranged below in sequence in order to see how they work together to refer to the funeral procession and to the burial rites. In the Old Kingdom example of the funeral procession cited above, the funeral procession consists of different episodes. It is hard, if not impossible, to determine how such episodes can be arranged, but what is known from the Old kingdom tomb scenes is that the funeral started from the place of embalmment and followed a course or a path until it reached the necropolis. During the procession there were several ritual acts taking place. The Old Kingdom procession was accompanied by recitation of ritual texts the aim of which is to mediate the deceased's passage to become an *3ḫ*. The nature of such recited texts is unknown, as the images do not provide information about the texts. The procession is also accompanied by presentations of offerings, an embalmer, two kites and a lector priest.

In Chapter Two we have seen that the scenes on the lid and case of the coffin of *p3-dj-jmn* focus on the following themes.

1-On the upper part of the lid are representations of scarabs, falcons and two jackals. The two jackals are described as *jnpw ḫntj sḥ-nṯr nb dw3t* "Anubis Foremost of the Booth of the God, Lord of the Underworld," and he is also addressed at the middle part of the lid as *jnpw ḫnty imntt* "Anubis Foremost of the West."

2- The middle part is occupied by the sky goddess Nut with outstretched wings.

3-The lower section of the middle part is divided into two parts by four columns of texts, in which the deceased asks Nut to spread her wings over him and to make him exist like the Imperishable and Unwearying Stars. Nut covers the deceased as if she is embracing him, and in this role she is acting as his mother. He also addresses Anubis, saying that the gods are happy with the arrival of the deceased in the necropolis. In the last speech of the deceased on this part of the coffin, he asks the gods to give him offerings.

4- The deceased is shown presenting offerings to the gods.

5- The offering scenes are preceded by a formula in which the deceased is described as a Revered One with a god or a goddess

6- The two borders of the lid are covered by the speeches of Nut and Geb.

These speeches on the lid are different forms of *Bitten* in which the gods and goddess addressed by the deceased are arranged in a particular way. These speeches are also accompanied by offering scenes in which the deceased offers unguents and vases of different kinds to deities. The deities are arranged such that Osiris is facing Anubis, Isis is facing Nephthys and finally Hapi is facing Duamutef. These deities form a kind of protection for the deceased whose body is placed within the coffin. The frequent use of unguent vases might be related to the anointing scenes in the ritual of the Opening of the Mouth, and when it is related or connected with the Four Sons of Horus, they represent the Canopic Jars.[399] The use of vases also might be related to an offering ritual in which these vases were presented.

The first problem facing us when trying to determine the sequence of the scenes on the lid is, from which part should we start reading them? As mentioned above, Hornung argues that the sequence of the scenes on such coffins should start from the lower part of the lid at the feet. He also argues that scenes referring to the journey of Re, with whom the deceased is identified, from the depth of the underworld until he shines in the sky run from the lower part of the lid to its upper part (from bottom to the top of the lid). That is why, for instance, we see the images of the scarab at the top and the scenes of the underworld at the feet.[400] The coffin might have been placed in two ways. The first is the standing position, and in this case the images placed at the feet of the lid are inverted compared to the rest of the decorations. For us the scenes might look upside down, but for the deceased who is looking down at his feet these scenes would be in the correct orientation. The other possibility is that the coffin was placed flat on the ground, and in this case the scenes should be read in a different way. The east side wall of the case would represent the front side, and the west side wall is the back of the coffin.

[397] Willems, *Chests of Life*, 148ff.
[398] Wilson, *JNES* 3(1944), 201-18.
[399] Van Walsem, *The Coffin of Djedmonthuiufankh,* 131.
[400] Hornung, *Innerrhoder Geschichtsfreund* 28 (1984), 8.

The scenes on the lid of the outer coffin represent the deceased's journey from the place of embalmment to his burial place, which is also envisaged as a journey through the sky. The path of the journey is the body of the sky goddess Nut who spreads her wings over the deceased. This is complemented by the speech of the deceased to the goddess, asking her to spread her wings over him and to make him like the Imperishable and Unwearying Stars, which means that the body of the goddess is a place of passage for the deceased. By travelling in the body of the goddess, the deceased will become an Imperishable Star. Nut here plays the role of the mother goddess who is embodied in the coffin. The role of the goddess as a mother of the deceased Osiris is explicit in the following text:

My beloved son, Osiris N.,
Come and rest in me!
I am your mother who protects you daily.
I protect your body from all evil,
I guard your body from all evil.
I make your flesh perfectly hale[401]

By covering the deceased with her body, the goddess Nut promises the deceased that he will be reborn as a star. In one of the Late Period texts we read:

I place you within me, I bear you a second time,
That you may go out and in among the Imperishable Stars
and be elevated alive and rejuvenated like the sun god, daily.
........I surrounded you in my name 'coffin'.
I give you the sweet breath of the north wind,
......your existence lasts forever, O Osiris N.[402]

By entering the body of the sky goddess Nut, the deceased is reborn again in the womb of his mother, the sky goddess Nut. The journey is envisaged as his resurrection as well as a journey into the sky. Both resurrection and travelling through the goddess's body refer to the path of the deceased's procession.

The speech of the deceased to Anubis telling him that the gods of the necropolis are happy when Shu shines in the sky is also an indication of the arrival of the funeral procession of the deceased in the necropolis. In this speech the deceased is envisaged as Shu, who is filling the space between the earth god Geb and the sky goddess Nut. Nut's body is envisaged here also as the path of the funeral procession, which is modeled on the journey of Re in the body of his mother Nut. The procession is also accompanied by the presentation of offerings, although it is not clear in which part of the procession this took place.

The scarab at the upper part of the lid is a symbol of the final phase of the journey of the god from the depth of the underworld until he rises in the morning in the sky. It is also a sign of the final stage in the procession, where the deceased reaches the necropolis, which is also represented on the right hand side wall of the case, where the deceased is shown presenting offerings to Hathor who comes out of the mountain and his tomb is depicted behind her. The final destination in the journey of the sun god Re, with whom the deceased is identified, is described by his arrival at the necropolis where the gods are happy to see him shine as Shu. The presence of Anubis also might refer to the embalmer who accompanied the funeral procession in the Old Kingdom tomb scenes. The two *ba* birds flanking the pectoral and presenting offerings with the inscriptions above them reading *ʿnḫ wsjr* might reflect the two kites accompanying the funeral procession. These two kites, who represent Isis and Nephthys, will appear again on the two sides of the case near the head of the deceased. So, the sequence of the funeral procession on the lid can be arranged as follows:

The scarab and the two jackals are reference to the final stages in the procession, where the scarab is a symbol of the arrival of the deceased at the necropolis, which is also the final phase of the god's movement from the underworld into the sky. The deceased's arrival at the necropolis is compared with the god's arrival in the sky. The path of the deceased's funeral procession is envisaged as the god's path in the body of the sky goddess Nut. The procession is accompanied by the presentation of offerings, which is clear from the scenes in which the deceased presents offerings to various deities. The two *ba* birds are also depicted presenting offerings. The act of presenting these offering is also obvious from the captions that accompany the offering scenes. When the tomb has been reached, there should have been offering lists read and the sacrifice should have been made: that might be indicated by the use of *ḏd mdw* formulae on the sides of the lid.

The images on the lid only represent the conclusion of the funeral procession; the rest of the procession and how it is envisaged as the journey of Re in the day and night skies are represented on the two sides of the case. In the next few pages I will argue how the journey of Re in the two skies is envisaged as the resurrection of Osiris, and how the rest of the scenes deal with the arrival of the deceased at the necropolis, and the burial rites.

#### *4.2.2. The Case of the Outer Coffin and the Burial Rites*

According to the tale of Sinuhe, the burial rites start in the place of embalming from the night that precedes the burial. In this tale, the king promises Sinuhe a good burial, saying:

A night will be prepared for you with ointment and wrappings from the hands of the weaving goddess. A funeral procession will be carried out for you on the day of burial.[403]

In this night a number of ritual actions and recitations took place. The enactment of the ritual was an enactment of the myth in which both Re cosmology and the myth of Osiris and how he was murdered and ritually reintegrated played the prominent role. How are Re cosmology and the myth of Osiris incorporated in the case decorations

[401] Assmann, *Death and Salvation*, 170.
[402] Assmann, *Death and Salvation*, 170.
[403] The translation uses Parkinson, *The Tale of Siunhe*, 36.

and texts, and how can we determine that the outer case decorations refer to both? The images and texts on exterior walls of the outer coffin allude to two important sets of rituals. The first is the rituals that took place in the night before burial, in which Osiris is vindicated. The second set is the burial rituals and arriving at the tomb, which are modeled on the night and day journeys of Re.

On the two sides of the case near the head end stands Nephthys on the right and the Goddess of the West above the head of the deceased. Isis is mentioned in the text that occurs on the left hand side wall near the head. Nephthys is shown raising her hands in a gesture of adoration. Isis, mentioned in the texts, and Nephthys, represented at the head of the deceased, reminds us of the two goddesses who sit at the two sides of the bier attending the mummy of the god in the place of embalming. The sequence of the scenes runs from the external left hand side wall to the external right hand side wall of the coffin.

The upper edge on the left hand side wall is ornamented by a single register of inscriptions in which the deceased is directing his speech to Anubis as patron of the necropolis. This side of the coffin, when it is placed flat on the ground, represents the west. This side on Middle Kingdom coffins is ornamented by an offering formula for Anubis as patron of the necropolis, and thus good burial in the west is ensured. It can also refer to the west and the underworld.[404] In ancient Egyptian thought, the west is connected with the underworld and the night journey of the sun god Re. The speech of the deceased also continues describing how the gods are happy when Shu (the deceased) arrives in the netherworld and in the sky. Horus is described as the son of Isis who is in his office, which also alludes to how Osiris was vindicated and as a result was appointed as the king of the underworld and his son Horus was proclaimed as a king.

The first scene on this side shows the deceased standing in front of the emblem of the west making adoration. He is also followed by the Sons of Horus. The captions that accompany the scene mention both Osiris as Lord of the West and Anubis as the Great God, Lord of the Underworld. This scene could be described as an introduction to what follows, stressing the fact that this side refers to both the west and the underworld.

The second scene deals with both the resurrection of Osiris and the journey of the sun god Re from the depth of the underworld. The resurrection of Osiris took place in the place of embalmment in the night before the burial. The same scene represents also the nocturnal journey of the sun god Re. As mentioned above, in Chapter Two, the cosmological scene refers to the creation process in which the sun god Re faces his enemies. According to the Egyptian vision of cosmos, the act of creation was repeated every day in the appearance of the sun at the eastern horizon. This act was preceded by the conflict with Apep, the primeval enemy of the sun god Re. The sun god Re overcame his enemy by the aid of fire, which burnt and destroyed Apep, and also with the aid of knives.[405] The victory of the sun god Re over his enemies refers at the same time to the victory of Osiris over Seth, over death. The night preceding the burial was full of rituals, the aim of which was the resurrection and the reintegration of the body of Osiris, who had been cut into pieces by Seth, the enemy of Osiris. The number of the beings within the cosmological circle is twelve, which might allude to the twelve hours of the night.[406]The two small discs refer to the two eastern and western extremes of the journey of the sun through the twelve hours of the day or night. The dots may mark the course of the sun from the east to the west. The figure of the mummy with the head of a scarab might also refer to Osiris in his solar aspects. The barque with a solar deity with the sun disc on his head above the scarab also refers to the same aspects of the deceased, who is identified with both gods. The mummy being attended by Isis and Nephthys also refers to the two goddesses as protecting and attending the deceased Osiris in his solar aspects. The goddesses were placed to the left and right respectively; Isis facing the mummy and Nephthys protecting the mummy from behind, just as they were depicted on Middle Kingdom coffins.

The creation process of the sun here refers at the same time to the resurrection process of Osiris, in which Isis and Nephthys play a prominent role. The ceremonies in the place of embalmment were recorded in the column texts in Middle Kingdom Coffin Texts. In these texts, gods pronouncing their speeches and their roles are played by priests and priestesses attending the mummy in the place of embalmment. Some speeches are also recorded on the lid and, as in the case of the outer coffin of *P3-dj-jmn*, could be evidence that they refer to the rituals that took place on the mummy and the coffin on the night before burial.

After the conclusion of these nightly rituals, which are here symbolized by the night journey of Re, the coffin was placed on a sledge and then taken in procession to the tomb. The act of moving the coffin from the place of embalmment to the sledge is compared to the sunrise, here represented by the mummy with the head of a scarab. This scene is separated from the next by a speech for Geb addressing the deceased as the legal heir of Osiris and son of Isis. The burial rites include also the presentation of offerings, which is clear where the deceased is represented presenting offerings to the recumbent cows and the seated gods. These cows are also the ones who will provide the deceased with food and nourishment. Although it might look as if the deceased is making offerings in the necropolis or at the burial place, the text that accompanies the scenes reads:

*ḳbḥw ḥtp ḏf3w jmj dw3t ḫntj jmntt dj=s ḥtpw*

[404] Willems, *Chests of Life*, 124.

[405] For how the knives and fire were used as tools of getting rid of Apep, see Abbas, *The Lake of Knives and the Lake of Fire*, 11-2.
[406] Niwinski, *GM* 109 (1989), 60.

Making libation and giving offering (to) those who are in the underworld by the Foremost of the West that she may give offerings.

So the deceased, as Re, is still in his nocturnal journey in the netherworld and has not yet come to the moment when he shines like Re in the morning. The final scene that completes the nocturnal cycle is the scene of the Tree Goddess, described in the text as Nut who gives offerings to Osiris Foremost of the West.

The right-hand side wall represents the day journey of the sun god Re, in which the deceased takes part. The cosmological scene on the right-hand side wall also relates the same story of the resurrection and rebirth. The arrival of the deceased in the necropolis is envisaged here as the appearance of Shu in the sky. Describing the deceased as Shu might also refer to the deceased as standing between earth and the sky, and thus he is not only Osiris but Re at the same time. He is Shu filling the space between the two spheres and thus he is sharing in the daily cycle of the sun. The falcons on the right and left, with their titles, refer to the deceased as sharing the aspects of both Osiris and Re. It looks as if the mummy inside the coffin is embraced by Osiris, who is represented on the floor board of the coffin, and by the sky goddess Nut on the top (she is the lid itself). He is not only Osiris; he is also an incarnation of the sun god who travels in an eternal process through the visible day sky and the invisible night sky.[407]

Upon the deceased's reaching the necropolis, offerings are presented. The deceased in the next scene is shown accompanied by Isis and Anubis and making offerings to the emblem of Osiris. Afterward, he is also shown presenting offerings to the goddess Hathor, who is coming out of the mountain with the tomb of the deceased behind her. The speeches on the right side wall of the outer coffin are also important. The first speech on that part is for Thoth and comes after the scene of Nephthys with upraised arms. In this speech Thoth is described as the Lord of the God's words and the scribe of Maat and the Great Ennead. The rest of the speech relates also the myth of how Re was saved on the day of beheading on the primeval mound. According to the myth, the sun god Re, in his journey through the underworld and before he shines on the eastern horizon, has to defeat his primeval enemies. These enemies took different shapes; they could be described as turtles, or even as Apep. The place where the sun god Re defeated his enemies is the Island of Fire.[408]

The deceased, as Osiris in his journey from death to resurrection, is faced with an enemy who is compared to Apep in Egyptian ritual texts. This enemy is Seth, who murdered Osiris and cut his body into pieces. The mutilation caused to the body of Osiris is overcome by the aid of the rites that take place in the place of embalmment in the night before burial. These rites are dynamic and repetitive[409] and could be envisaged as a journey by water or as a creation process in which the deceased, as a follower of a god, takes different forms focusing on a multiplicity of constituent parts making up the individual personality or identity.[410] These rites focus also on the reassembly and reintegration of the individual, who has disintegrated at death.[411] All these themes are represented in ritual texts during the different periods of Egyptian history. On the coffin of *P3-dj-jmn*, these themes are represented in images and caption of texts.

Although some might argue that the reconstruction of the funeral procession ritual from the images is impossible and there is no direct reference to such a ritual on the lid, it is impossible to imagine that these images were just placed randomly on the lid. The absence of the ritual acts does not mean that the images on the lid do not refer to rituals. The ritual is also preserved in images referring to the mythical sphere of the ritual. The images refer to the myth of the god who travels through the body of the sky goddess Nut, with no reference to any ritual actions, but these images still allude to the ritual of the funeral procession.

Although there is no object frieze as on Middle Kingdom coffins, we have instead items that were included in this object frieze, in the unguents and vases on the lid. There are also no ritual directions, but what is clear is that there must have been ritual texts recited over the coffin and the deceased within it. These recited texts are alluded to in the divine speeches of the gods and goddesses on the lid. Here the burial, as a rite of passage, is mixed with the passage of the soul to the sky and to the netherworld ruled by Osiris, or even by a cyclical and continuous passage through the night and day skies in the divine company of Re.[412] These rites are related to the ritual texts referred to as the *Stundenwachen*.[413]

#### *4.2.3. The Floor Board of the Case of the Outer Coffin and the ḳbḥw Offering Ritual*

In Chapter Two it has been argued that the image of Osiris on the floor board of the case refers to the offering of fresh or cold water to the deceased. The images and the texts on the floor board have been related to an offering ritual in which *ḳbḥw* water is offered to the deceased. It has also been argued that this offering of cold water represents an episode of a larger ritual in which the resurrection of the deceased is accomplished. The whole decoration program on the floor board of the outer case ensures the resurrection of the deceased, in which offering the *ḳbḥw* water plays an important part. The water offered to the deceased, which has been depicted in

[407] Niwinski, *GM* 109 (1989), 54.

[408] Abbas, *The Lake of Knives and the Lake of Fire*, 47-8.

[409] Servjean, *Djet et Neheh. Une histoire du temps* égyptien.

[410] Assmann, *Death and Salvation*, 87-112; Eyre, in: Poo (ed.), *Rethinking Ghosts in World Religions*, 33-46.

[411] Assmann, *Death and Salvation*, 23-38.

[412] Federn, *JNES* 19/4 (1960), 249; Assmann, *Ägyptische Geheimnisse*, 165-74; *Death and Salvation*, 392-8. See also Smith, *Traversing Eternity*, 7 on becoming Osiris in the afterlife meant becoming one of his community worshippers or one of his followers, see also Smith, in: Backes et al, *Totenbuch-Forschungen*, 325-37.

[413] Pries, *Die Stundenwachen in Osiriskuklt*, 10-26.

the image of Osiris with water signs on his body, mediates the passage of the deceased from death to resurrection. This water is the living substance that comes from the body of Osiris and will be offered to him in ritual. The deceased, who shares in the cycle of death and resurrection of the god, will be revitalized with this water. The cycle of the resurrection of the deceased is also completed by the surrounding scenes on the two sides of the flanking walls of the inner case and the head of Osiris.

For the deceased whose body is placed on this floor board, drinking the *ḳbḥw* water offered to Osiris means he drinks the vital fluid of Osiris, and as a result he partakes of the god's immortality.[414] When the body of the deceased is placed on the floor board, he is then embraced by Osiris from the bottom and by the sky goddess Nut from above on the lid, and thus the coffin becomes a cosmos for the deceased.

### *4.3. The Inner Coffin and the Judgment of the Dead*

Scenes and divine speeches of the gods dealing with the resurrection and the journey of Horus to his father Osiris are depicted on the lid of the inner coffin of *P3-dj-jmn*.[415] The images on the lid of the inner coffin focus on how the deceased Osiris's body is ritually integrated by the aid of the triangular constellation of Isis, Nephthys and Horus. In the Coffin Texts, the ceremony of the judgment of the dead occurred at the end of the embalming ritual. The night before burial was concluded with a wake that was celebrated with offerings, libations, censing, purification and most importantly the recitation of ritual texts. These recitations confront us with the concept of the judgment of the dead, which was still largely based on a royal model of the mythic lawsuit between Horus and Seth. According to the myth, Osiris was vindicated against Seth and thus became the king of the netherworld, while Horus, the legal heir of the throne of his father Osiris, became the king of Egypt. The ordinary deceased would go through the same cycle of events as those experienced by Osiris. He would be vindicated against Seth-death and become one of the followers of Osiris. The deceased bears the same titles of Osiris along with his own name, titles, and epithet of *m3ᶜ-ḫrw* "justified" or vindicated," or *jm3ḫj* "Revered One."

The deceased in ancient Egypt faced two kinds of death. The first is caused by Seth, who has dismembered his body and isolated him from his family. The deceased Osiris could be cured from this death by the combined efforts of Isis, Nephthys, Horus, Anubis and Thoth. After the great efforts of theses deities, the deceased's body is reassembled and with this the deceased Osiris has escaped the first death, but Seth continues to threaten the decease even after he has been vindicated. He continues to threaten his offerings with annihilation, described by Assmann as the second death. For that reason, Seth had to be confronted, humiliated and punished. All these acts were done to Seth in the ritual of the judgment of the dead. The deceased's vindication in the lawsuit of Heliopolis and getting rid of his sins were envisaged as his victory over death in the image of Seth. In Assmann's words this vindication of the deceased is described as:

> 'Victory over the enemy had the same meaning as acquittal from the accusation of sin, and therein lay the distinctive common ground of the older and the newer concept'.[416]

The Coffin Texts give us an insight into the ritual enactment of the judgment of the dead in the form of liturgical recitation. The liturgical recitation connects the vindication of the deceased in the judgment of the dead with the process of embalming and mummification. Guilt, sin, accusation are treated as decay and impurity and also as harmful substances that should be eliminated. By removing these harmful substances, the deceased is vindicated. With this concept, removing the decay and the impurity is described by Assmann as the 'physical mummification' and getting rid of sins is described as a 'moral mummification'.[417] It looks as if, after the embalmer finished his work on the corpse, the deceased was then taken to a priest who extended the work of purification and the preservation of the deceased. After the priest's work on the mummy, the deceased gains the status of being *sᶜḥ*, which could be described as the last stage in the whole mummification process, in which the deceased undergoes the judgment of the dead, after which he becomes one of the followers of Osiris.[418]

This ritualised model of the judgment of the dead is different from the model that occurs in BD Chapter 125. In this model of the judgment of the dead the deceased is not plaintiff but defendant. He has to vindicate himself in front of the judges and to recite a long list of transgressions and testify that he has not committed them. His heart is weighed against the feather of *Maat*. If he is found guilty he will be eaten by a monster who is here the personification of Seth or the second death described above, but here the monster *ᶜmᶜm* does not stand for evil as Seth but for defense against evil.[419]

This brief introduction to the judgment of the dead as a ritual is important because in the exterior decorations and texts of the inner coffin of *P3-dj-jmn* the cycle of death and resurrection is repeated more than once. That is because the different episodes of the judgment of the dead are envisaged as a cycle of death and resurrection. The deceased's vindication, as we will see, is envisaged as his resurrection. Being vindicated also means being victorious over death-Seth. The two different ways of dealing with the judgment of the dead are found on the lid and case of the inner coffin of *P3-dj-jmn*. The Middle Kingdom judgment of the dead as a ritual is depicted on the lid of the inner coffin of *P3-dj-jmn*, while the model

---

[414] Delia, *JARCE* 29 (1992), 183; Kettel, In: *Hommages Leclant* III, 318-20; Assmann, *Death and Salvation*, 357-8; *Totenliturgien* II, 96-7; in: *Hommages Fayza Haikal*, 19.

[415] See above, Chapter Three.

[416] Assmann, *Death and Salvation*, 73.

[417] Assmann, *Death and Salvation*, 74.

[418] Assmann, *Death and Salvation*, 75

[419] Assmann, *Death and Salvation*, 75.

of the judgment of the dead that is common in BD Chapter 125 is found on the case of the same coffin.

### *4.3.1. The Ritual of the Judgment of the Dead on the Lid of the Inner Coffin*

In Chapter Three we have seen that the images and texts on the lid of the inner coffin allude to the journey of Horus to resuscitate his father Osiris, who is shown lying on a bier with all signs of royalty, attended by Isis and Nephthys. The lid is also covered with divine speeches of the gods and goddesses, which have been described as taking place in the *Stundenwachen*. These divine speeches are pronounced by deities whose roles are played by priests reciting these liturgical texts in the place of embalming.

These speeches on the lid can be compared with the divine speeches of the column gods on Middle Kingdom coffins, which relate the acts of the priests in the place of embalmment and include the pronouncing of a judgment for the deceased. This judgment of the dead is modeled on the mythical trial between Horus and Seth. The liturgical nature of these speeches is evident from the use of *ḏd mdw* "recitation," which indicates that there must have been recitations taking place.

The scenes and text on the lid are bordered by the two speeches of the goddesses Neith and Serqet, running from down the elbow to the end of the feet. At the feet edges are two texts that mention Isis and Neith. The middle part of the lid is occupied by texts that mention Osiris, Ptah-Sokar, Neith, Serqet, Hapi, Anubis and Geb. There is also a speech by the deceased asking the goddess Nut to spread her wings over him and to make him like the Imperishable Stars and the Unwearying Stars so that he will not die again in the necropolis near the Great Ennead. He also appears on the lid as the Venerated One with different deities. These gods are not very different from the column gods on the lid of the coffin of Merenptah or the column gods on Middle Kingdom coffins. They can be described as the Great Ennead who led the judgment of the dead, in which Osiris was vindicated against Seth. The recitation took place in the *Stundenwachen* around the bier of the deceased, who is depicted here attended by Nephthys and Isis.

The main scene on the lid of the inner coffin of *P3-dj-jmn* is the bier of Osiris, where Isis and Nephthys are represented at the feet and head ends and Horus hovers over the body of his father Osiris. The surrounding scenes complement the roles of the deities around the bier. Horus as the son of Osiris is also depicted in a boat upon which is a shrine housing Osiris, and he is travelling between two trajectories symbolizing the west and east, as represented by the two lion's heads emerging from the wings of Horus. The two cobras surrounding the boat are named as Neith and Serqet. This scene might refer to Horus, who is travelling in a boat towards the abode of his father to resurrect him. This theme of the son who travels in a boat crossing a body of water occurs in the ferryman spells cited above, where the son is asked about the aim of his journey, and he replies that he is in his way to awaken his dead father.[420]

The vindication of Osiris against Seth took place in the lawsuit of Heliopolis, where Horus summoned the court in Heliopolis and that court was on his side. Osiris was crowned as king of the netherworld, while Horus was appointed as King of Egypt.[421] This complex of thoughts is referred to in the texts and representations of the journey to Sais. According to the inscriptions of Merenptah, after the mummification process finished Osiris was justified and crowned as king in the presence of the two Enneads and the Two State Chapels. When Osiris reached Sais, his enemies were destroyed. The text columns' gods are mentioned individually, stating their positions to the left and right, head and feet of the deceased. The Ennead features as a court of justice, and they are depicted at the corners of the coffin to protect the deceased. Most probably the role of the gods in the court of justice was played by priests attending the mummy of the deceased. Thus the journey to Sais seems to incorporate Osiris' victory over his enemies and his coronation as a king in the netherworld.[422]

The journey of Sais is hinted at in the speeches of the goddess Neith on different parts of the lid. She appears on the border of the coffin as mother of the god, Eye of Re and Mistress of the House of Life. She is then asked to give offerings to Osiris. She appears at the foot end and she is also described as the mother of the god. The deceased is also described as the Revered or Venerated One with the Goddess Neith, mother of the god. On the inscription of the coffin of Merenptah, the goddess Neith is described as the mother of the king and the embodiment of the coffin. She addresses her son Merenptah in a long speech in which the king is first described as inside the womb of his mother Neith, who represents the coffin itself. The rest of the text deals with the actions taking place in the place of embalmment, where the rituals are performed by Isis and Nephthys and the Four Sons of Horus. Then the goddess Neith places other gods—Shu, Tefnut, Geb and Nut—to the left and right of the deceased. These deities proclaim Merenptah to be a king, after which he appears at the temple of Neith at Sais. All these sequences of events, according to Assmann, are taking place in the *Stundenwachen*, the nightly wake before burial.[423] The gods of the columns in the inscriptions of Merenptah appear as priests, or as Willems says, 'priests playing divine roles'.[424] The role of the goddess Neith as mother of the coffin is also complemented by the role of the sky goddess Nut on the lid. She is depicted on the lid with her outstretched wings. The speeches of the goddess Neith on the different parts of the lid indicate that there might have been a judgment that is pronounced by the goddess and also might refer at the same time to a journey taking place to Sais.

---

[420] See above, 37.
[421] Grieshammer, *Jenseitsgericht*, 111-5; Willems, *Chests of Life*, 148-9.
[422] Willems, Chests of Life, 150.
[423] Assmann, *MDAIK* 28.1 (1973), 47-73.
[424] Willems, *Chests of Life*, 142.

The other gods and goddesses on the lid are arranged such that Isis and Nephthys are placed at the two sides of the bier with Horus on the top. Under the bier the goddess Nut is shown flanking the bier as if she is carrying it. The Four Sons of Horus are depicted under the two wings of the goddess Nut as supporting the sky and attending the bier. Neith and Serqet are shown at the two borders of the lid as if flanking the whole composition. Isis and Neith appear again at the foot end with their speeches. Horus, son of Osiris, appears more than once on the different sides of the lid. The middle part of the lid is occupied by texts that mention Osiris, Ptah-Sokar, Neith, Serqet, Hapi, Anubis and Geb. These gods and goddesses might form the Ennead who occurs among the inscriptions on the lid. On the lid the deceased's arrival to the west is envisaged as his crossing of the sky. The gods of the necropolis are also happy when he reaches the necropolis where he will not die again in the necropolis with the Ennead. The reference to not dying again might allude to the second death referred to by Assmann, which the deceased will escape by undergoing the judgment of the dead, whose judges are the Ennead.

The Ennead here also might refer to the gods who are forming protection around the body of the deceased Osiris who is depicted lying on his bier. The presence of offerings around Osiris and the different kinds of crowns under the bier is evidence that the god has been vindicated and received the *wrrt* crown as a sign of his victory over his brother Seth. This is clear in the speech of Thoth on the case of the inner coffin, as we will see later in this chapter. The image of the scarab under the collar with a sun disc is also a reference to the sunrise. Sunrise means that the god has been victorious over the demons of the night, and for the deceased Osiris means that he has been justified. Osiris is also described on the lid as *ꜥnḫ wsjr*, the living Osiris, which also can be a sign that Osiris is now not dead but alive and now the ruler of the underworld, which is the main aim of the judgment of the dead ritual.

### *4.3.2. The Case of the Inner Coffin as the Hall of the Judgment of the Dead*

The scenes and texts on the case of the inner coffin are arranged so as to make the case look like the hall of the judgment of the dead. The scenes on the case start from the part behind the head of the deceased and then proceed to the external left hand side wall. As on the case of the outer coffin, along the upper edge of the case runs a horizontal text. It is a speech by the deceased in which he is addressing Anubis, telling him that all the gods are in festival as Shu shines in the sky and in the netherworld. The speech also relates that Isis is protecting the limbs of Horus, who is standing in his office, and it ends with a plea for divine offerings. This part, as argued above, is decorated on Middle Kingdom coffins with an offering formula dedicated to Anubis as patron of the necropolis. The scene under the ornamental text starts with the part behind the head of the deceased. Behind the head of the deceased stands a goddess with upraised arms. The sequence of the scenes then starts from the left hand side wall of the case. The first scene on this side shows the deceased in front of the emblems of Osiris and Anubis. The scene is separated from the previous one by a speech for Geb and from the following scene by a speech for the goddess Neith and Nephthys. Neith is also described here as the Mother of the God and Nephthys as the God's Sister.

The scene following is the cosmological image described in detail in Chapter Three, which deals with the resurrection of the deceased, shown here as Shu filling the space between the earth and the sky.[425] The gods and goddesses are arranged in this scene as follows. Osiris is described as Lord of the West and Duat, the Great God and Lord of the sky. Being Lord of the two spheres, earth and sky, means that Osiris is filing the space between Nut, in whose body he travels to the heavenly spheres, and Geb in whose body is the earthly netherworld. Isis is also described here as the Lady of the West and Nephthys as the God's Sister. The final speech on this side is for Thoth who is described here as the Scribe of Maat and of the Great Ennead of the Great Temple (the Great temple of Heliopolis).

The next scene shows the deceased being introduced to Osiris, Foremost of the West. The deceased is shown accompanied by a lioness goddess and Isis. He is introduced to Osiris, who is shown seated on a throne while Thoth records the event. This scene is also accompanied by texts and speeches. The first text is for Osiris, who is described as Osiris, Foremost of the West, the Great God, and the living One. Thoth is also mentioned here as Lord of Maat, Foremost of the Divine Booth, which is in sky and earth. The speech on this part is for Duamutef, Lord of the Sky, Son of Osiris, the Great God, and Lord of the Sacred Land, Who is in the Middle of the shrine of Wenennefer, Lord of the West that he may give offerings. The final scene on this part of the case shows the deceased and his *ba* drinking water from the Tree Goddess. The deities named in the scene are Osiris, who is described as Osiris Lord of the West, Nephthys as the God's Sister and finally Isis as Foremost of the West. The speech in this scene is for the goddess Nut, who is described as Nut the Great, Mother of the God Foremost of the West, Eye of Re, and Mistress of the Beautiful House, that she may give offerings to Osiris, Lord of Abydos, the Great God.

On the external right hand side wall the scenes begin from the part behind the head of the deceased. There is a horizontal inscription running along the upper edge of the case as on the left hand side wall. The text is a speech by the deceased, which he directs to Osiris as "the the God and Lord of the Sacred Land who dwells in Abydos, Great Sovereign, Lord of the Necropolis, the King of the Living who is beloved by the Great Ennead, Lord of the White Crown who takes possession of the Red Crown, who nurses all those of the Great Mansion! He who speaks in the Hall of Maat beside the Lord of Maat, truly sacred beside the Lord of Maat, Sacred of Seat in

[425] See above, 49-50.

Southern Heliopolis, Lord of Offering in northern Heliopolis, Great of Name, may his offering be much in the presence of Atum".

The sequence of the scenes on this part of the lid starts near the head of the deceased, where he is represented in a festive garment presenting offerings to the emblem of Osiris. There is a text behind the kneeling goddess describing her as Nephthys, God's Sister, Lady of the West, Osiris the Great God, Lord of the sky and earth. The second scene near the shoulders is for Osiris, who is shown seated on a throne and flanked by Isis and Maat. He is described as Osiris Lord of the West. The speech in that scene is for Neith the Great Mother of the God Foremost of the West that she may give offerings. The next scene is a judgment scene. There is a speech for Osiris in this scene reading: "A speech by Osiris, the Great God, Foremost of the West, Nefertem, Protector of the Two Lands and Potent Heir of Wenennefer". The other speech on this side of the coffin is for the deceased, saying "A speech by the Revered One with Anubis, Foremost of the West, Wenennefer Ruler of the Living, King and Lord ."

The final scene in this part shows the deceased kneeling and making offering for Hathor who is shown coming out of the mountain. She is described as Hathor Lady of the Sacred Land (Necropolis), the Eye of Re and Mistress of the West, that she may give offerings. The final speech on this part is for Hathor and reads:

A speech by Hathor, Lady of Sacred of Seat in Southern Helipolis and Lady of Offering in Northern Heliopolis, that she may give offerings to Osiris, Lord of Abydos.

The images and texts on the exterior of the case of the inner coffin of *P3-dj-jmn* are related to the judgment of the dead. In Chapter Three we have seen that the judgment of the dead as a ritual was incorporated in the journey to Sais, in which the goddess Neith plays a prominent role. She speaks to her son who is pictured inside the coffin as a mother and also as a protector. Here on the exterior of the inner case the goddess appears more than once, with different speeches. The deceased on the lid is described as a Venerated One with Neith. At the edge of the feet of the lid of the coffin there is a speech for the goddess in which she is described as a mother of the king and Lady of the West. She also occurs at the border of the lid as a mother who gives thousands of various offerings to the deceased. Along with Isis, Nephthys, and Serqet, Neith protects the Four Sons of Horus. These different deities on the lid, as argued above, pronounce their speeches in the night before burial in the place of embalmment.

In the first speech on the exterior left side wall Isis is described as the one who protects the limbs of Horus, who stands here for Osiris. The judgment of the dead, as argued above, comes at the end of the embalming ritual when the body has received *sꜥḥ* status. This process of collecting the dismembered body of Osiris is the task of Isis and Nephthys with Anubis, all of whom are addressed on this part of the case. The resurrection of Osiris is ensured by the final act of vindication which is accomplished by undergoing the judgment of the dead. The scene following is described in Chapter Three as a resurrection scene. In this scene the resurrection of the deceased is envisaged as the journey of Re in the body of the sky goddess Nut. The deceased is here envisaged as Shu filling the space between earth and sky, which means that the scene is referring to the two spheres of the journey of Re, in the day sky and in the night sky, in which the deceased participates. This scene is important here because it can be described as a wakeup call for the deceased to go to the judgment of the dead. This might also be compared with similar calls in the Pyramid and Coffin Texts, in which deceased is asked to wake up (*rs*). The recollecting of the body of Osiris and the union of its different parts can be also indicated by the two *sm3-t3wj* symbols over which stand Isis and Nephthys.

After the deceased gains his integrity, he is introduced to the Lord of the West Osiris. He is accompanied by Isis, Duamutef, a serpent-headed goddess and Thoth. The speech of Thoth that precedes the scene of the hall of Osiris relates that Thoth is the scribe of the Great Ennead who plays the major role in the vindication of Osiris against Seth in the Great Temple of Heliopolis. Thoth is also described as Lord of Maat, which is also related to the judgment of the dead.

The texts and images on the right side wall of the inner case show the deceased speaking to Osiris, describing him as the Lord of Maat and the one who is loved by the Great Ennead. The hall of Maat, as a place where the judgment of the dead takes place, is also described here with the Ennead and Heliopolis. All these are signs of the judgment of the dead, which was designed on the lawsuit of Heliopolis. Atum, as the Lord of this lawsuit, is also mentioned here. The next scene is showing the deceased in a festive garment in front of the emblem of the Osiris is an indication of his arrival in the presence of Osiris.

The scene following shows Osiris on his throne flanked by Isis and Maat and sitting on a throne with two mythical animals at its base. This scene can be considered as an introduction to the main scene of the hall of the judgment of Osiris. Neith is also described as mother of the god and she is asked to give offerings to Osiris.

The next scene is the judgment of the dead itself, in which Osiris is shown sitting on his throne. The deceased is shown in festive garment approaching the hall of the judgment of the dead. The scale with the heart of the deceased is also shown, while Thoth stands in front of Osiris and Isis at his back. After being vindicated in the judgment of the dead, the deceased is shown entering the west and welcomed by the goddess Hathor Lady of the Sacred Land.

It can be concluded that the lid of the inner coffin of *P3-dj-jmn* represents the ritualized model of the judgment of the dead, which was designed on the lawsuit between Seth and Horus. The decorations on the exterior walls of the case represent the other model of the judgment of the dead, in which the deceased's heart is weighed on a scale against the feather of Maat. The existence of the two models of the judgment of the dead on the lid and case of the inner coffin of *P3-dj-jmn* might also be related to the fact that the deceased had to escape the two phases of death described above. The repetition of the scenes of rebirth and resurrection on the two sides of the inner case might also be connected with the first and second death of the deceased.

Like the ancient Egyptian ritual texts, the images on the two coffins of *P3-dj-jmn* do not refer to a coherent set of rituals. However, the scenes on the two coffins are repetitive and draw on different metaphors. It is known that the ancient Egyptian ritual texts survived in textual corpora and the focus is on the speaking of the word, which is highly allusive to their explanation of the myth to accompany the ritual action. In the coffin of *P3-dj-jmn* the images seem to play the same role of the word, or more precisely the spoken word. They are also highly allusive to the myth to accompany the ritual action. It is impossible to envisage the image being placed on the coffin sides without having ritual functions. We have the illustrated versions of rituals on the sides of the coffins, and what is missing is the spoken word that accompanied the performance of such rituals. These images can be described as the ritual actions that should have been accompanied by recitation of ritual texts. The evidence for the existence of such spoken words to accompany the ritual is the use of the *ḏd mdw* formula on different parts of the coffin. Ritual texts intended for recitation are designated by the formulaic heading *ḏd mdw* "saying of words." [426]

The images on the two coffins can also be described as a service-book used by the ritualist in the course of performing ritual, which also does not contain a coherent set of images but discrete units of ritual images rather than continuous ritual images. The resurrection of Osiris and his coronation are all represented on the coffin sides in images, and not in texts as they were on Middle Kingdom Coffin Texts. These images relating the process of death and resurrection are repeated on the coffin sides. The images show also how the enactment of the myth in ritual set in motion a continuous process that was necessary for the deceased to share in the daily cycle of death and resurrection of both Re and Osiris. The deceased within the coffin has several roles to play in the myth of death and resurrection of Osiris. He is Osiris, who is resurrected by the aid of Isis, Nephthys and Horus. In his journey to the netherworld near the eastern horizon, he plays the role of Horus, the son of Osiris who travels towards the shrine of his father Osiris to embalm him and bring him back to life.[427] In this case the deceased takes on the role of the father Osiris and Horus, his son. The mummification and resurrection of the deceased father Osiris was envisaged as his coronation. As a result, Osiris became the king of the underworld and Horus became the king of Egypt.[428] The cycle of death and resurrection of the deceased was also incorporated in the daily cycle of the day and night journeys of Re in the sky. That might explain the existence of the images of a boat, scarabs and sun discs on the different sides of the coffin.

#### 4.3.3. *The Floor Board of the Case of the Inner Coffin and the Embrace of the Goddess of the West*

The floor board of the case of the inner coffin is occupied by the figure of the goddess of the West. She is also identified as Isis and as Hathor. The Four Sons of Horus and the goddess of the West with the two cow horns might also refer to the ascent of the god to the sky. The deceased in the coffin is then embraced by the goddess of the West from the bottom and by Nut from the top. He is thus filling the space between earth and sky and has free movement in the whole cosmos.

### 4.4. *The Mummy Cover*

The mummy cover is placed directly on the mummy and could be considered as a second lid for the inner coffin. The scenes and images on the mummy cover of *P3-dj-jmn* show the god in his final stage of resurrection. The first scene under the collar shows a scarab wearing the *Atef* crown. Attached to the scarab with the *Atef* crown is a heart amulet. The placing of the heart amulet attached to the solar disc might refer to the identification of the heart (here as a symbol of Osiris) with the sun. It is also a symbol of resurrection and the union between the solar and Osirian aspects of the deceased, which also guarantees the eternal renewal of the universe.[429]

The images and texts on the mummy cover all work together to ensure that the deceased has already become the legitimate Osiris who has gained his justification from the gods in the court of Maat.[430] This also can be evident in the use of the heart amulet mentioned above. The deceased is here identified as Osiris who has overcome death and passed the final trial and is now among the company of the gods as one of their followers. He is then able to go forth by day,[431] which is evident in the use of the scarab. The scenes on the the mummy cover show Osiris as a justified deceased, and that might be complemented by the image of the heart amulet. The heart amulet can also be a sign for the ritual of erecting the mummy in front of the tomb on a sand bank; thus exposed to the sun, the deceased is identified with the sun god Re himself.[432] The surrounding images and icons also help in understanding the reason why a heart amulet was placed on this part of the mummy cover.

---

[426] Eyre, *The Cannibal Hymn*, 27

[427] Willems, in: *Essays te Velde*, 366.

[428] Willems, in: *Essays te Velde*, 358

[429] Sousa, *JARCE* 43(2007), 63; Niwinski, *JEOL* 30 (1987-1988), 87-106. For other examples where the heart amulet is depicted on the chest of coffins dating to the 21st Dynasty, see Sousa, *JARCE* 43 (2007), 63, n.21.

[430] For instance, the a mulet which is drawn on the *Weskh* collar of Pinedjem II and in the middle of which there is a heart amulet; see Niwinski, *21st Dynasty Coffins from Thebes*, 67-96.

[431] Sousa, *JARCE* 43 (2007), 66.

[432] Sousa, *JARCE* 43 (2007), 63-4.

The middle part is divided into registers. The first from the top shows two falcons flanking the emblem of Nefertem. It is interesting to note that the emblem of Nefertem is placed on the mummy cover; this also has a symbolic meaning. Nefertem is the symbol of rebirth, also evident from his name. Depicting the emblem of Nefertem flanked by the emblems of Osiris and at the same time flanked by the Isis and Nephthys is a sign that the rebirth of the new god is also envisaged as the resurrection of Osiris. The head of the goddess Nut has the emblem of Hathor, two cow horns with a sun disc between them, which refers to the goddess as the one who will elevate the god to the sky, also confirmed by the wish of the deceased to be covered and received by the sky goddess Nut.

The rest of the scenes on the mummy cover show the deceased Osiris dressed and having all the signs of royality, with the *Atef* crown on his head. This also might refer to the god with whom the deceased is identified as a vindicated being. The entire decoration program on the mummy cover shows the deceased in his final stages of resurrection. He is Osiris with the *Atef* crown and Re as a scarab, also wearing the *Atef* crown, and finally Nefertem.

So, the mummy cover with all the symbolic signs on it can be described as representing the final stage in the rituals taking place on the mummy of the deceased and his coffin before interment. He is shown as Nefertem surrounded by Isis and Nephthys and in this aspect he is the newborn god who comes into being as Nefertem surrounded by the two *Benu* birds. He is Re coming out of depth of the underworld in the shape of a scarab. He is also Osiris with the *Atef* crown; the heart could also be attributed to him. He is born young in the identity of both Osiris and Re, which is one of the most important aspects of this period. The deceased's passage of birth and resurrection is represented here in the use of many icons on the mummy cover that connect him with both Re and Osiris.

### 4.5. *Ritual Images and Ritual Texts*

The images on the two coffins cannot be envisaged as purely mythical; they also allude to certain rituals. These images might explain the ritual actions that accompanied the recitations of the ritual texts. As argued above, these images are repetitive, possibly because they refer to the very complicated cycle of death and resurrection of Osiris that is represented in the journey of the sun god Re in day and night skies. The Solar-Osirian unity is also very clear in the images on the two coffins. We have seen that there are cosmological scenes that have been modified to fit in the context of this unity. For instance, the famous cosmological scene in which Shu stands between the sky and earth, which is purely solar, has been modified to refer also to the cycle of the death and resurrection of Osiris. The funeral procession of the deceased has also been modelled on the journey of the sun god Re in the sky. Like the Egyptian religious texts of the afterlife, the images and texts on the two coffins of *P3-dj-jmn* hardly adhere to one particular doctrine, Solar or Osirian. The images on the two coffins provide the deceased with the characteristics of Re and at the same time with those of Osiris. Both Osiris and Re were considered as the sons of the sky goddess Nut and their existence depended on rebirth. That is why, as Willems argues, Osiris's rebirth and resurrection is envisaged as the sunrise. These concepts of sunrise and resurrection of Re and Osiris became very clear during the New Kingdom, especially when the body of the sun god Re merged with that of Osiris. Osiris in his journey from death to resurrection is Re in his journey from the depth of the underworld until he shines in the day sky.[433] Every deceased shared in this cycle of death and resurrection of both gods. This idea is expressed in the images and texts on the two coffins of *P3-dj-jmn*.

The images on the two coffins can be described as texts that should be read. The scene of pouring water by the deceased to the seated figure of Osiris in the middle part of the lid of the inner coffin illustrates the fact that there might have been ritual texts recited and the images replace these texts. The same can be also said of the scene of Osiris on the floor board of the case of the outer coffin. The text describes the act of pouring *ḳbḥw* to Osiris, which has been described as having a long history dating back to the Pyramid Texts. All that was recited in texts has just been abbreviated in the image of Osiris with water signs on his body.

The ritual environment is integration between actions and recitations, which have been transmitted on the sides of the two coffins in images and in captions of texts; they cannot be separated from each other and need to be approached as a unity. Texts and images on the two coffins recreate the essence of the actions taking place in the performance of rituals depicted on the sides of the coffins. They provide a record of the rituals performed on or for the deceased. In spite of the extensive record of such ritual actions and recitations placed in texts and images on the coffins sides, the record of such rituals is still incomplete. This record can be described as episodic and the material record of such rituals on the coffins is still representative and not narrative.

The decoration program can also be described as having a wider function rather being purely pictorial representation of rituals or its material recreation. These images, with the aid of texts, are highly allusive in referring to recitations of rituals, but they can also be described as simply decorative. As argued above, the coffins during this period served as tombs, and the coffin sides can also be described simply as tomb walls. In this way the scenes and images were placed on these walls as decorative elements, but at the same time they can also be used as a writing surface, on which the scenes and texts are placed or inscribed according to the rules that are derived from a literary tradition or motivation rather than a representational one. The decorations on the two coffins concern the coffin as a living thing in itself, as a

[433] Willems, *Chests of Life*, 150.

representation of the cosmos or part of it, in which the deceased remains. It is also a place in which the gods are immanent as well, and in which the interaction between human and gods takes place. In this sense the sides of the two coffins can be read as a book rather than being simply pictures.[434] It is also not surprising to see that the decoration corpus on the coffin sides can also be considered as a service-book containing images that are diverse in nature and intended to be used on different ritual occasions. The integration between the texts and the images symbolises the essence of an object or recreates the essence of action.[435]

There are some scenes that are repeated more than once on the coffin sides, in particularly those of rebirth and resurrection. For instance, the scene of the Shu filling the space between Geb and Nut is repeated twice on the two cases of the inner and outer coffins. This might be explained in terms of the repeated cycle of death and resurrection in which the deceased takes part. The deceased, as a follower of the god, faces the same ordeals, and his every passage is envisaged as a journey from death and resurrection. The journey from the place of embalming to the necropolis, for instance, is envisaged as the death and resurrection of Osiris and equally is envisaged as the journey of Re across the sky. The sequence of these ritual images on the coffin sides was also not intended to be merely narrative, though it can be difficult to relate them to one another. Nonethess, by comparing parallel data from different textual sources we can a reach a meaningful interpretation of these images on the coffins.[436] These scenes can provide us with the raw material of what actually was carried out in the cult of the dead or in the funerary rituals connected with the integrity of the deceased, whose body has disintegrated at death. They also can be viewed as ritual papyri that provide material for a service book, even though these scenes still do not provide complete, direct record of each individual ritual that was performed.

---

[434] Graefe, in: Quaegebeur (ed.), *Ritual and Sacrifice*, 143-56, where he stresses on the scenes on temple walls are to read as texts, similar Dercahin, in: Loprieno (ed.), *Ancient Egyptian Literature*, 359 on the temple art as literary composition. Derchain-Urtel, in: Quaegebeur (ed.), *Ritual and Sacrifice*, 99-105 on an analysis between illustration and text as literary composition; see also Assmann, in: Bildermann et al, *Interpretation in Religion*, 87-109. See also Eyre, *The Cannibal Hymn*, 36-40 on the iconic representation on the ritual of the Cannibal Hymn.

[435] Bickel, *Cosmogonie*, 100-1.

[436] For the difficulty of ritual narrative on different sources, see Eyre, *The Cannibal Hymn*, 39, n. 15 and the reference cited there.

## Bibliography


Abbas, E., *The Lake of Knives and the Lake of Fire: Studies in the Topography of Passage in Ancient Egyptian Religious Literature,* BAR 2144, Oxford, 2010.

Abbas, E., 'Crossing of the Lake Ritual', in Corbelli, J., D. Boatright, and C. Malleson (eds), *Current Research in Egyptology 2009: Proceedings of the Tenth Annual Symposium, University of Liverpool,* Oxford, 2010, 1-14.

Allen, J. P., *The Inflection of the Verb in the Pyramid Texts*, BAe 2, Malibu, 1984.

Allen, J. P., J. Assmann, A. B. Lloyd, R. K. Ritner and D. P. Silverman, *Religion and Philosophy in Ancient Egypt*, YES 3, New Haven, 1989.

Allen, J. P., J. Assmann, A. B. Lloyd, R. K. Ritner and D. P. Silverman, 'Reading a Pyramid', in: *Hommages Leclant* I, 1-25.

Allen, J. P., J. Assmann, A. B. Lloyd, R. K. Ritner and D. P. Silverman, The Ancient *Egyptian Pyramid Texts*, WAW 23, Atlanta, 2005.

Altmann, V., *Die Kultfrevel des Seth: Die Gefährdung der göttlichen Ordnung in zwei Vernichtungsritualen der ägyptischen Spätzeit (Urk. VI)*, Studien zur spätägyptischen Religion I, Wiesbaden, 2010.

Assmann, J., *Liturgische Lieder an den Sonnengott*: *Untersuchungen zur ägyptischen Hymnik* I, MÄS 19, Berlin, 1969.

Assmann, J., 'Die Inschrift auf dem äuβeren Sarkophagdeckel des Merenptah', *MDAIK* 28.1 (1972), 47-73.

Assmann, J., 'Neith spricht als Mutter und Sarg. Interpretation und metrisch Analyse der Sargdecklinschrift des Merenptah', *MDAIK* 28.2 (1972), 115-139.

Assmann, J., *Grabung im Asasif: 1963 – 1970. Band. VI. Das Grab der Mutirdis*, Mainz am Rhein, 1977.

Assmann, J., *Sonnenhymnen in thebanischen Gräbern*, Theben 1, Mainz am Rhein, 1983.

Assmann, J., 'Egyptian Mortuary Liturgies', in: Israelit-Groll, S. (ed.), *Studies in Egyptology presented to Miriam Lichtheim*, 2 vols, Jerusalem, 1990, I, 1-45.

Assmann, J., 'Semiosis and Interpretation in Ancient Egyptian Ritual', in: Bildermann, S. and A. Scharfstein (eds), *Interpretation in Religion*, Philosophy and Religion, vol. 2, Leiden and New York, 1992, 87-109.

Assmann, J., *Tod und Jenseits im Alten Ägypten*, Munich, 2001.

Assmann, J. and M. Bommas, *Altägyptische Totenliturgien*, vol. I, *Totenliturgien in den Sargtexten des Mitteleren Reiches*, Supplemente zu den Schriften der Heidelberger Akademie der Wissenschaften, Philosophisch-historische Klasse 14, Heidelberg, 2002.

Assmann, J., 'Das Leichensekret des Osiris: Zur kultischen Bedeutung des Wassers im alten Ägypten', in: *Hommages Fayza Haikal*, 5-16.

Assmann, J., *Theologie und Weisheit im Alten Ägypten*, Munich, 2004.

Assmann, J., *Ägyptische Geheimnisse*, Munich, 2004.

Assmann, J., *Death and Salvation in Ancient Egypt*, translated from German by D. Lorton, Ithaca and London, 2005.

Assmann, J., M. Bommas and A. Kucharek, *Altägyptische Totenliturgien,* vol. II, *Totenliturgien und Totensprüche in Grabinschriften des Neuen Reiches*, Supplemente zu den Schriften der Heidelberger Akademie der Wissenschaften, Philosophisch-historische Klasse 17, Heidelberg, 2005.

Assmann, J., M. Bommas and A. Kucharek, *Altägyptische Totenliturgien,* vol. III, *Osirisliturgien in Papyri der Spätzeit*, Supplemente zu den Schriften der Heidelberger Akademie der Wissenschaften, Philosophisch-historische Klasse 20, Heidelberg, 2008.

Aston, D. A., *Burial Assemblages of Dynasty 21–25. Chronology – Typology – Developments,* Österreichische Akademie der Wissenschaften, Denkschriften der Gesamtakademie LIV, Contributions to the Chronology of the East Mediterranean XXI, Vienna, 2009.

Baines, J., 'Egyptian Myth and Discourse: Myth, Gods, and the Early Written Iconographical Record', *JNES* 50 (1991), 81-105.

Beinlich, H., *Die "Osirisreliquien". Zum Motive der Körperzergliederung in der altägyptischen Religion*, ÄA 42, Wiesbaden, 1984.

Bell, C., *Ritual: Perspectives and Dimensions*, New York, 1997.

Bettum, A., *Death as an Eternal Process: A case Study of a 21st Dynasty Coffin at the University Museum of Cultural Heritage in Oslo.*
www.duo.uio.no/sok/work.html?WORKID=20317

Bickel, S., *La cosmogonie égyptienne avant le Nouvel Empire*, OBO 134, Freiburg and Göttingen, 1994.

Billing, A., *Nut: The Goddess of Life in Text and Iconography*, Uppsala, 2002.

Blackman, A. M., 'The Significance of Incense and Libation in Funerary and Temple Ritual', *ZÄS* 50 (1912), 69-75.

Bleiberg, E., 'East is East and West is West: A Note on Coffin Decoration at Asyut', in: *Studies Redford*, 113-120.

Bourriau, D. J., 'Change of Body Position in Egyptian Burials from the mid XIIth Dynasty until the Early XVIIIth Dynasty', in: Willems, H. (ed.), *Social Aspects of Funerary Culture in the Egyptian Old and Middle Kingdoms*, Leuven, 2001, 1-20.

Brunner, H., 'Illustrierte Bücher im alten Ägypten, in Wort und Bild', in: Röllig, W. (ed.), *Das hörende Herz. Kleine Schriften zur Religions-und Geistesgeschichte Ägypten*, OBO 80, Freibourg, 1988, 363-384.

Brunton, G., *Qau and Badari*, vol. III, BSAE 50, London, 1930.

Ciccarello, M. and J. Romer, *Theban Royal Tombs Project: A preliminary Report of the recent Work in the Tomb of Ramesses X and XI in the Valley of the Kings*, The Brooklyn Museum Theban Expedition, New York, 1979.

Coenen, M. and A. Kucharek, 'New Findings on the Lamentations of Isis and Nephthys', *GM* 193 (2003), 45-50.

Cooney, K. M., 'Changing Burial Practices at the End of the New Kingdom: Defensive Adaptations in Tomb Commissions, Coffin Commissions, Coffin Decoration, and Mummification', *JARCE* 47 (2011), 3-44.

Corteggiani, J. P., 'La "butte de la Décollation" à Héliopolis', *BIFAO* 95 (1995), 141-151.

Daressy, G., 'Les sepultures des prètres d'Ammon à Deir el-Bahari', *ASAE* 1(1900), 141-148.

Daressy, G., 'Les Cercueils des Prêtres d'Ammon (Deuxième Trouvaille de Deir el-Bahari)', *ASAE* 8 (1907), 3–38.

Daressy, G., *Cercueils des Cachettes royales* (CGC), Cairo, 1909.

Davies, N. de Garis, *The Tomb of Nakht at Thebes*, New York, 1917.

Davis, W. M., *The Canonical Tradition in Ancient Egyptian Art*, Cambridge, 1989.

Derchain, P., 'Théologie et literature', in: Loprieno, A. (ed.), *Ancient Egyptian literature: History and Forms*, Probleme der Ägyptologie 10, Leiden, 1996, 351-360.

Derchain-Urtel, M. T., 'Les scènes rituelles des temples d'époque gréco-romaine en Égypte et les règles du jeu "Domino"', in: Quaegebeur. J. (ed.), *Ritual and Sacrifice in the Ancient Near East: Proceedings of the International Conference organized by the Katholieke Universiteit Leuven from the 17th to the 20th of April 1991*, OLA 55, Leuven, 1993, 99-105.

Dodson, A., 'A Twenty-First Dynasty Private Reburial at Thebes', *JEA* 77 (1991), 180-182.

Egberts, A., 'Action, Speech, and Interpretation: Some Reflections on the Classification of Ancient Egyptian Liturgical Texts', in: Eyre, C. (ed.), *Proceedings of the Seventh International Congress of Egyptologists*, OLA 82, Leuven, 1998, 357-363.

Egner, R., and E. Haslauer, *Särge dr Dritten Zwischenzeit I*, Corpus Antiquitatum Aegyptiacarum Kunsthistorisches Museum: Wien Ägyptisch-Orientalische Sammlung 10, Mainz am Rhein, 1994.

El-Sayed, R., 'Les sept vaches célètes, leur taureau et les quatre gouvernails d'aprés les données de documents divers', *MDAIK* 36 (1980), 375-385.

Englund, G., 'Propos sur l'iconographie d'un sarcophage de la 21e dynastie', *Boreas* 6 (1974), 37-69.

Englund, G., 'L'horizon et quoi encore', *Boreas* 13 (1984), 47-54.

Englund, G., 'Interior Iconography of the Coffin of Khonsu-mes', *Medelhavsmuseet Bulletin* 20 (1985), 33-41.

Eschweiler, P., *Bildzauber im alten Ägypten: Die Verwendung von Bildern und Gegenständen in magischen Handlungen nach den Texten des Mittleren und Neuen Reiches*, OBO 137, Freiburg, 1994.

Eyre, C. J., *The Cannibal Hymn: a Cultural and Literary Study*, Liverpool, 2002.

Eyre, C. J., 'Belief and the Dead in Pharaonic Egypt', in Poo, M. (ed.), *Rethinking Ghosts in World Religions*, Studies in the History of Religions 123, Leiden, 2009, 33-46.

Eyre, C. J., 'Funeral, Initiations and Ritual of Life in Pharaonic Egypt', in: Alice, M., and J. Patrier (eds), *Life, Death, and Coming of Age in Antiquity: Individual Rites of Passage in the Ancient Near East and its Surroundings/ Vivre, grandir et mourir dans l'antiquité: rites de passage individuels au Proche-Orient ancien et ses environs* (forthcoming).

Federn, W., The 'Transformations' in the Coffin Texts: a new approach", *JNES* 19/4 (1960), 241-257.

Faulkner, R.O., The *Papyrus Bremner-Rhind*, BAe 3, Brussels, 1933.

Faulkner, R.O., 'The Lamentations of Isis and Nephthys', in: *Mélanges Maspero* I, MIFAO 66, Cairo, 1935-1938, 337-348.

Faulkner, R.O., 'The Papyrus Bremner-Rhind-I', *JEA* 22 (1936), 121-40.

Faulkner, R.O., 'The Papyrus Bremner-Rhind-II', *JEA* 23 (1937), 10-16.

Faulkner, R.O., 'The Papyrus Bremner-Rhind-III', *JEA* 23 (1937), 166-85.

Faulkner, R.O., 'The Papyrus Bremner-Rhind-IV', *JEA* 24 (1938), 41-53.

Faulkner, R.O., *The Ancient Egyptian Pyramid Texts. Supplement of Hieroglyphic Texts,* Oxford, 1969.

Faulkner, R.O., *The Ancient Egyptian Coffin Texts*, 3 vols, Warminster, 1973-78.

Faulkner, R.O., *The Ancient Egyptian Book of the Dead*, London, 1985.

Frandsen, P. J., 'The Letter to Ikhtay's Coffin: O. Louvre Inv. NO. 698', in: Demarèe, R. J., and A. Egberts (eds), *Village Voices*, Leiden, 1992, 31-50.

Gee, J., 'The Use of Daily Temple Liturgy in the Book of the Dead', in: Backes, B., M. Munro and S. Stöhr (eds), *Totenbuch-Forschungen: Gesammelte Beiträge des 2. Internationalen Totenbuch-Symposiums 2005*, SAT 11, Wiesbaden, 2006, 73-86.

Giddy, L. L., *The Anubieion at Saqqara*, vol. II*: The Cemeteries*, MEES 56, London, 1992.

Goebs, K., 'Zerstörung als Erneuerung in der Totenliteratur: Eine kosmische Interpretation des Kannibalenspruchs', *GM* 194 (2003), 29-49.

Goebs, K., *Crowns in Egyptian Funerary literature*, Oxford, 2008.

Goff, B. L., *Symbols of Ancient Egypt in the Late Period: The Twenty First Dynasty*, Paris and New York, 1979.

Graefe, E. and G. Belova (eds), *The Royal Cache TT 320: A re-examination*, Cairo, 2010.

Graefe, E., 'Die Deutung der Sogenannten "Opfergaben" der Ritualszenen ägyptischer Tempel als "Schriftzeichen"', in: Quaegebeur. J. (ed.), *Ritual and Sacrifice in the Ancient Near East: Proceedings of the International Conference organized by the Katholieke Universiteit Leuven from the 17th to the 20th of April 1991*, Leiden, OLA 55, Leuven, 1993, 143-156.

Grieshammer, R., *Das Jenseitsgericht in den Sargtexten*, ÄA 20, Wiesbaden, 1970.

Harpur, Y., 'Further Reliefs from the Chapel of *Rʿ-ḥtp* at Meydum', *JEA* 73(1987), 197-200.

Hartwig, M. K., *Tomb Painting and Identity in Ancient Thebes, 1419-1372 BCE.* Monumenta Aegyptiaca 10, Série Imago 2, Brussels, 2004.

Hayes, W. C., *Royal Sarcophagi of the XVIII Dynasty*, Princeton, 1935.

Hermsen, E., *Lebensbaumsymbolik im Alten Ägypten: Eine Untersuchung*, Arbeitsmaterialien zur Religionsgeschichte, Köln, 1981.

Heyne, A. K., 'Die Szene mit der Kuh auf Särgen der 21. Dynastie, in: *Fs Hornung*, 57-68.

Hofmann, A., *Das Grab des Neferrenpet*, Theban 9, Wiesbaden, 1995.

Hölscher, U, *The Excavation of Medient Habu,V. Post-Ramessid Remains*, Chicago, 1954.

Hornung, E. Staehelin, E., *Skarabäen und andere Siegelamulette aus Basler Sammlungen*, Mainz, 1976.

Hornung, E. 'Der ägyptische Sarg im Heimatmuseum Appenzell', *Innerrhoder Geschichtsfreund* 28 (1984), 1-9.

Hornung, E. *Texte zum Amduat*, 3 vols, Aegyptiaca Helvetica 3, 14, and 15, Geneva, 1987-1992 and 1994.

Hornung, E. and T. Abt (eds), *The Ancient Egyptian Amduat: The Book of the Hidden Chamber*, Zurich, 2007.

Ikram, S. and A. Dodson, *The Mummy in Ancient Egypt: Equipping the Dead for Eternity*, New York, 1998.

Janssen, J., *Commodity Prices from the Ramesside Period: an Economic Study of the Village of Necropolis Workmen at Thebes*, Leiden, 1975.

Jansen-Winkeln, K., 'Ein Anruf an den Sarg', *DE* 30 (1994), 55-63.

Jansen-Winkeln, K., 'Horizont und Verklärtheit: Zur Bedeutung der Wurzel *ꜣḫ*', *SAK* 23 (1996), 201-215.

Jequier, G., *Les frises d'objets des sarcophages du Moyen Empire,* Cairo, 1921.

Kanawati, N., *The Tomb and its Significance in Ancient Egypt*, Cairo, 1987.

Keel, O., 'Ägyptische Baumgöttinnen der 18-21. Dynastie', in: Keel, O. (ed.), *Das Recht der Bilder gesehen zu werden: Drei Fallstudien zur Methode der Interpretation altorientalischer Bilder*, OBO 122, Freibourg, 1992.

Kikuchi, T., 'Die Thebanische Nekropole der 21. Dynastie-Zum Wandel der Nekropole und zum Totenglauben der Ägypter', *MDAIK* 58 (2002), 343-371.

Kitchen, K., *The Third Intermediate Period in Egypt (1100-650 BC)*, Warminster, 1973.

Koeing, Y., 'Between Order and Disorder: a Case of Sacred Philology', in: Kousoulis, P. (ed.), *Ancient Egyptian Demonology. Studies on the Boundaries between the Demonic and the Divine in Ancient Egyptian Magic*, OLA 175, Leuven, 2011, 121-128.

Lapp, G., *Die Opferformel des Alten Reichs*, DAIK Sonderschrift 21, Mainz am Rhein, 1986.

Lapp, G., *The Papyrus of Nu*, Catalogue of the Books of the Dead in the British Museum I, London, 1997.

Leahy, A., 'The Libyan Period in Egypt: An Essay in Interpretation', *Libyan Studies* 16 (1985), 51-65.

Leclant, J., 'Les textes des pyramides', in *Textes et Langages de l'Égypte pharaonique,* 3 vols, BdÉ 64, Cairo, 1972, II, 37-52.

Leclant, J. (ed.), *Les Textes de la Pyramide de Pepy I* $^{er}$; 2 vols, MIFAO 118/1-2, Cairo, 2001.

Leitz, C., *Lexikon der Ägyptischen Götter und Götterbezeichnungen* V, OLA 114, Leiden, 2002.

Lichtheim, M., *Ancient Egyptian literature*. vol. II: *The New Kingdom*, California and London, 1984.

Liptay, É., *Coffins and Coffin Fragments of the Third Intermediate Period,* Catalogues of the Egyptian Collections in Budapest Museum of the Fine Arts, Budapest, 2011.

Lull, J., 'A Scene from the Book of the Dead Belonging to a Private Twenty-First Dynasty Tomb in Tanis (Tomb of *ꜥnḫ.f-n-Jmnw*), *JEA* 87 (2001), 180-186.

Lüscher, B., *Untersuchungen zu Totenbuch Spruch 151*, SAT 2, Wiesbaden, 1998.

Mace, A. C., *The Early Dynastic Cemeteries of Nag-ed-Der II*, Leipzig, 1903.

Maraite, E., 'Le cône de Parfum dans làncienne Egypte', in: Obsomer, C. and A-L Oosthoek, *Amosiadès: Mélanges offerts au Professeur Claude Vandersleyen par ses anciens ètudiants*, Louvain-la-Neuve, 1992, 213-219.

McDowell, A. G., *Village Life in Ancient Egypt: Laundry Lists and Love Songs*, Oxford, 1999.

Minas-Nerpel, M., *Der Gott Chepri: Untersuchungen zu Schriftzeugnissen und ikonographischen Quellen vom Alten Reich bis in griechisch-römische Zeit*, OLA 154, Leiden, 2006.

Montet, P., *Les Constructions et le tombeau de Chéchanq III à Tanis*, Paris, 1960.

Munro, I., *Das Totenbuch des Nacht-Amun aus der Ramessidenzeit (pBerlin P. 3002),* HAT 4, 1997.

Münster, M., *Untersuchungen zur Göttin Isis*, MÄS 11, Berlin, 1968.

Nelson, M. 'The Ramessum Necropolis', in: Strudwick, N. and J. H. Taylor (eds), *The Theban Necropolis: Past, Present and Future*, London, 2003, 88-94.

Niwinski, A., 'Untersuchungen zur ägyptischen religiösen Ikonographie der 21. Dynastie', *GM* 49 (1981), 47-59;

Niwinski, A., Untersuchungen zur ägyptischen religiösen Ikonographie der 21. Dynastie/2: Der Entwicklungsprozess der thebanischen ikonographischen Sonnenlaufmotive zwischen der 18. und der 21. Dynastie' *GM* 65 (1983), 75-90.

Niwinski, A., 'The Bab el-Gusus Tomb and the Royal Cache at Deir el-Bahri', *JEA* 70 (1984), 73-81.

Niwinski, A., *21st Dynasty Coffins from Thebes, Chronological and Typological Studies*, Theben 5, Mainz am Rhein, 1988.

Niwinski, A., Untersuchungen zur ägyptischen religiösen Ikonographie der 21. Dynastie/3: Mummy in the Coffin as the Central Element of Iconographic Reflection of the Theology of the 21st Dynasty in Theben' *GM* 109 (1989), 53-66.

Niwinski, A., 'The 21st Dynasty Religious Iconography Project Exemplified by the Scene with Three Deities Standing on a Serpent', in: Schoske, S., H. Altenmüller and D. Wildung (eds), *Linguistik,*

*Philologie, Religion. Akten des Vierten Internationalen Ägyptologen-Kongresses München 1985*, SAK Beihefte 1-4, Hamburg, 1988-1991, III, 305-314.
Niwinski, A., *Studies on the Illustrated Theban Funerary Papyri of the 11 and 10 centuries B.C*, OBO 86, Freiburg, 1989.
Niwinski, A., 'The Solar-Osirian Unity as Principle of the Theology of the State of Amun in Thebes in the 21st Dynasty', *JEOL* 30 (1989), 89-106.
Niwinski, A., *La seconde trouvaille de Deir el-Bahari (Sarcophages)* (CG 6029-6068), Cairo, 1995.
Niwinski, A., 'Coffins from the Tomb of Iurdudef-a Reconsideration. The Problem of Some Crude Coffins from the Memphite Area and Middle Egypt', *BiOr* 53 (1996), 324-363.
Niwinski, A., 'Les périodes whm-mswt dans l'histoire de l'Eypte: un essai comparatif', *BSFE* 136 (1996), 5-26.
Niwinski, A., *Catalogue General of Egyptian Antiquities of the Cairo Museum Numbers 6069-6082, The Second Find of Deir El-Bahri (Coffins)*, 2nd vol.1st Fascicle, Cairo, 1999.
Niwinski, A., 'Iconography of the 21st Dynasty: Its Main Features, Levels of Attestation, the Media and their Diffusion', in: Uehlinger, C. (ed.), *Images as Media: Sources for the Cultural History of the Near East and the Eastern Mediterranean (1st millennium BCE)*, OBO 175, Freiburg, 2000, 21-43.
Niwinski, A., 'The Twenty-first Dynasty on the Eve of the Twenty-first Century', in: Hawass, Z. and L. P. Brock (eds), *Egyptology at the Dawn of the Twenty-first Century*: *Proceedings of the Eighth International Congress of Egyptologists, Cairo, 2000*, II, Cairo and New York, 2003, 416-422.
Niwinski, A., 'The Book of the Dead on the Coffins of the 21st Dynasty'in: Backes, B., M. Munro and S. Stöhr (eds), *Totenbuch-Forschungen: Gesammelte Beiträge des 2. Internationalen Totenbuch-Symposiums 2005*, SAT 11, Wiesbaden, 2006, 245-264.
Niwinski, A., 'The so called Chapters 141-142 and 148 on the Coffins of the 21st Dynasty from Thebes; In: *Fs Irmtraut Munro*, 133-162.
O'Connor, D., 'The Interpretation of the Old Kingdom Pyramid Complex', in: *Fs Stadelmann*, 135-144.
Ogdon, J., 'A New Dramatic Argument in the Coffin Texts (Spells 30-37)', in: *L'Egyptologie en 1979: axes prioritaires de recherché*, 2 vols, Colloques Internationaux du Centre National de la Recherche Scientifique 595, Paris, 1982, II, 37-43.
Op de Beeck, L., 'Relating Middle Kingdom Pottery Vessels to Funerary Rituals', *ZÄS* 134 (2007), 157-165.
Otto, E., 'Abydos-Emblem', *LÄ* 1 (1979), 47-48.
Padgham, J., *A New Interpretation of the Cone on the Head in the New Kingdom Egyptian Tomb Scenes*, BAR 2431, Oxford, 2012.
Parkinson, R.B., *The Tale of Sinuhe and Other Ancient Egyptian Poems 1940-1640 BC*, Oxford, 1997.
Piankoff, A. and N. Rambova, *Mythological Papyri*, 2 vols, Egyptian Religious Texts and Representations 3, New York, 1957.
Pinch, G., *Votive Offerings to Hathor*, Oxford, 1993.
Pries, A. H., *Die Stundenwachen im Osiriskult. Eine Studie zur Tradition und späten Rezeption von Ritualen im Alten Ägypten*, Studien zur spätägyptischen Religion 2, Wiesbaden, 2011.
Quack, J., 'Apopis, Nabelschnur des Re', *SAK* 34 (2006), 377-379.
Quibell, J. E, *The Ramesseum*, London, 1898.
Quibell, J. E. and A. G. K. Hayter, *Teti Pyramid, North Side*, Cairo, 1927.
Raven, M. J., 'Egyptian Concepts on the Orientation of the Human Body', *JEA* 94 (2005), 37-53.
Reeves, N. and R. H. Wilkinson, *The Complete Valley of the Kings: Tombs and Treasures of Egypt's Greatest Pharaohs*, New York, 1996.
Refai, H., 'Überlegungen zur Baumgöttin', *BIFAO* 100 (2000), 383-392.
Roeder, H., *Mit dem Auge sehen: Studien zur Semantik der Herrschaft in den Toten- und Kulttexten*, SAGA 16, Heidelberg, 1996.
Sabbahy, L., *Egyptian Museum Collections around the world: Studies for the Centennial of the Egyptian Museum*, Cairo, 2002.
Sabbahy, L., 'A note on the Goddess Selekt as Protector of Rebirth' *RdÉ* 54 (2003), 286-287.
Saleh, M., *Das Totenbuch in den thebanischen Beamtengräbern des Neuen Reiches: Texte und Vignetten*, AV 46, Mainz am Rhein, 1984.
Schäfer, H., *Priestergräber und andere Grabfunde vom Totentempl des Ne-user-re*, WVDOG 8, Leipzig, 1908.
Schneider, H. D., *Shabits: An Introduction to the History of Ancient Egyptian Funerary Statuettes*, 3 vols., Leiden, 1977.
Schneider, H. D., *Life and Death under the Pharaohs: Egyptian Art from the National Museum of Antiquities in Leiden*, The Netherlands, 1998.
Schot, E., 'Goldhaus', *LÄ* II (1977), 739-740.
Seele, K. C., *The Tomb of Tianefer at Thebes*, OIP 86, Chicago, 1959.
Servajean, F., *Djet et Neheh. Une histoire du temps* égyptien, Orientalia Monspeliensia XVIII, Montpellier, 2007.
Sethe, K., *Die altägyptischen Pyramidentexte*, 3 vols, Lepizig, 1908-1922.
Seyfried, K. J., 'Entwicklung in der Grabarchitektur des neuen Reiches als eine weitere Quelle für theologische Konzeptionen der Ramessidenzeit', in: Assmann, J., G. Burkard, and V. Davies (eds), *Problems and Priorities in Egyptian Archaeology*, London, 1987, 219-253.
Sheikholeslami, C. M., 'The Burials of the Priests of Montu at Deir el-Bahri in the Theban Necropolis', in: Strudwick, N. and J. H. Taylor (eds), *The Theban Necropolis: Past, Present and Future*, London, 2003, 131-137.
Silverman, D., 'Textual Criticism in the Coffin Texts', in: Allen et al., *Religion and Philosophy in Ancient Egypt*, 29-53.
Singleton, D., 'An Investigation of Two Twenty-first Dynasty Painted Coffin Lids (EA 24792 and EA 35287) for Evidence of Material and Workshop

Practices;, in: Strudwick, N. and J. H. Taylor (eds), *The Theban Necropolis: Past, Present and Future*, London, 2003, 83-87.
Smith, M., *The Liturgy of Opening the Mouth for Breathing*, Oxford, 1993.
Smith, M., *Papyrus Harkness (MMA 31.9.7)*, Oxford, 2005.
Smith, M., 'Osiris NN or Osiris of NN', in: Backes, B., M. Munro and S. Stöhr (eds), *Totenbuch-Forschungen: Gesammelte Beiträge des 2. Internationalen Totenbuch-Symposiums 2005*, SAT 11, Wiesbaden, 2006, 325-337.
Smith, M., *Traversing Eternity: Texts for the Afterlife from Ptolemaic and Roman Egypt*, Oxford, 2009.
Sousa, R., 'The Meaning of the Heart Amulets in Egyptian Art', *JARCE* 43 (2007), 59-70.
Smith, M.,,'The Coffin of an Anonymous Woman from Bab El Gassus (A.4) in Sociedade de Geografia de Lisboa', *JARCE* 46 (2010), 189-204.
Speiser, C., 'Serket, Protectrice des Enfants à Naitre et des Defunts a Renaitre', *RdE* 52 (2001), 251-264.
Taylor, J. H., 'The Third Intermediate Period', in: Shaw, I (ed.), *The Oxford history of ancient Egypt*, Oxford and New York, 2000, 333-369.
Taylor, J. H., *Death and the afterlife in ancient Egypt*, London, 2001.
Taylor, J. H., 'Patterns of Colouring on Ancient Egyptian Coffins from the New Kingdom to the Twenty-sixth Dynasty: an Overview', in: Davies W. V (ed.), *Colour and Painting in Ancient Egypt*, London, 2001, 164-181.
Taylor, J. H., 'Theban Coffins from the Twenty-second to the Twenty-sixth Dynasty: dating and synthesis of development' in: Strudwick, N. and J. H. Taylor (eds), *The Theban Necropolis: Past, Present and Future*, London, 2003, 95-121.
Taylor, J. H., 'The Coffin of Padiashaikhet', in: Sowada, K.N. and B.G. Ockinga (eds), *Egyptian art in the Nicholson Museum, Sydney*, Sydney, 2006, 263-291.
Taylor, J. H., 'Changes in the Afterlife', in: Wendrich, W. (ed.), *Egyptian Archaeology*, Blackwell Studies in Global Archaeology, Oxford, 2010.
Thomas, E., *The Royal Necropolis of Thebes*, Princeton, 1966.
Van Dijk, J., 'The Amarna Period and the Later New Kingdom', in: Shaw, I. (ed.), *The Oxford History of Ancient Egypt*, Oxford and New York, 2000, 272-313.
Van Gennep, A., *The Rites of Passage*, translated from French by M. B. Vizedom and G. L. Caffee, Chicago, 1975.
Van Walsem, R., *The Coffin of Djedmonthuiufankh in the National Museum of Antiquities at Leiden: Technical and Iconographical/Iconological Aspects*, 2 vols, EU 10, Leiden, 1997.
Vischak, D., 'Common Ground between Pyramid Texts and Old Kingdom Tomb Design: The Case of Ankhmahor', *JARCE* 40 (2003), 133-157.
von Falck, M., 'Text-und Bildprogramm ägyptischer Särge und Sarkophage der 18. Dynastie: Genese und Weiterleben', *SAK* 34 (2006), 125-140.
Von Leiven, A., 'Book of the Dead of the Living: BD Spells as Temple Texts', *JEA* 98 (2012), 249-269.
Waitkus, W., 'Zur Deutung einiger apotropäischer Götter in den Gräbern im Tal der Königinnen und im Grabe Ramses III', *GM* 99 (1987), 51-82.
Weidner, S., *Lotos im alten Ägypten, Pfaffenweiler: Vorarbeiten zu einer kulturgeschichte von Nympaea Lotus, Nympaea coerulea und Nelumbo nucifera in der dynastischen Zeit*, 1985.
Willems, H., *Chests of Life*, Leiden, 1988.
Willems, H., 'The Shu-Spells in Practice', in: Willems (ed.), *The World of the Coffin Texts*, 197-209.
Willems, H., *The Coffin of Heqata (Cairo JDE 36418): A Case Study of Egyptian Funerary Culture of Early Middle Kingdom,* OLA 70, Leuven, 1996.
Willems, H., (ed.), *The World of the Coffin Texts. Proceedings of the Symposium held on the Occasion of the 100th Birthday of Adriaan de Buck. Leiden, December 17-19, 1992*, EU 9, Leiden, 1996.
Willems, H., 'The Embalmer Embalmed. Remarks on the Meaning of the Decoration of Some Middle Kingdom Coffins, in: *Essays te Velde*, 343-372.
Willems, H., (ed.), *Social Aspects of Funerary Culture in the Egyptian Old and Middle Kingdoms. Proceedings of the International Symposium held at Leiden University 6-7 June 1996*, OLA 103, Leuven, 2001.
Willems, H., 'The Social and Ritual Context of a Mortuary Liturgy of the Middle Kingdom (CT Spells 30-41)', in: Willems (ed.), *Social Aspects*, 253-272.
Winkler, A., 'The Efflux that Issued from Osiris: A Study on *rḏw* in the Pyramid Texts', *GM* 211 (2006), 125-139.
Winlock, H. E., *Bas-Reliefs from the Temple of Rameses I at Abydos*, New York, 1912.
Wilson, J, A., 'Funeral Services of the Egyptian Old Kingdom', *JNES* 3 (1944), 201-218.
Zandee, J.,'Sargtexte um über Wasser zu verfügen (Coffin Texts V 8-22; Sprüche 356-362)', *JEOL* 24 (1976), 1-47.

**Plates**

Pl. I.

The Lid of the Outer Coffin

Pl. II

1. The External Left Side Wall of the Case of the Outer Coffin

2. The External Right Side Wall of the Case of the Outer Coffin

Pl. III

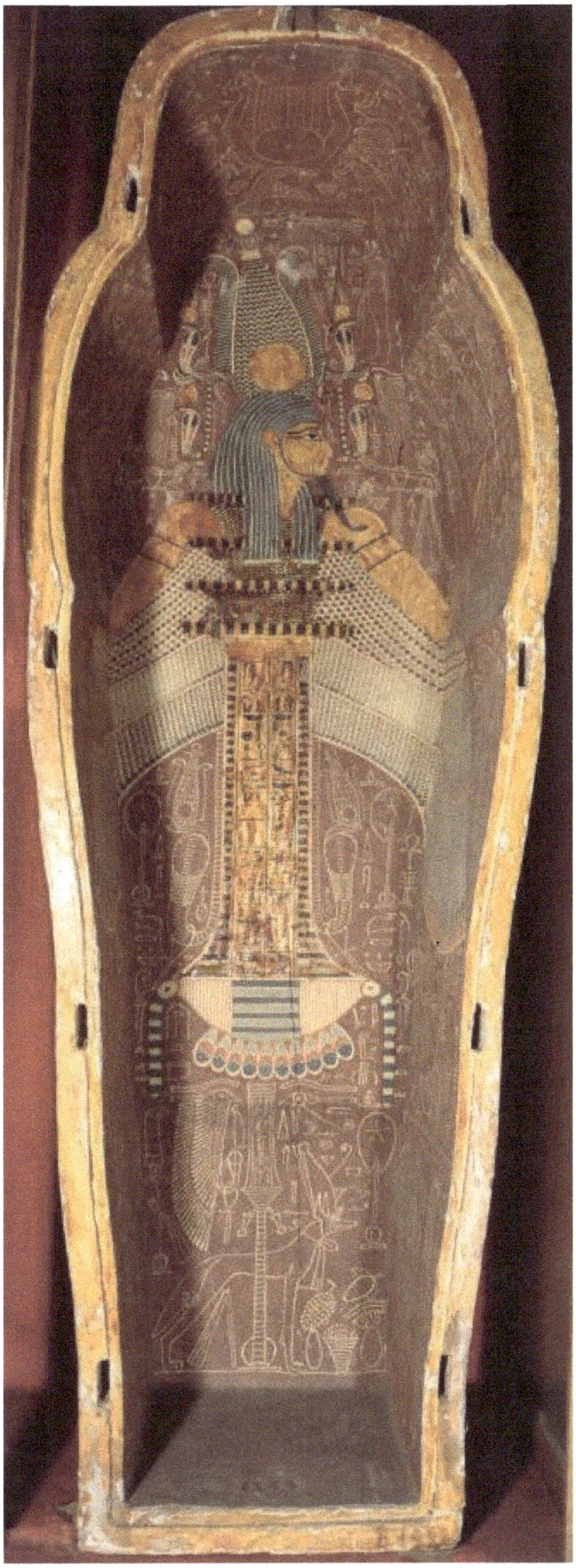

The Inner Decorations of the Case of the Outer Coffin

The Lid of the Inner Coffin

Pl. V

1. The External Left Side Wall of the Case of the Inner Coffin

2. External Right Side Wall of the Case of the Inner Coffin

Pl. VI

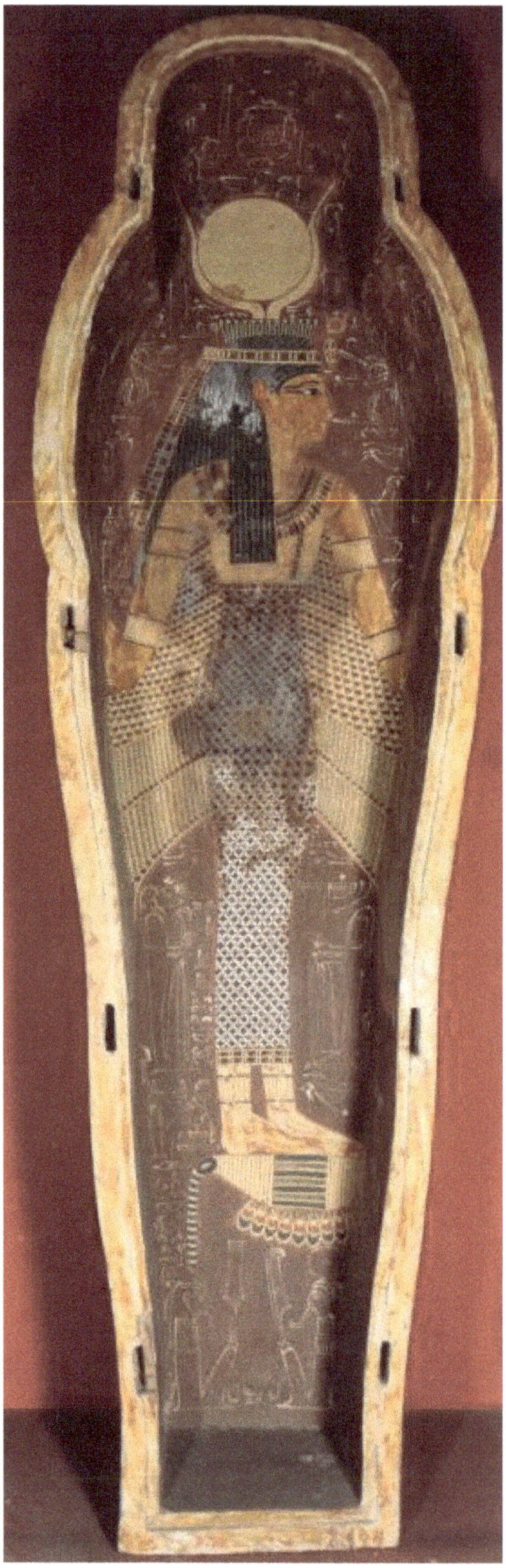

The Inner Decorations of the Case of the Inner Coffin

Pl. VII

The Mummy Cover

www.ingramcontent.com/pod-product-compliance
Lightning Source LLC
Chambersburg PA
CBHW041708290426
44108CB00027B/2900